TSA Past Paper
Worked Solutions

Volumes I & II

Joseph Nelson

Rohan Agarwal

About the Author

Rohan is the **Director of Operations** at *UniAdmissions* and is responsible for its technical and commercial arms. He graduated from Gonville and Caius College, Cambridge and is a fully qualified doctor. Over the last five years, he has tutored hundreds of successful Oxbridge and Medical applicants. He has also authored ten books on admissions tests and interviews.

Rohan has taught physiology to undergraduates and interviewed medical school applicants for Cambridge. He has published research on bone physiology and writes education articles for the Independent and Huffington Post. In his spare time, Rohan enjoys playing the piano and table tennis.

THE BASICS

What are TSA Past Papers?

Thousands of students take the TSA exam each year. These exam papers are then released online to help future students prepare for the exam. Before 2013, these papers were not publically available meaning that students had to rely on the specimen papers and other resources for practice. However, since their release in 2013, TSA past papers have become an invaluable resource in any student's preparation.

Where can I get TSA Past Papers?

This book does not include TSA past paper questions because it would be over 1,000 pages long! However, TSA past papers from 2008 are available for free from the official TSA website. To save you the hassle of downloading lots of files, we've put them all into one easy-to-access (and free!) folder for you at **www.uniadmissions.co.uk/tsa-past-papers**.

At the time of publication, the 2018 paper has not been released so this book only contains answers for 2008 – 2017. An updated version will be made available once the 2018 paper is released.

How should I use TSA Past Papers?

TSA Past papers are one the best ways to prepare for the TSA. Careful use of them can dramatically boost your scores in a short period of time. The way you use them will depend on your learning style and how much time you have until the exam date but in general, you should try to do at least 2008 – 2015 once. If time permits, do them twice- practice really does make perfect!

How should I prepare for the TSA?

Although this is a cliché, the best way to prepare for the exam is to start early – ideally by September at the latest for TSA Oxford and by October for TSA Cambridge. 4 weeks of preparation is usually sufficient for the majority of students. If you're organised, you can follow the schema below:

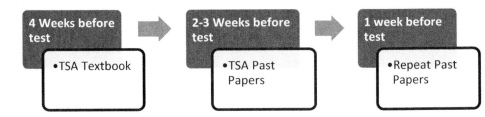

This paradigm allows you to focus your preparation and not 'waste' past papers. In general, aim to get a textbook that has lots of practice questions e.g. *The Ultimate TSA Guide* (**www.uniadmissions.co.uk/tsa-book**) – this allows you to rapidly identify any weaknesses that you might have e.g. identifying flaws, spatial awareness etc.

You are strongly advised to get a copy of '*The Ultimate TSA Guide*' which has 300 practice questions– you can get a free copy by following the instructions at the back of this book.

Finally, it's then time to move onto past papers. The number of TSA papers you can do will depend on the time you have available but you should try to do each paper at least once. If you have time, repeat each paper (choose a different essay question). Practice really does make perfect!

If you find that you've exhausted all past papers, there are an additional six mock papers available in *TSA Practice Papers* (flick to the back to get a free copy).

How should I use this book?

This book is designed to accelerate your learning from TSA past papers. Avoid the urge to have this book open alongside a past paper you're seeing for the first time. The TSA is difficult because of the intense time pressure it puts you under – the best way of replicating this is by doing past papers under strict exam conditions (no half measures!). Don't start out by doing past papers (see previous page) as this 'wastes' papers.

Once you've finished, take a break and then mark your answers. Then, review the questions that you got wrong followed by ones which you found tough/spent too much time on. This is the best way to learn and with practice, you should find yourself steadily improving. You should keep a track of your scores on the previous page so you can track your progress.

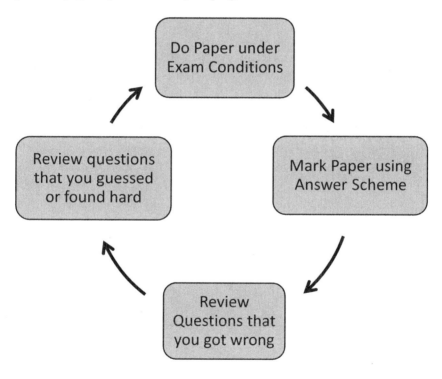

Scoring Tables

Use these to keep a record of your scores – you can then easily see which paper you should attempt next (always the one with the lowest score).

SECTION 1	1st Attempt	2nd Attempt	3rd Attempt
2008			
2009			
2010			
2011			
2012			
2013			
2014			
2015			
2016			
2017			

Extra Practice

If you're blessed with a good memory, you might remember the answers to certain questions in the past papers – making it less useful to repeat them again. If you want to tackle extra mock papers which are fully up-to-date then check out *TSA Practice Papers* for **six** full mock papers with worked solutions (flick to the back for a free copy).

SECTION 1	1st Attempt	2nd Attempt	3rd Attempt
Practice Paper A			
Practice Paper B			
Practice Paper C			
Practice Paper D			
Practice Paper E			
Practice Paper F			

2008

Section 1

Question 1: C

The passage discusses how measuring wealth relative to average income measures inequality, not poverty. It then goes on to describe a situation where under this flawed definition, a pay rise for some leads to some being described as in "poverty" (where this may not be the case), and how in some societies, there is such widespread poverty that using average income describes very few as being in poverty (though there are many in poverty).

Both A) and C) are valid conclusions from this passage, but we can see that the statement in A) goes on to support that in C). Thus A) is an intermediate conclusion, and C) is the main conclusion of this passage. D) Is a reason given in the passage to support these conclusions, and thus is not a conclusion in itself.
E) is an irrelevant statement, whilst B) is not a valid conclusion as the passage has made no reference to whether there is a suitable definition of poverty, it has simply refuted one possibility. This does *not* mean there are no others.

Question 2: C

Let a Child fare be C, and an Adult fare be A. We see from the question that 1 adult far plus 2 child fares is £1.20. Thus: $A+2C=120$(pence)

We also see that C is greater than 0.5A. Thus, 2C must be greater than A, so A must be less than half of 120. Thus, the answer cannot be D) or E), as A is at least half of 120 in both these answers.

We also see that C is less than A. Thus, if $A+2C=120$, 3 times A must be *more* than 120. Thus, A must be more than 40. This means the answer cannot be A) or B), because in these answers A is not more than 40. Thus, we can see that the answer must be C).

Question 3: D

The passage discusses how the number of drug-related road deaths has increased more than drink-driving deaths in recent years, and concludes that this means the drink-driving campaigns have been successful, and it is now time to begin campaigns against drug-related driving.

Answer D) correctly points out that this reasoning is flawed. Just because Drug-driving has increased more does *not* mean the campaigns have been successful. We have no information on how much drink-driving deaths would have increased without the campaigns. This is the information we need to conclude that the campaigns have been successful. Observing that one problem is bigger does not mean another thing is not a problem. B) and E) are completely irrelevant statements, and thus are not flaws.

A) And C) both refer to the possibility that a campaign against driving on drugs may not be as successful as one against drunk-driving. These would weaken the argument, if true, but they are not *flaws* because they do not mean the argument's conclusions are invalid. A) and C) could be described as counter arguments, but are not logical flaws with the argument's reasoning.

Question 4: B

The passage discusses how socialist politicians are often criticised as being hypocritical for objecting to inequalities in wealth whilst enjoying above-average wealth. It then goes on to refute this criticism as invalid by claiming there is no hypocrisy in enjoying high levels of wealth whilst still arguing for a fairer society.
If all these reasons are true, they give us good cause to believe that one *therefore can* be a socialist (and thus argue for less inequality in wealth) whilst enjoying high levels of personal wealth. Thus, B) is the answer.

E) is the opposite of this conclusion, and directly goes against the thread of the argument, thus E) is not a valid conclusion from the passage.

Equally, the argument makes no claims of what socialists with wealth should do about those in even wealthier positions, so A) is incorrect and cannot be concluded from this argument.

Equally, the argument says nothing about whether wealth inequality is immoral, or who is most effective at fighting it. Thus, C) and D) are also incorrect.

Question 5: D

The passage discusses how the University has implemented improved safety features on areas of its campus, which will help to make those areas safer. It then describes how the council owns the lake, so the University has not been able to implement safety features in this area. It concludes on the basis of these reasons that the lake will be a dangerous area, and should be avoided by lone students at night.

However, this argument is flawed, as it assumes that the only thing making an area safer is the University's safety measures. The council could have put its own safety features in place, which may be just as good as the University's and this would make the conclusion invalid. Answer D) correctly illustrates this flaw.

Answers C) and E) are irrelevant. Whether students would pass the lake regularly, or the reasons behind the safety features, do not affect whether the area will be dangerous without the implementation of the safety features. Thus C) and E) do not affect the argument's conclusion.

Answer B) would actually strengthen the argument. If the council consider the lake as part of the campus it would suggest they have not implemented any safety features of their own, thus reinforcing the notion it may be dangerous.

Answer A) is not an assumption because it does not need to be true for the conclusion to be valid. Even if students do look after their own safety, the notion of avoiding walking around the lake alone at night might still be valid (in fact this may *be* a measure students could take to ensure their own safety).

Question 6: D

Since the rear wheel is 2.5m in circumference, it will complete a full rotation every 2.5m. Equally, the front wheel will complete a full rotation every 2m.
We know the tyre valves are beginning at the bottom of the wheels, so they will be in this position again after each complete rotation.

Thus, we are simply looking for the lowest common multiple of 2 and 2.5. This will give us the number of metres after which each wheel will have rotated a whole number of times, and will both be at the bottom at the same time.

The lowest common multiple of these numbers is 10. After this distance, the front wheel will have completed 5 rotations, and the rear wheel will have made 4 complete rotations.

Question 7: E

The Question tells us that the last letter of each 5-digit code signifies which item this set of letters represents the code for, and that B represents the Bicycle lock combination. We see that the last 5-digit code ends with a B - D F G C B

Thus, D F G C represents the 4-digit code for the bicycle lock. Now we simply look at each letter and see which letter of the alphabet it is:

-   D is the 4th letter
-   F is the 6th letter
-   G is the 7th letter
-   C is the 3rd letter

Thus, we end up with 4673 as our combination. We are told that each 4-letter code is written in *reverse* with respect to the actual number code, so we know the bicycle lock combination is 3764.

Question 8: A

We can see in the top view a smaller square shape in the centre of the sculpture. This could be either a raised feature, going *out* of the sculpture, or an indent, going *into* the sculpture.

We can see from the top view that all the sides are flat, with nothing projecting out of them. However, we cannot see if any of the sides have any indented features, so we cannot judge if this might be the case.

A final thing we can see from the top view is that the edges of the top face, around the central feature on the top are all flat, with no indents or raised features.

View B) is possible, as it simply shows featureless sides, and a raised feature on top, which is possible.

View C) is possible because the top feature could be an indent, which would not be visible from the sides, and the sides could have indents represented by the square seen in view C).

View D) is possible as it shows a raised feature on top, which could be the feature in the top view, and a feature in the sides which could be an indent. This is possible from the information given in the top view.

E) is a possible view because it simply shows featureless sides, and the feature on the top may be an indent, which would not be visible from the sides.

A) is not a possible view because it shows indents along the top edge, other than the central feature. We can see from the top view that apart from the central feature, the top is all featureless, with no indents. Thus A) is not possible.

Question 9: C

The passage discusses how in evolution, organs do not develop to be large unless they are used. Based on this fact, the passage describes how whale brains are much larger than our own, and concludes that sperm whales must therefore possess great intelligence, perhaps beyond our own understanding.

Answers A) and B) are irrelevant. Language does not necessarily equal intelligence (so B) is wrong), and the fact that intelligence is possible without large brains does not mean that large brains do not give intelligence (as implied in the passage).

D) and E) actually strengthen the argument. D), by saying the large brains are not related to the large size of sperm whales, reinforces the idea they might be for intelligence, whilst E) reinforces the notion their intelligence may be beyond our understanding.

C) however, weakens the argument, because if the brains may be used for something else then their size does not necessarily mean they are used for intelligence, thus weakening the argument.

Question 10: C

The passage can be summarised very simply. It argues that Mrs Jackson **will** resign if Mrs List is promoted, and then argues that if Mrs List is **not** promoted, Mrs Jackson will **not** resign.

Answer C) directly contradicts how this reason leads on to this conclusion. It points out that the conclusion is invalid because it does not follow on that Mrs Jackson **won't** resign if Mrs List is not promoted. Thus, C) correctly identifies a flaw in the argument.

A), B) and E) are completely irrelevant because they have no effect on the fact that Mrs Jackson will resign if Mrs List is promoted, or whether this means she will not resign if Mrs List is not promoted. Thus, they are not flaws with the argument.

D) is not a flaw because the argument directly states that Mrs Jackson **will** resign if Mrs List is promoted. Therefore, we assume there is no a chance that she won't, as it has been directly stated in the argument that she will.

Question 11: D
The passage discusses how there is evidence that Cannabis has therapeutic uses in certain medical scenarios, and that it should thus be legal. It goes on to say this means doctors being allowed to prescribe cannabis would help those with the relevant medical conditions. It then goes on to say legalising cannabis prescriptions would also allow large-scale studies to establish if the supposed benefit is real.

If we accept all of these reasons as true, we have good reason to believe doctors should be allowed to prescribe cannabis. Thus, D) is the main conclusion of the passage.

B) is a reason given in this argument which supports the main conclusion.

A) and C) are not conclusions or reasons given in the passage. Both could be said to strengthen the conclusion, if true, by providing further reasons why current laws should be changed. However, neither can be concluded from the passage, and are thus irrelevant to what the main conclusion is.

E) is an irrelevant statement with no effect on the argument's reasoning or its conclusion.

Question 12: C
Let the normal rate be termed Y, and the overtime rate be termed Z.
We know from the Question that Pierre worked 30 sessions at normal rate, and 10 at overtime rate, and earned 700 euros. Thus, $30Y + 10Z = 700$
Equally, we know that Mark worked 20 sessions at the normal rate, and 5 at overtime rate, and earned 425 euros. Thus, $20Y + 5Z = 425$
By subtracting the 2nd equation from the first, we can see that:
$30Y - 20Y + 10Z - 5Z = 700 - 425$
$10Y + 5Z = 275$
We can then subtract this new equation from the equation formed from Mark's work, to work out the normal rate. Thus:
$20Y - 10Y + 5Z - 5Z = 425 - 275$
$10Y = 150. Thus\ Y = 15$
Now that we know Y, we can now use either waiter's working patter and pay to calculate z.
Let us use Pierre's work and pay. We see that 30Y+10Z=700. Thus, $30 times\ 15 + 10Z = 700$
$30\ times\ 15\ is\ 450. Thus, 450 + 10Z = 700$
Thus $10Z = 700 - 450$, which is 250.
If 10Z=250, Z must equal 25.
Thus, the overtime rate is 25.

Question 13: E

This question is simpler than it appears on first glance.

We are calculating the number of wins, so we need to combine the away wins and home wins into one figure. Since they are next to each other on the pie chart we can easily do this visually.

Now, if we examine the amount of the chart made up of "wins", and the amount of the chart made up of "draws" (both home and away combined), we can see that roughly ¾ of the pie chart is made up of some form of "wins". We can verify this by examining the angle between the boundary of "Home Wins" and "Away Draws", and the boundary between "Away wins" and "Home Draws". This angle appears to be 90 degrees. This verifies that ¾ of the pie chart is made up of wins, whilst the other quarter is made up of draws.

Three quarters of 24 is 18.

Question 14: E

We can readily see that when this net is folded up, the face with the cross will be adjacent to the 4 faces with thick grey lines, and that the thin diagonal line will be on the opposite side. Most of the incorrect answers can be discounted in terms of what faces will be adjacent to each other:

Shapes A) and B) cannot be made because the 2 non-diagonal thick grey lines *must* be located on opposite sides of the box (separated by the cross as seen in the Net) and cannot be adjacent.

Shape C) cannot be made because the face with the thin diagonal line *must* be opposite the face with the cross, and cannot be adjacent.

Shape D) and Shape E) both present faces adjacent to each other in a possible combination, so we must now examine the orientations these faces will be to each other when folded

Shape D) is not possible because the orientations of the diagonal lines are incorrect. We can see that there are definitely possible combinations in which one of the thick grey diagonal line will be orientated with one of the vertical or horizontal thick grey lines as shown in view D). However, we see that in order for this to be achieved, the thin diagonal line must be *perpendicular* to the thick grey diagonal line from the viewpoint in question, *not* parallel as shown in view D).

Shape E) is possible. We can readily see if we turn the net upside down that we now have the Cross, with one thick grey line continuing upwards from the top of the cross, and one thick grey diagonal line radiating away from the bottom-right corner of the cross. This is exactly the view shown in E). Thus, E) is possible. Hence E) is the answer.

Question 15: D

The passage describes how random drug testing in prisons has caused prisoners to switch from Cannabis to Heroin, as it stays in the system for much less time. It describes how since drug testing was introduced, cannabis use has decreases but heroin use has increased. From this, we can conclude that drug testing **hasn't** solved the issue of drug use in prisons, because heroin use has increased. Thus D) is a valid conclusion from the passage.

The fact that it hasn't solved the issue does not mean that it **can't** solve the issue, so C) is not a valid conclusion. Equally, we cannot conclude that the method needs to be improved, so A) is incorrect.

The other 2 answers concern incorrect statistical inference. The fact that cannabis has increased and heroin has decreased does not mean heroin use is now higher, so B) is incorrect. Equally, the fact that heroin encourages intimidation doesn't mean that doubling heroin use will increase intimidation by the same amount (we have no information on *how much* heroin increases intimidation).

Question 16: D

The passage concludes that doctors must deceive their patients in some medical scenarios. The reasons given to support this are that patients have a right to know the truth, but in some scenarios the patient's health would be better served by not knowing the truth.

We can see that this reasoning only supports this conclusion if we accept the statement in D) as true. At no point has D) been stated, so it is therefore an assumption on which the argument rests.

E) is the opposite idea to the assumption in D), and if true, E) would invalidate the argument. Thus E) is not an assumption.

C) is irrelevant as it refers to a situation where a patient would be upset, and not where their health would worsen from knowing the truth. B) is also irrelevant in a similar way, referring to a situation where patients would be frightened, not risking their health.

A) is completely irrelevant, as what patients accept about a doctor's responsibilities does not affect how doctors should respect whether their right to know the truth is more important than their health.

Question 17: A

The passage concludes that tits that tear paper are searching for food, on the basis that they use a similar method to tear paper as they do to strip tree bark and search for food.

However, if we accept A) as true, then it seems the tits are choosing to tear paper *instead* of taking food which is readily visible and available, weakening the conclusion that tearing paper *is* a search for food.

B) is not correct because the fact that humans know does not mean that the tits themselves know that no food is forthcoming.

C) is incorrect because the fact that families feed them does not mean that the birds will not search for more food.

D) is an irrelevant statement, and thus incorrect.

E) is not correct because the fact that animals engage in pointless activities does not necessarily mean that this activity is pointless and not functional.

Question 18: E

With a rate of inflation of 10%, a car worth 500 Bols a year ago will now be worth 550 Bols (we assume for this question that the car's value has not degraded due to damage or wear and tear).

80% of 550 Bols is 440 Bols. Thus he will receive 440 Bols for his old car.

The new car will be worth 550 Bols, as it is an identical model, and with an inflation rate of 10%, something worth 500 Bols a year ago will now be worth 550 Bols.

550-440=110. Thus, Evitan will need to contribute 110 Bols towards purchasing the new vehicle.

Question 19: B

Answering this question first requires understanding how to read the table.

The left-hand side of the table describes the percentage *change* of industrial growth for the last year. Thus, we only need to consider the Latest figure, as this gives us the percentage change that the question refers to.

The right-hand side of the table describes the percentage *of the population* unemployed. Thus, to calculate the *change* in percentage unemployed we need to subtract the current figure from the figure a year ago.

Working these 2 figures out for the UK we see that it had a percentage increase of industrial production of 4.2%, as seen in the table, and that the % of the population unemployed fell from 10 to 8.8, a fall of 1.2.

Thus, we are seeking a country with a percentage increase in industrial production of >4.2, and a percentage *fall* in unemployed of more than 1.2 (i.e. a percentage change of less than minus 1.2).

We see that all countries except the Netherlands and Belgium had a percentage change in industrial production of more than 4.2. However, of these countries, only Canada *also* had a fall in the % of people unemployed of more than 1.2

Question 20: B

First we should pick out the distances mentioned for the towns the two drivers have travelled to, in order to get an idea of where the towns are with respect to each other.

➢ Barneyville is 5km West, and 15km South of Abbeytown

➢ Carloston is 5km East of Barneyville.

➢ Denburgh is 5km South of Barneyville.

➢ Easterby is 10km East and 15km North of Denburgh.

We know that Ahmed is in Carloston, and Wayne is in Easterby. From the distances mentioned above, we can work out how far away Carloston is with respect to Easterby:

➢ Carloston is 5km East of Barneyville.

➢ Easterby is 10km East and 10km North of Barneyville (Denburgh is 5km south of Barneyville, and 0km East or West. Easterby is 10km East and 15km North of Denburgh)

➢ Thus, Easterby must be 5km East and 10km North of Carloston.

We know that all roads run directly North-South or East-west, so in order to get between these two towns, one driver must drive a 5km stretch, and then a 10km stretch. Thus, a total of 15km must be driven.

Question 21: D

The passage discusses how a study has found that those with more control over their work have lower levels of a particular stress-related disease. It then concludes that in order to reduce stress-related disease, we must give workers more control over their work.

The argument has confused cause and correlation twice. It has assumed that a lower incidence of heart disease is *because* of a lower incidence of stress, and not simply correlated with it. Answer D) correctly illustrates this flaw.

Answer A) is not a flaw because the argument does not imply the government is serious, it simply comments on what must happen if it is.

B) is not a flaw because whether workers wish to have more control is irrelevant to whether more control over work reduces stress-related disease.

C) is irrelevant as practical limitations of a policy do not affect what results this police will have *if* it is implemented.

E) is also irrelevant. Reducing the amount of stress-related disease among white-collar workers would still reduce the overall incidence. Thus, whether other groups are also affected is irrelevant.

Question 22: B

The passage can be summarised as arguing that "A can happen if B happens. B has not happened, so A cannot happen". Although this is incorrect, we are still able to assess which of the answers follow this pattern.

➢ Answer B) follows this pattern, where "A" is curing a headache, and "B" is being willing to try acupuncture.

➢ Answers A) and C) both follow a pattern of "A can happen if B does. B happens, therefore A will happen". (In C), "A" is avoiding being overweight)

➢ D) can be summarised as "A happens if B does. A already happens so we do not need B".

➢ E) can be summarised as "A happens if B happens. A is happening, so B must be happening".

None of these are the same as the reasoning used in the passage.

Question 23: C

The passage refers to a principle where *actions* bring more responsibility for a given scenario than a *failure to act*. This is because when an action is taken, the result would not have happened without the action from the person in question. However, when an action *fails* to be taken, the consequences would have happened anyway without the existence of the person who failed to act.

➢ Answer C) directly follows this principle, stating that those who break the law are more responsible than those who fail to prevent them from doing so.

➢ Answer A) follows an opposite principle, stating that the government is responsible for high crime rates through its *failure to act*, rather than through any given action.

➢ Answer B) simply states that a situation is happening, so clearly prisons are failing to prevent this situation. This does not give any claims on whether the prisons are therefore *responsible* for the situation.

➢ Answers D) and E) are irrelevant scenarios, which bear no relevance to the principle.

Question 24: D

First we need to work out how many performances will be carried out in the course of 1 full week. We see that there are 6 evening performances (one for each day except Sunday), and that in addition to this there are 3 Matinee performances (Wednesday, Thursday and Saturday). This gives a total of 9 performances in the course of each full week.

Now we need to work out how many complete weeks there are in each month. 7 goes into 31 fully 4 times, with 3 left over. Thus, there will be 4 full weeks each month. This gives a total of 36 performances.

Then, there are 3 leftover days at the end of each month, which will contain extra shows. The maximum number of shows which occur in a 3 day period is either the period from Wednesday to Friday, or the period from Thursday to Saturday. In each of these 3 day periods there are a total of 5 performances.

Thus, the *maximum* number of performances that can occur in a month is 41.

Question 25: D

To calculate the number of days of labour that peter must pay for, we simply calculate the area of the filled in grey blocks, which represent a number of days of labour, and how many individual workers need to be present for those days. We can see that for all tasks except brickwork, only one row is filled in, so only one worker needs to be present.

➢ Preparing foundation lasts for 6 days, and one labourer, so accounts for 6 days labour in pay.

➢ Brickwork lasts for 9 days, and involves 2 labourers, so accounts for 18 days of labour in pay.

➢ Roofing lasts for 16 days, and involves 1 labourer, so accounts for 16 days of labour in pay.

➢ Glasswork lasts for 10 days, and involves 1 labourer, so accounts for 10 days of labour in pay.

➢ Decorating lasts for 8 days, and involves 1 labourer1, so accounts for 8 days of labour in pay.

This gives a total of 58 days of labour that must be paid for.

Now we examine how many is the maximum number of workers that may be on site at any one time. We can quickly see that there are 2 points when 3 roles are being carried out at the same time (Days 12-13 and Days 20-21)

One of these sets of days (Days 12-13) involves brickwork and 2 other jobs. We have already seen that brickwork requires two labourers, whilst all other jobs require 1 labourer. Thus, at this point there will be 4 labourers on site at 1 time.

Thus the answer is D), 58 and 4.

Question 26: B

This question holds a simple answer, and is designed to test your ability to think logically and clearly under time pressures.

The tile shown has 1 fully rounded curve, and shape made out of straight lines, which looks like a square with part of the corner cut off.

We can immediately see from examining the possible answers that Answer B) shows four tiles (Bottom-left, Middle-left, Bottom-Middle and the Middle tile) which only have rounded curves. Thus, this pattern cannot be made with tiles identical to that shown in the Question.

Question 27: C

The passage discusses how market forces have always limited the adverse effects of the environment on food production. However, it then goes on to say that we are not changing the environment irreversibly, with changes that will be permanent. The passage says how this will cause devastating effects on world agriculture, such that market forces alone cannot prevent a global famine.

Thus, the argument mentions Answers A), B), D) and E) as reasons throughout the passage.

The argument then brings all these reasons together and concludes that some form of planned intervention is necessary. Thus, we can see how answers A), B), D) and E) all come together to support the statement in C). Thus, C) is the main conclusion of this passage, and all the other answers are reasons given to support this conclusion.

Question 28: A

The passage discusses plants being genetically modified to produce pesticides. However, it then discusses how pesticides lose their effectiveness if used continually, thanks to development of resistance in the pests, and that they remain effective only if there are gaps in which they are not used. It then finishes off by saying that the plants which produce pesticide will produce them continuously, without these gaps.

If all these factors are true, we have good cause to believe that the Pesticides produced by these plants will become ineffective against pests. Thus A) is the answer.

Nothing in the passage says anything about plants becoming contaminated with pesticides, so B) is not a conclusion.
All the other answers actually argue *weaken* the conclusion given in A), or contradict stated reasons in the passage. Thus, none of these are valid conclusions from the passage.

Question 29: D

The passage states that recycling is not the best answer to the problem of garbage disposal. It backs this up by describing how most bottles in America are constructed of PET. It then discusses how this material is not safe when recycled, due to the absorbance of other chemicals which may then leach into food and drink stored in the recycled product.

We can see that this conclusion that recycling is not the best solution relies on an assumption that there is little use for recycled PET other than food/drink containers. If there are other, safe uses, then the potential carcinogenicity described is no longer a reason not to recycle. Since the argument has provided no other reasons why recycling is not the best solution, its conclusion is no longer valid from its reasoning. Thus, D) correctly identifies an assumption in the passage.

The passage says nothing about the pros/cons of burning plastic, reducing plastic production, the exhaustion of landfill space or whether soft drink bottles should be made of other material. Thus, none of the other answers affect the argument's conclusion, and thus they are not assumptions.

Question 30: B

We can see from the information given that 8 bricks are required to cover an area of 40cm by 40cm.

40cm by 40cm is 1600cm^2.

The area of the whole driveway is 550cm by 400cm. This is 220,000cm^2

220,000cm^2 divided by 1600cm^2 is 137.5 (140 times 1600 is 224,000. 2.5 times 1600 is 4000).

Thus, the amount of bricks required will be 8 times 137.5. 140 times 8 is 1120. 2.5 times 8 is 20.

Thus, 1100 bricks will be needed to cover the entire driveway.

Question 31: B

The ratio is currently 1/3 Sand to 2/3 Coir. Thus, there is currently 5kg of Sand present in the mixture, and 10kg of Coir.

The target ratio is 3/5 sand to 2/5 Coir. Since we are only adding sand, the actual amount of coir will stay the same. Thus, 2/5 of the entire weight of the new compost will be 10kg.

If 10kg is 2/5 of the entire weight of the new compost, then the full weight must be 25kg. Since 3/5 is Sand, this means there needs to be 15kg of Sand to make the new mixture.

Thus, 15kg of sand is needed, and 5kg is present. Thus, 10kg of Sand must be added to make the new compost. Hence, the answer is B).

Question 32: E

If the second stage begins with 4 quarter finals then the number of teams progressing through to the second stage must be 8, as there will be 2 teams in each of the 4 quarter finals. To progress through to the next round, you must have won your group, so there must be 8 group winners and hence 8 groups. The teams are divided into equal groups, so the number of teams starting the competition must be a multiple of 8. The two multiples of 8 given as possible answers are 8 and 72. If the competition started with 8 teams then there would be 1 in each group and hence no need for the first stage at all, so this cannot be the answer. Hence the only possible solution of the 5 given is 72. Hence the solution is E.

Question 33: C

The passage argues catalytic converters were created to tackle one kind of pollution, but in fact create another. It argues that converters do this by removing certain pollutants that usually serve to reduce the levels of ground-level ozone. The passage claims that since such ozone is a major cause of choking smogs, people with breathing difficulties affected by it will be worse off if more catalytic converters are used.

We can see that this conclusion (that catalytic converters indirectly cause breathing difficulties) is weakened by the statement in C), which suggests that catalytic converters remove other pollutants that also cause breathing difficulties. If this is the case, it's overall effect on breathing difficulties may be neutral or a positive one (if the pollutants it removes are more potent than ground-level ozone). Thus C) weakens the argument, and the answer is B).

A), B), D) and E) are all irrelevant in that they do not affect whether increasing the number of catalytic converters in cars will increase the incidence of breathing difficulties, via indirectly increasing the amount of ground-level ozone.

Question 34: A

The passage discusses how membership of the EU *has resulted* in growth and stability in the EU members. It then discusses how it is desirable for previous Eastern Bloc members to become more prosperous and stable, and concludes that they should therefore join the EU.

Answer A) points out that this conclusion relies on the former Eastern Bloc countries having the same potential as the current EU members. If they do not, there is no guarantee that membership of the EU would have the same effect, and thus the argument's conclusion is invalid. Hence, the answer is A).

Answers B) and D) appear to be flaws, but are not upon closer inspection. Answer B) relates to other non EU members also being prosperous and stable, whilst D) refers to exclusion from the EU not necessarily resulting in lack of prosperity/stability. Neither of these statements necessarily means that EU membership would not bring prosperity and stability, and thus they do not affect how the argument's reasons support its conclusion.

C) and E) are completely irrelevant statements which have no effect on whether EU membership brings prosperity and/or stability. Thus they are not flaws.

Question 35: A

The passage argues that the driver's attempt to disable his main competitor and thus ensure victory was fair. It argues that the other driver would have done the same, that the driver was acting as anyone else would, and that he was defending an earned lead. All of these reasons, if true, give us good cause to believe that the main driver's actions were not unfair. Thus, A) correctly identifies the main conclusion of this passage.

B) is an irrelevant statement, as the rewards have no effect on whether the driver's actions were fair, and the fact that there are rewards is simply a stated fact, and not a conclusion.

C) is not a valid conclusion from the passage, and in fact disagrees with the passage, as the passage claims the actions "may have been dangerous and irresponsible". Thus C) is not a conclusion to the argument, and appears to be a counter-argument to the passage.

D) and E) are both reasons given in the passage to support the main conclusion, which is that given in Answer A).

Question 36: B

Firstly we need to calculate what time the first flight arrives in Dubai, as this is not given. We are told that the wait time in Dubai is 5 hours and 15 minutes, and the flight leaves Dubai at 14:30 on Saturday. Hence the flight from London must arrive at 09:15 Dubai time on Saturday (5 hours and 15 minutes before 14:30).

Now we can work out the time spent in the air for each flight. The first flight departs London at 22:30 on Friday and arrives in Dubai at 09:15 on Saturday, both given in local times. If Dubai is 4 hours ahead of London, then 09:15 in Dubai will be 05:15 in London. Hence the flight is in the air from 22:30 until 05:15 the next morning, London time. This is 6 hours 45 minutes.

The second flight departs Dubai at 14:30 on Saturday and arrives in Kampala at 20:45 on Saturday, both given in local times. If Kampala is 1 hour behind Dubai then 20:45 in Kampala will be 21:45 in Dubai. Hence the flight is in the air from 14:30 until 21:45, Dubai time. This is 7 hours and 15 minutes. The total time spent in the air is hence 6 hours 45 minutes + 7 hours 15 minutes, which is 14 hours. Hence the solution is B.

Question 37: B

If each pen must be accessible from at least one side, the most efficient way to pen the sheep in is to have them in rows of 2, as this means most of the hurdles are being used to pen in more than one sheep. If the sheep are in 2 rows of 8 then 3 lots of 8 hurdles will be needed to pen them in one direction, and 9 lots of 2 will be needed in the other direction as shown below.

Hence the minimum number of hurdles required is 3x8 + 2x9 = 24 + 18 = 42. Hence the solution is B.

Question 38: C

The answer to this question is best illustrated by a diagram:
This is a representation of the ribbon folded in half:

If this is then folded in half again, it will look somewhat like this:

If we cut through the middle of here as shown by the dotted line, and consider the pieces we will get starting from the top left and following the ribbon, there will be 1 of 1m, 1 of 2m, 1 of 2m, 1 of 2m, then 1 of 1m. Hence there will be 3 pieces of 2m and 2 of 1m. Hence the answer is C.

Question 39: E

The passage discusses how ecotourism *should* provide a sustainable alternative to the overuse of natural resources, but then describes how it actually causes a range of problems in wildlife, such as new diseases, stress and reduced breeding success. From this information, we can infer that whatever benefits ecotourism provides are outweighed by these negative consequences. This is especially true because the argument implies that ecotourism *should* provide a sustainable alternative, which carries an implication that in truth it doesn't. Thus E) can be reliable inferred.

We cannot imply anything about the nature of the changes observes such as new diseases and altered behaviour patterns, so the suggestion in A) that they may not be apparent to a casual observer *cannot* reliably be concluded from the passage.

C) and D) are irrelevant statements on which we have no information (e.g. we do not know if the stressed dolphins become frenetic when near fishing boats), thus neither of these can be reliably inferred.

Equally, the passage is actually implying that ecotourism projects *are not* sustainable thanks to the harm caused to wildlife. Thus, B) cannot be reliably inferred.

Question 40: A

The passage claims that his lack of care about winning *fully explain* why he did not win the open championship.

We can readily see that this conclusion rests entirely on an assumption that if he had cared more about winning, he would have won. If this is not true, then this conclusion that the lack of care*fully explains* the loss is not valid. Thus A) correctly identifies an assumption in the passage.

B) and C) are both invalid conclusions from the passage. The idea that lack of care was all that stopped Van de Velde winning is *not* enough to assume that caring enough is *sufficient* to win major championships. There are probably many other things required, which Van de Velde possessed (such as a good level of skill). Equally, we cannot state that there *is* nothing worse than losing from the suggestion that this belief needs to be held in order to win championships.

E) is also an invalid conclusion from the passage. The idea that Van de Velde would have won the championship if he'd cared more about winning does suggest that he should have cared more about losing **if** he wants to win the championship.

D) is an irrelevant statement for which the passage provides no information.

Thus, only A) is an assumption in this passage, and the answer is A).

Question 41: B

The passage describes how extended warranties for electrical items are poor value for money, because the average cost of repair per customer is less than the price of the warranty. It then concludes that customers would be well advised to not purchase the extended warranties due to the poor value for money.

Answers A), C) D) and E) all strengthen this conclusion by reinforcing the notion that the warranties are poor value for money.

Answer B) is the only answer which weakens this conclusion. If the actual cost for many people is 0, then it may be that the average cost of repairs *if a repair is needed* is greater than the cost of the warranty. Thus, the warranties may actually be *good* value for money if a repair is required. Thus, B) weakens the argument.

Question 42: C

➢ For a parcel which requires 24c postage, they will require 4 6c stamps.
➢ For a parcel which requires 30c postage, they will require 1 30c stamp
➢ For a parcel which requires 72c postage, they will require 2 6c stamps and 2 30c stamps

(Note: the 30c and 72c postages could be made using other combinations but it is specified in the question that we use the minimum number of stamps on each parcel.

The parcels are sent in about equal numbers, so the proportion of stamps needed will be the proportion that would be needed if 1 parcel of each postage is sent.

If 1 parcel which requires each amount of postage is sent, then 6 6c stamps and 3 30c stamps will be required (adding up the amounts given above). Hence 2 6c stamps are needed for every 1 30c stamp. Hence the solution is C.

Question 43: C

The Goats came 3rd in League B, so they will play in the 4th quarterfinal and hence, if they are to progress to the final, the 2nd semi-final. Hence their opponents in the final must come from the 1st semi-final. In the first semi-final, the winners of the 1st quarterfinal play the winners of the 2nd quarterfinal; hence the teams that could potentially play The Goats in the final are those who play in the first two quarterfinals. This is the winners of League A (The Scorpions), 4th place in League B (The Archers), 3rd place in League A (The Bearers) or the runners up in League B (The Bulls). Hence the teams The Goats may face in the final are The Scorpions, The Archers, The Bearers and The Bulls. Hence the solution is C.

Question 44: E

One piece of carpet is 4m x 6m and the other is 4m x 4m. The total amount of carpet is 40 square metres. We can rule each of the other 4 rooms out in turn.

The Snooker Room is 8m by 6m, 48 square metres, so there is not physically enough carpet to use it in this room, as there would be a 4m x 2m gap somewhere.

The Breakfast Room is 7m by 5m, 35 square metres. Although there is physically enough carpet for this room, carpeting this room with it would require more than one join as whichever way the larger piece of carpet is laid, the smaller piece cannot cover the space that is left without being cut into two pieces.

The Dining Room is 6m by 6m, 36 square metres. Although there is physically enough carpet for this room, carpeting this room with it would require more than one join as whichever way the larger piece of carpet is laid, the smaller piece cannot cover the space that is left without being cut into two pieces.

The Living Room is 8m by 5m, 40 square metres. Although there is physically enough carpet for this room, carpeting this room with it would require more than one join as whichever way the larger piece of carpet is laid, the smaller piece cannot cover the space that is left without being cut into two pieces.

The Library is 9m by 4m, 36 square metres. We can use the carpet for this room because by laying the carpet end to end we can cover both the length and the width of the room with the carpet available, with only one join.

Question 45: A

The passage discusses how a number of farm animals have been found killed in fields, and that the injuries suggest a large predator is responsible, which locals claim is some form of big cat. The passage then discusses how official investigations have refuted these claims, and say that the sightings were of big cats. However, the argument claims the investigations are flawed in that although the sightings may be explained by domestic cats, the injuries cannot be, and concludes that big cats such as pumas must therefore be responsible.

This last statement is supported if we accept all the other reasons in the argument as being true, and thus this is the main conclusion of the passage. Thus A) correctly identifies the main conclusion of the passage.

C) is a reason given in the passage to support this main conclusion, and is not a conclusion in itself.

D) and E) are irrelevant statements which do not affect the argument's conclusion, and are not conclusions in themselves.

B), meanwhile, is a direct contradiction of the results of the investigations, which is conceded as being true by the passage. Thus, it is not in any way a conclusion from the passage.

Question 46: A
The passage can be summarised as claiming that "A" and "B" are needed for "C".
Although we have "B", we do not have "A", so we cannot get/do "C".
Only answer A) follows this same structure. Here "A" is having enough time to get to the station, "B" is having enough time to find the platform, and "C" is catching the train.

Answer B) refers to a situation where "A" and "B" are both needed for "C", but in instance *neither* of "A" and "B" has been provided, so "C" cannot happen. This is different from *just one* of "A" and "B" being missing, so "C" cannot happen.
Answer E) refers to a situation where *either* "A" or "B" is sufficient for "C", but neither have been provided, so "C" can't happen. Again this is different from the question.

Answer C) refers to a situation where only one criterion needs to be fulfilled (i.e. the tide holding back for long enough for the truck to arrive), but it cannot be. This is different from needing two criteria, as in the question.

Answer D) refers to a completely different setting where one of two options needs to be used to carry out "C", and one of the options cannot be used, so the other must be.
Hence, the answer is A)

Question 47: B
The passage illustrates a principle where only those who use a certain service should have to pay towards its upkeep, and how nobody who does not use the service should have to pay for it.
Answer B) follows this same principle, suggesting that those who do not visit London should not have to pay towards the subsidisation of the London transport system.
Answers C) and D) both refer to a principle where all people should provide a contribution to services which are beneficial, even if they do not use them themselves. Thus, these two answers illustrate an opposite principle to that in the question.

Answers A) and E) do not really refer to a principle at all, and simply describe possible outcomes from not subsidising art galleries. These answers are probably provided to distract you, and test you ability to focus on the *principle* at hand (whether people should pay towards a service they don't use) rather than the *situation* at hand (art galleries).

Question 48: C
➢ The winner receives $100 for lifting 80kg.
➢ He then receives another $10 for having lifted 85kg.
➢ He then receives another $15 for having lifted 90kg.
➢ He then receives another $20 for having lifted 95kg.
➢ He then receives another $25 for having lifted 100kg.
➢ He then receives another $30 for having lifted 105kg.
➢ He then receives another $35 for having lifted 110kg.
➢ Hence his total prize money is $100 + $10 + $15 + $20 + $25 + $30 +$35 = $235.
➢ Hence the solution is C.

Question 49: D
Energy costs can be considered Gas + Electricity + Coal + Logs. We can add the costs of these up for each month and this elicits:

January: 125	May: 180	September: 0
February: 160	June: 80	October: 70
March: 40	July: 80	November: 0
April: 120	August: 80	December: 85

The highest of these is May, at 180. Hence the solution is D.

Question 50: D
The only boxes on the right hand side as Vinod looks at the boxes are directly in front of Sarah, so this pile of boxes must be 3 high. One of the piles in the middle as Vinod looks at the boxes must be 4 high but none can be more than 4 high, and one of the piles on the left as Vinod looks at the boxes must be 2 high but none can be more than 2 high.

We have already ascertained from the view than Vinod has that the pile of boxes in front of Sarah must be 3 high, so the middle pile as Sarah looks at the boxes must be at least 3 high. Hence D cannot be the view that Sarah sees as the middle pile is only 2 high. Hence the solution is D.

END OF SECTION

Section 2

When, if ever, is forgiveness wrong?

This is a complex philosophical question based on an empirical issue. In order to answer this question, which I would not advise unless you have a solid and wide philosophical background, it is vital that one has a sound understanding of the different ways that the term 'wrong' can be interpreted. Explore and define this term in as clear a manner as possible (some pointers are given below). Failure to either define this word concretely and clearly, or to stray from the definition introduced in the opening paragraph will result in an essay which is vague and weak in terms of argument – the worst possible characteristics of a philosophy essay.

Introduction

➤ Definitions - to write a good essay, it is vital that two words are clearly defined, and that the definitions are followed throughout. Those words are 'forgiveness' and 'wrong'

➤ A good idea would be to use a case (if possible from real life) to illustrate your argument – such as, for example, a murder.

➤ Lay out your argument and give a good idea of the direction you are going to take.

Forgiveness

➤ Consider a clear definition of forgiveness – for example 'to stop feeling angry or resentful towards (someone) for an offence, flaw, or mistake'.

➤ A good idea would be to explore what forgiveness is in terms of victim and perpetrator– namely that the perpetrator commits an act which in some way harms the victim, and forgiveness is a decision by the victim to accept what had happened.

➤ It might also be a good idea to contrast forgiveness with reconciliation – reconciliation goes beyond forgiveness in that the forgiveness is the acceptance of a bad act, whereas reconciliation is the restoration of good relations.

➤ A key element of forgiveness, which should be explored is the idea of repentance on the part of the perpetrator.

Wrong

> Consider a clear definition of wrong. Explore the idea of wrongness in different senses – for example in the context of justice and the law, or a more personal interpretation.

Possible arguments

> One possible approach is to flip the question, from 'when is forgiveness wrong' to 'when is forgiveness right?' A way to answer could be to refer back to your example and think of instances where forgiveness is right – such as for example when the perpetrator has shown remorse.

> The idea of remorse serves as a good focal point to build your argument around – namely forgiveness can only be 'right' when the perpetrator shows remorse.

> A counter argument to this could be that certain crimes are unforgivable (give examples), no matter how much remorse is shown

Conclusion

> Summarize the main points made on each side of the argument in the essay.

> Link back to the original definitions you gave – is there any way that the definitions could be changed, and, if so, would that lead to a different conclusion? For example you may come to one conclusion if you focus on a moral definition of the word wrong, but perhaps, if you take a more legalistic definition of the word you may come to the conclusion which is the opposite of what you had previously. This is a useful perspective to introduce when you conclude your essay as it shows wider thinking around the topic.

> A key thing to keep in mind is that this is a humanities and not a science question meaning that there is not a definite answer.

Should parking fines be based on the driver's income?

This essay is relatively simple to answer if structured correctly due to the availability of arguments both for and against the point. However, it is important that the arguments you use are measured and focused in approach – merely writing down every single argument you can think of will not lead to a good essay as you will fail to achieve sufficient depth or clarity of thought.

It is therefore very important with this question to have a clear and concise opening paragraph in which you introduce the reader to the arguments that you are about to make. As well as framing the essay well, this has the additional benefit of helping you keep the rest of the essay structured.

Introduction

➢ Identify the key concepts in the question – namely justice/punishment and fines - and explain them in relation to the question. In this case parking fines are in place to prevent a negative action from taking place (bad parking) and the level of the fine – the key point of the question – determines the effectiveness of the fine.

➢ If parking fines were £10,000, people would be very careful to park correctly. However, there is another element to this question – justice. Parking incorrectly is a problem, but it is important that the punishment reflects the severity of the crime. This is why parking fines are limited.

➢ Another thing to consider and explore is relative income - £10,000 means a lot more to someone earning £20,000 a year than to someone who earns £2 million.

Possible arguments in favour

Equality of impact of law

➢ This is the idea of relative income. The purpose of a fine is to ensure that the offender faces the consequences of their actions. The extent to which a financial penalty feels like a negative consequence is relative to someone's income; not to the amount that the fine is.

➢ Therefore, if you make fines proportional to the income someone has, everybody feels the impact of the punishment equally, rather than the poor facing a relatively larger punishment than the rich.

Deters the rich

➢ Another purpose of fines is to provide a deterrent. If fines are applied at a flat rate regardless of income, they must be low enough not to be unaffordable for those who do not earn much money. Consequently, they are set so low that they fail to have a deterrent effect on the richest in society, who are easily able to afford to break the law. A variable rate would avoid this problem.

Possible arguments against

Flat rate is more just

➢ A fine ought to be proportionate to the severity of the crime committed, not the income of the offender. It is fundamental that the justice system should treat all offenders equally; if two people commit the same crime in the same circumstances but one is richer than the other then they have caused the same amount of harm so should pay the same price for that harm. Having a richer person pay more implies that crimes by the rich are necessarily more harmful to society regardless of what the crime actually is.

Conclusion

➢ Summarize points made on both sides of the argument concisely and draw ends together.

➢ One option is to have an open ended conclusion – if one values justice then parking fines should not be based on income, however if one values the effectiveness of the law, then parking dines should be based on income.

"The cause of gender inequality is in the hands of men, but the solution is in the hands of women." Do you agree?

Although this question, at first, appears complex, the question is made easier to answer simply because the statement involved is extreme. As a result, and as we shall see below, it is very easy to take the statement at the heart of this question apart and analyse each section individually. As well as helping to create a more clear structure to your essay which is often difficult with these philosophical questions, it also makes it far easier to answer the question and make a convincing argument. However, in dissecting this quite extreme statement, it is very important that the conclusion you reach is not equally extreme in nature. It is tempting to simply refute the statement, as such a refutation is easy to make. What makes a better response is the formulation of a counter statement which you can argue better sums up the reality of the situation.

Introduction

➢ One possible approach is to contextualise the argument by firstly defining what is meant by gender inequality.

➢ One meaning could be a financial one – women are paid less than men for the same job. Another could be that it is an issue of power – there are fewer women in positions of power than men.

➢ If at all possible, introduce a figure from the news – for example only 32% of MPs are female, or for every £1 a man earns a woman earns 80p.

Argument

➢ In this case it is very importantly to look very closely at the statement. It is clear that there are two parts:
   1. The cause of gender inequality is in the hands of men
   2. The solution is in the hands of women

➢ A good approach would be to split the statement up into these parts and to then assess each part individually. (It is perfectly acceptable to agree with one and disagree with the other)

➢ A possible argument for 1) is that men occupy the majority of positions of power, and for 2) that it is only through campaigning for themselves that women will be able to overcome gender equality.

➢ Another approach could be to reverse and then critically assess the statements– i.e.:
   1. The cause of gender equality is in the hands of women
   2. The solution of gender equality is in the hands of men

➢ Possible arguments in favour of these statements could be that 3) gender equality still exists because women have not campaigned hard enough or 4) men dominate the power structure of society, therefore only they have the power to change it. (NB. these are both counter arguments to points 1) and 2).

➢ It is quite obvious that the way the question is worded leads to arguments which focus solely on one gender or the other either causing or giving the solution to gender inequality. How likely is it that this is the case? Another option could be that it is either the fault of neither gender, it is simply the result of biology, or that it is the result of both genders.

Conclusion

➢ Summarize the main points made on each side of the argument in the essay.
➢ Link back to the original quote – play with it if you need to.
➢ You may wish to come to a decision either way, or it is equally fine to sit somewhere in the middle, so long as this is fairly justified

END OF PAPER

2009

Section 1

Question 1: D

The argument discusses various reasons why people should be allowed to work beyond the current compulsory retirement age, and then strikes down a possible reason why the compulsory retirement age should continue to be enforced (the notion of struggling to get rid of inefficient elder employees). If we accept all these given reasons as true, it gives us good cause to accept the statement in D), thus answer D) correctly identifies the main conclusion.

Answers B) and E) are both reasons given in the passage to support this conclusion.

Answer A), meanwhile cannot be reliably concluded from the passage as the passage makes no reference to the fairness of the current compulsory retirement age. Answer C) is also irrelevant as the argument suggests the retirement age should be *abolished*, not raised.

Question 2: C

If 5cm is folded up on each side, the box is 40cm by 40cm on the bottom (50cm minus two lots of 5cm). It is 5cm high. Hence the volume is 5 x 40 x 40 cm, which is 8000cm^3. Hence the answer is C.

Question 3: D

The argument describes some biological tendencies of boys and girls, and how these may be causing the differences in performance between boys and girls in school. It then goes on to conclude that this means failing teachers cannot be responsible.

D) correctly points out that just because biological tendencies may be causative, does not mean they are entirely responsible for the observed phenomenon. Thus D) correctly identifies a flaw in the argument's reasoning.

A), B) and E) are irrelevant to how the argument's reasons lead on to its conclusions, so are not flaws. Meanwhile, Answer C) is not relevant because the argument is discussing how the inferior verbal and emotional skills of boys are causative, and makes no reference to the effect of their greater skills in calculating and planning.

Question 4: B

The argument discusses how shortening the length of degrees would produce lower quality graduates, and then states that any move which results in lower quality graduates should be resisted by Universities. From this, it readily follows on that Universities should thus oppose the shortening of degree lengths from 3 years to 2 years, so B) is the correct answer.

Answers A) and E) are completely irrelevant to the argument's reasoning, so cannot be concluded. Answer C) is also irrelevant as the argument describes how universities should *resist* the move, making no reference to whether they are proposing it.

Answer D) is irrelevant because the argument refers to what *Universities* should do, not students.

Question 5: E

The passage describes how there are 2 options for treating depression: drugs, which alter the chemical balance of the brain, and psychotherapy. It then concludes that if we do not wish to alter the brain's chemical balance, we should choose psychotherapy. At no point is it stated that psychotherapy does not alter the chemical balance of the brain, and we can see that if this is not true, then this conclusion is no longer valid. Thus, E) is the answer.

A), B) and D) are all completely irrelevant, as the argument makes no reference to the causes of depression or which treatment is more effective.

C) is also irrelevant, since the argument refers to *if* we do not wish to alter the chemical balance, and it is stated that drug treatments do this, so the situation in C) is not relevant.

Question 6: C

Last time Jenny put petrol in the car, it had 5 litres in and she bought $6 worth of fuel at a cost of 60c per litre, which is 10 litres. Hence after filling it up, it had 15 litres in. She then drove 50km. Her car travels 100km on 8 litres of petrol, hence travelling 50km will use 4 litres of petrol. Hence the next time she goes to fill it up, it will have 11 litres in (15 minus 4). Since the tank holds 50 litres, Jenny will put 39 litres of fuel in (50 minus 11) if she fills it right up. At 50c per litre, 39 litres of fuel will cost $19.50. Hence the answer is C.

Question 7: E

To answer this question, halve the amounts in the "Period 1" column and compare these new amounts to the amounts in the "Period 2" and "Period 3" columns. We are looking for a row where half the amount in the period 1 column is less than the amount in both the "Period 2" and "Period 3" column. The only row where this is the case is the row for Belgium. Hence the answer is E.

Question 8: D

Imagine the 3 sections of the shape from left to right in the original diagram are named x, y and z.

Shape A can be made by rotating sections x and z inwards in to meet in the middle. Shape B can be made by rotating section x in to meet the bottom of section y and then rotating the whole shape 180 degrees. Shape C can be made by rotating sections x and z round to point upwards.

Shape E can be made by rotating section z in to meet the bottom of section y and then rotating section x in to meet the side of section z.

Shape D cannot be made because if either section x or section z is rotated in to make the hexagonal shape, the other cannot then be in the position on the top due to where it is attached. Therefore the only shape that cannot be made is shape D. Therefore the answer is D.

Question 9: E

The passage discusses how Zoos do not showcase animals exhibiting normal behaviour, and then concludes that it would be preferable to abandon zoos, and instead use the money to protect natural habitats. If the statement in E) is true, then it follows on that the money spent on Zoos already boosts the populations of animals in natural habitats, through re-introduction of animals bred in captivity. This weakens how the argument's reasons lead on to its conclusion, as there now seems little point in abandoning zoos in order to boost/aid natural habitats. Thus E) is the answer.

D) is irrelevant, whilst A) actually strengthens the argument by reinforcing the notion that animals in cramped conditions become neurotic.

Question 10: C

The passage discusses how tests have shown that after intense use of memory, the brain sections responsible for memory are observed to increase in size, and thus the brain increases in size and power when used for a certain purpose. It then concludes that in order that taking part in many IQ tests will boost an individual's IQ. However, this is not a reliable conclusion because nothing in argument states that what applies to memory will also apply to general brain function. Thus, C) correctly identifies a flaw in the argument.

D) is irrelevant to the argument's conclusion. We do not need to have a certain number to accept the premise that many IQ tests will *increase* the brain's power, because no specific quantity of increase is given. E) is a direct refutation of the argument's conclusion and not a flaw. B) is irrelevant to the argument's conclusion, so it is not a flaw.

Answer A) is not correct because the argument has referred to multiple observations, with the London taxi drivers simply given as an *example*. Thus, we do not need them to be representative for the argument's conclusion to be valid, and A) is thus not a flaw.

Question 11: C

The passage discusses how many concerns about expert opinion are justified. Answers D) and E) are simply reasons/facts stated in the passage to support this conclusion, and are not conclusions in themselves. Answer A) is a statement of this conclusion.

The passage then describes how in many cases expert *evidence* is reliable, and not subjective to opinion, and how it would not be desirable for this to be discounted because of justifiable concerns over expert opinions. Answer B) is a statement of this conclusion.

Both of these conclusions go on to support the statement given in C), that we should therefore seek to distinguish expert opinion and expert evidence. Thus, A) and B) are *intermediate* conclusions, whilst C) is the *main* conclusion of this passage. Thus, C) is the answer.

Question 12: B

The round trip takes 4 ½ hours and Ionnais can walk twice as fast on the way back as on the way there. Therefore the trip back takes half as long as the trip there. If we denote the time taken to get BACK FROM the post office as t, then the time taken to get there is 2t. Hence the total time there and back equals $t + 2t = 3t$. Hence $3t = 4 ½$ hours, so $t = 1 ½$ hours. Hence we know that it takes Ionnais 1 ½ hours to do the journey at 4km an hour. Walking at 4km an hour for 1 ½ hours would result in a distance of 6km being travelled. Hence Ionnais lives 6km from the post office. Hence the answer is B.

Question 13: B

We can work out how much 100 minutes of call time will cost on each of the 15 packages given as follows:

	High User	Medium User	Low User
Activering	$50 + (100 \times 0.05) = £55^*$	$20 + (100 \times 0.30) = £50$	$100 \times 0.60 = £60$
Bellaphone	$55 + (100 \times 0.05) = £60$	$20 + (100 \times 0.25) = £45^*$	$100 \times 0.60 = £60$
Canconnect	$60 + (100 \times 0.05) = £65$	$20 + (100 \times 0.35) = £55$	$100 \times 0.55 = £55^*$
Dialfast	$65 + (100 \times 0.05) = £70$	$10 + (100 \times 0.45) = £55$	$5 + (100 \times 0.45) = £50^*$
Engaged	$70 + (100 \times 0.05) = £75$	$10 + (100 \times 0.40) = £50^*$	$100 \times 0.70 = £70$

The lowest cost package is the Bellaphone medium user package, hence the answer is B.

Note: Some of the options can be ruled out without calculation to save time.
For example, the high user packages for all providers apart from Activering are clearly more expensive than the Activering high user package given that the fixed charge is higher and the call charge is the same.

Likewise, the Engaged and Bellaphone medium user tariffs are the only medium user tariffs that need to be calculated because others have the same fixed rental but have a higher call charge.

The low user tariffs for Canconnect and Dialfast are the only low user tariffs that need to be calculated for the same reason. The packages that need to be calculated are asterisked in the table.

Question 14: E

We can write two simultaneous equations to work out how much food is needed for each small chicken and each large chicken. Let the amount of feed needed for a small chicken per day be S & the amount needed for a large chicken per day be L.

1) $100 = L + 2S$
2) $175 = 2L + 3S$

Equation 1 can be rewritten as $2L=200-4S$, and equation 2 as $2L=175-3S$. Therefore $200-4S=175-3S$.

We can rearrange this to $200-175=4S-3S$, hence $S=25$. Substituting this back into equation 1 elicits $100=L+50$, so $L=50$.

So a small chicken needs 25 pellets per day and a large chicken needs 50 pellets per day. Now let's look at the statements:

A is true because a small chicken needs 25 pellets per day and so 30 will last for longer than a day.

B is true because a large chicken needs only 50 pellets per day so 70 will be enough for one day

C is true because a large chicken needs 50 pellets per day and a small chicken needs 25, and 50 is twice 25

D is true because two large chickens would need 100 pellets (50 x 2) and four small chickens would need 100 pellets (25 x 4), making a total of 200 pellets.

E is false because three large chickens would need 150 pellets (50 x 3) and ten small chickens would need 250 pellets (25 x 10), making a total of 400 pellets.

Hence E is the only untrue statement.

Question 15: A

The passages discusses in depth how different types of dishonest acts are committed by different children for different reasons. From this, we can readily conclude that motives behind one child committing a certain dishonest act will not necessarily be there for a different dishonest act. Thus, we can reliably refute the assumption that a child dishonest in one situation may be dishonest in another, and thus A) can be reliably concluded.

Answers D) and E) are incorrect as the argument makes no reference to an overall reason underlying all dishonest acts. In fact, the argument refutes the existence of such a reason.

C) is also incorrect as the argument makes no claim as to what should happen in response to dishonest acts. The argument also makes no claim that *all* reasons for cheating are complex, so B) is incorrect.

Question 16: E

The passage gives many reasons why the hard shoulders should not be utilised to relieve congestion, but then states that the main reason is to maintain Britain's good record of safety on motorways. At no point is it stated that this record is somewhat attributable to the hard shoulders, and if this is not the case this conclusion is no longer valid. Thus, E) correctly identifies an assumption in the argument.

All the other statements are irrelevant, because they have no effect on this conclusion that the hard shoulder should be kept open to maintain the safety record of the motorways. We can readily see that none of the other answers are required to be true for this conclusion to be valid. Thus, none of the other answers are assumptions.

Question 17: C

The passage discusses how speed-reading works, and states that this is of limited use for students as it does not allow a deep understanding of the text to be achieved. We can see that the statement in C) contradicts the suggestion that reading at speed does not lead to a deep understanding, and in fact suggests the opposite. Thus, C) weakens the argument's conclusion.

Answers A) and D) both reinforce the suggestion that speed-reading does not lead to a sufficient understanding for students, and thus these would actually strengthen the argument's conclusion.

Answers B) and E) are irrelevant, as they do not refer to how speed-reading affects a person's understanding of a given text.

Question 18: B

The boy spends at least half his money, so 50c, on gobstoppers. He then spends at least a quarter, so at least 25c, on fruit chews. Fruit chews are 3c each so the minimum he spends on fruit chews is 27c. This leaves 23c for him to spend on other things. We know that he spends at least a tenth of his money, so 10c, on bubble gum. Therefore he spends between 10c and 23c inclusive on bubble gum. At 2c each, this is from 5 to 11 pieces. Hence the answer is B.

Question 19: D

We can go through the calendar and see how many consecutive days in any of the countries are public holidays by observation. From January to March, the longest period of consecutive bank holidays is 5 days. This stretch of holidays occurs from May the 9th (which is a Holiday in Denmark) to May 13th (A holiday in several countries). We see that each day between these 2 dates is a public holiday in at least 1 country. Hence, the Answer is D)

Question 20: A

We can see that Pulley A is half the size of Pulley B. Thus, for every 2 complete rotations of A, B will rotate once if rotating at the same speed (As determined by the Belt connecting Pulley A and the outer pulley of Pulley B)

This means the inside pulley of Pulley B will also rotate once for every 2 complete rotations by Pulley A (since both parts of Pulley B will rotate at the same speed).

We can see that Pulley C is 4 times bigger than the inner Pulley of Pulley B. Thus, for every 4 rotations by Pulley B, Pulley C will rotate once if rotating at the same speed.

Thus, in order to get the number of complete rotations by Pulley C, we divide the number of rotations of Pulley A by 2, then divide this number by 4.

Thus, for every 8 rotations of Pulley A, Pulley C will rotate once. Hence the answer is A).

Question 21: D

The passage discusses how the widespread prevalence of the English language is given as a reason for the poor performance at learning languages, since they have little need to speak other languages abroad. It then refutes this reason, saying that even amongst children who have never been abroad the English are poor at learning languages. It then concludes that this must mean the reason is actually that English schools are poor at teaching languages.

Answer D) correctly points out that there may be a whole host of other reasons behind this phenomenon, so the argument's conclusion is incorrect. Thus D) is the answer.

Answer B) actually strengthens the argument, by suggesting other languages are also widespread, thus reinforcing the notion that the widespread nature of English is not a reason for the poor performance of the English in learning languages. A) is irrelevant, as the reasons behind why English schools may be deficient at teaching languages (such as poor funding) do not affect the fact that they are deficient. E) is also irrelevant as the fact the English are poor at learning languages is a stated fact in the argument, which we thus accept as true for the purposes of a critical thinking assessment. Hence, it does not require proof in this context.

Answer C) is incorrect because the sample is given to refute the notion that lack of requirement to speak foreign languages abroad are the reason behind the poor performance of the English. Thus, the sample does not need to be representative of the population in order to be valid for its purpose.

Question 22: D

The passage's reasoning can be summarised as "If A happens, B will happen. If C happens, D will happen. We need D more than we need B, so C will happen". We can see that answer D) follows this same reasoning, with "B" being a pleasant house, and "D" being a pleasant me.

Answer A) differs in that it is stated we do not care about losing weight, not that one option is preferable to the other, thus we will follow the other option.

Answer B) differs in that learning to drive is stated as being needed, but claimed that this can be learned later. This is different from simply claiming it is less preferable/needed than the other option, as in the question.

Answers C) and E) both refer to negative consequences of *not* following one of the options, and thus are different from the question, which simply refers to a choice between 2 positive consequences.

Question 23: A

The passage discusses how users of mobile phones on trains and in restaurants would object if other passengers/customers were to cause noise and disruption to them, and therefore they should not cause disruption to others by using their phones. The principle here is that you should not do something to others that you would object being done to you. Answer A) follows this principle, that parents should not do to their children things that they would object having done to them.

Answers B), C) and E) are completely irrelevant to this principle, whilst Answer D) actually describes an opposite principle (namely that we should accept these annoyances for the sake of other's convenience).

Question 24: B

If Roger and the goalkeeper play the whole match, then there are 9 players on the pitch who are ones who are being "rotated". If there are 16 players in total, without Roger and the goalkeeper this is 14 players. Hence each player will play 9/14 of the whole match, which is 70 minutes. 1/14 of a 70 minute match is 5 minutes as 70 divided by 14 is 5. Hence 9/14 of the match is 45 minutes. Hence the answer is B.

Question 25: C

The question is how far behind June's time zone April lives, because we want to know how much later April thinks 23:30 on Wednesday is than June. April lives 5 hours behind London time and June lives 9 hours ahead. Hence the total time differences is 14 hours. Hence the answer is C.

Question 26: D

The distances from Nickel to the other towns are: 28km, 40km, 63km, 68km, 72km, 102km and 119km.

If the distance from Nickel to another town is 28km, it must be at the end of one of the 28km long roads as no other combination of roads adds up to 28km. Hence Nickel must be P, Q, W, V, S or T.

If the distance from Nickel to another town is 40km, it must also be at the end of one of the lengths of road where a 28km road is connected to a 12km road, as no other combination of roads adds up to 40km. Hence Nickel must be W, S, V or T.

If the distance from Nickel to another town is 63km, it must be also at the end either of the 63km road or at the end of the combination of connecting roads of length 23km, 12km and 28km. Hence Nickel must be T or W.

The distance from T to W is 68km so using this criteria the answer can still be either T or W. However there is no combination of roads from W that adds up to 72km. However, T to R is 72km. Hence the only town that can have this combination of distances to the other towns is T. Hence Nickel is town T. Hence the answer is D.

Question 27: E

The passage discusses how over-qualification is often cited as a reason for rejection, and then argues that there are no circumstances in which someone is actually over-qualified, and thus it should not be cited as a reason for rejection on a job application.

Answers A) and E) are both valid conclusions from this passage, which readily follow on from the reasons given. However, we can see that the statement in A), if true, goes on to support the statement in E), which is also a valid conclusion. Thus, A) is an intermediate conclusion, whilst E) is the main conclusion of this passage.

B) and C) are both restatements of reasons given in the passage, and are not conclusions. They do both go on to support the conclusions given in A) and E).

We can see that D) is required for the conclusion in E) to be valid. If D) is not true, then the fact that nobody can be overqualified for a job does not necessarily mean that employers should not list this as a reason for rejection. However, D) has not been stated. Thus, we can actually see that D) is an assumption in the passage, not a conclusion.

Question 28: D

The passage discusses how the generation born in the 1940s/1950s will have a good chance of living a long lifespan, due to a number of healthy habits they indulge in. It then discusses how the generation currently in their 20s/30s indulge in a number of unhealthy habits, and are thus likely to suffer from health problems and die sooner. We can see from this summary that we have only been given information on 2 generations, and thus we cannot conclude what trends are present among life length for different generations, and how these are likely to change on the whole. Thus, the statement in C) cannot be concluded, as it refers to a trend of "ever-increasing life expectancy", which we cannot conclude exists based on the information in the passage.

B) and E) are completely irrelevant as the passage makes no reference to the causes of such healthy/unhealthy habits, or the effects on the health service that will follow. Thus, B) and E) cannot be concluded.

However, we *can* conclude that it would be wise for the "big mac generation" to change their habits, as the passage has discussed how these will lead to decreased life span and more health problems. Thus, Answer D) can be reliably concluded.

Answer A), meanwhile, is actually an assumption in the passage. We can see that if this is not true, then the argument's conclusions are no longer valid. Thus, A) is an assumption and not a conclusion.

Question 29: B

The passage discusses how the law should be changed to allow people to sell their kidneys, because this would result in a greater number of successful kidney transplants. We can immediately see here that this relies on an assumption that some people would be willing to sell their Kidneys, and if this is not true, this conclusion is no longer valid. Thus we can readily see that B) is an assumption. Thus, the answer is B).

The passage then goes on to discuss why we should not be dissuaded by fears of rich patients exploiting poor donors, as this is no different from working in a dangerous occupation. Since the primary reason for changing the law has already been given, this additional discussion is no longer *required* to be true for the argument's conclusion to be valid. Thus, C) is not an assumption, as it is not required to be true for the conclusion to be valid.

D) and E) do not affect the conclusion. Whether foreign transplants are successful or not does not affect whether more donors in the UK would result in more successful transplants. Equally, the argument is referring to there being *more* successful transplants, so the notion of whether an adequate supply would be attained is irrelevant.

Answer A) is a completely irrelevant statement.

Question 30: E

If the month of January contains five Fridays, then it must either start on a Wednesday, Thursday or Friday and hence finish on a Friday, Saturday or Sunday. You can see this by writing out the possible combinations of 31 consecutive days starting on each day of the week and counting the Fridays as follows:

MTWTFSSMTWTFSSMTWTFSSMTWTFSSMTW
TWTFSSMTWTFSSMTWTFSSMTWTFSSMTWT
WTFSSMTWTFSSMTWTFSSMTWTFSSMTWTF
TFSSMTWTFSSMTWTFSSMTWTFSSMTWTFS
FSSMTWTFSSMTWTFSSMTWTFSSMTWTFSS
SSMTWTFSSMTWTFSSMTWTFSSMTWTFSSM
SMTWTFSSMTWTFSSMTWTFSSMTWTFSSMT

Hence A is definitely true, as Friday must either be the 1st, 2nd (if the month starts on Thursday) or 3rd (if the month starts on Wednesday). B also could be true because if the month starts on a Wednesday, there will be 5 Fridays (3rd, 10th, 17th, 24th and 31st). C is also definitely true because no matter which of the starting days of Wednesday, Thursday or Friday we pick there will only be 4 Tuesdays. D also could be true as if the month starts on a Friday, the 31st will be a Sunday and hence there will be 5. However, E cannot be true because if the 31st is a Monday, there are only 4 Fridays (7th, 14th, 21st, 28th). Hence the answer is E

Question 31: C

For the 45 weeks the restaurant is open, there are total overhead costs of £45000 (£36000 rent + £9000 other expenses). Hence the overheads cost £1000 a week. The total wages per week are £1200. Hence the total costs paid by the restaurant for all non-food expenses are £2200.

During each week the restaurant is open, it is open for 10 sessions at which on average 20 people eat, so 200 people eat there each week. The food for their meals costs another £1000. Hence the total expenses to the restaurant are £3200.

Splitting £3200 between 200 people is £16. Hence the owner must charge £16 for each meal to cover expenses. Hence the answer is C.

Question 32: C

➢   In map A, 2 stations have 2 connections and 3 stations have 3 connections.
➢   In map B, 2 stations have 2 connections and 3 stations have 3 connections.
➢   In map C, 1 station has 2 connections, 3 stations have 3 connections, and 1 station has 4 connections
➢   In map D, 2 stations have 2 connections and 3 stations have 3 connections.
➢   In map E, 2 stations have 2 connections and 3 stations have 3 connections.

Hence the one map that must be wrong is map C because it shows different connections to the others. Hence the answer is C.

Question 33: A

The passage discusses the timeframe in which batsmen observe a bowled ball and respond with a shot. It then discusses how science claims this is an impossible timeframe in which to react like this, concluding that this means science must be wrong, and failing to explain a phenomenon due to inherent limitations.

However, if we accept the statement in A) as true, then suddenly the claims of scientists seem much more reasonable. It may well be that there is not enough time to consciously react, and that instead a reflex response has to occur, which is much faster than a conscious response. Thus, Answer A) weakens how the reasons in the passage support its conclusion.

Answers C) and D) both strengthen the argument, as C) reinforces the notion of people reacting in timeframes which science claims are impossible, whilst D) reinforces the notion that science may have gaps and limitations which reduce its ability to explain phenomena.

E) is irrelevant as the claim is that such a reaction is *impossible*. The fact that it only happens *sometimes* does not affect the erroneous nature of this claim.

B) is completely irrelevant. It does not matter how the information was found out, this does not affect how correct the claims of scientists are about it.

Question 34: D

The passage argues that education standards are failing, and that government claims of improving standards are driven by tests simply becoming easier. The main evidence to support the notion that education standards are falling is that in recent tests almost half of students attained below average results.

However, D) correctly identifies that this is flawed evidence. If we calculate the average of the scores in a given test, we would expect it to be somewhere around the middle, with roughly half of people performing above-average, and roughly half performing below-average. Thus, this figure does not say anything about the quality of the test of the levels of attainment that students achieved. It merely confirms what we would expect due to how statistics work.

A) simply states the other side of the statistic given in the test, and thus does not affect the argument's reasoning.

B) and C) are irrelevant to the notion of whether standards are falling, and whether we need to return to teaching methods of the 1950s, so are not flaws.

E), meanwhile, correctly points out that there could be other explanations for falling standards, but is not a valid flaw. Just as we cannot conclude falling standards are due to failing teaching methods, neither can we conclude that they are due to changed social attitudes. If E) stated that the falling standards *could* be due to differing social attitudes, then this would be a valid flaw. However, since E) presents a fact that cannot be *certainly* concluded, it is not a valid flaw.

Question 35: B

The passage discusses how we may *admire* certain acts, but cannot refute that they are morally wrong. It argues that many acts (such as those stated) would be described as morally wrong by anyone who knew what this phrase meant, and thus some things can be shown to be morally wrong as much as the snow can be shown to be white.

From this, we can reliably conclude that the statements in B), C) and E) are true. Thus, these are all valid conclusions from this passage. However, we see that Answers C) and E) both go on to support the statement in Answer B). Thus, C) and E) are *intermediate conclusions* from the passage, whilst B) is the main conclusion.

Answers A) and D) are *not* valid conclusions from the passage. The passage discusses how certain acts are *definitely morally* wrong, but it is *possible* to admire them and think that they are right. Thus, we cannot conclude that such acts are *wrong*, only that they are *morally* wrong. Equally, there is nothing in the argument that means we can definitely state that they are *right*, we can only conclude it is *possible* to take this view. Thus, neither A) or D) can be reliably concluded from the passage.

Question 36: B

If 50 calories would be used from rowing 500m, then rowing 400m would use 40 calories (50 x 4/5)
If 55 calories would be used from rowing 500m, then rowing 600m would use 66 calories (55 x 6/5)
For the third session, 60 calories were used for the first 500m. For the remaining 300m: if 40 calories would be used from rowing 500m, then rowing 300m would use 24 calories (40 x 3/5).
Hence the total calories used is 40 + 66 + 60 + 24 = 190.
Hence the answer is B.

Question 37: D

The only factor relevant to whether the tree will obscure the block of flats is its height. The question also refers to *when the tree is fully grown*, thus growing time is irrelevant. Thus, we can safely ignore the columns detailing the features, growth speed and width, and just focus on the height of the trees. This simplifies the question considerably.

We can see that a bush 1.6m in height obscures a building 7m tall.

The new building to be obscured is 20m, which is roughly three times the height of the Bungalow. We know that the distance away from the observation point, and the observation point itself have remained the same. Thus, we know the new tree must be roughly three times the height of the bush to obscure the block of flats.

Three times 1.6 is 4.8. Thus, we look for a tree which is at least 4.8m high. We also know that Mrs Brown wishes the tree to be as small as possible whilst obscuring the flats, so we are looking for the smallest tree which is at least 4.8m high when fully grown. This is the Hornbeam. Thus, the Hornbeam would be the most suitable tree.

Question 38: D

We cannot infer anything about Northern Irish house prices from this graph unless we are given information about UK house prices as whether they are true or false depends on Northern Irish house prices not on the ratio of Northern Irish to UK house prices, so we cannot say for sure that A, B or E are true. We also cannot say that C is true because it is impossible to infer anything about UK house prices from this graph without knowing what happened to Northern Irish house prices. We can however say that D is definitely true because in some years, the gradient of the graph was positive (the line goes upwards) which means that in that year Northern Irish house prices rose as a percentage of the UK average in that year. Hence the answer is D.

Question 39: A

The passage states that policies to prevent drink driving often rely on severe penalties as a *deterrent*. It then claims that such policies are only a deterrent *if* people perceive a moderate or high chance of being caught for these offences, and that people *do not* perceive the chances of being caught are moderate or high. Thus, the *if* has not been satisfied, and we can readily conclude that severe penalties do not constitute an effective deterrent. Thus A) is the answer.

B) is not correct because the passage only claims that governments have *tended* to rely on severe penalties. Thus we cannot conclude that they have **not** tackled the problem of drink-driving.

C) and E) are incorrect as the passage makes no reference to what the actual chances of being caught are, or whether other policies would be more effective. Stating that one policy is not effective does *not* necessarily mean that another will be effective.

D) is incorrect because the passage has discussed how severe penalties are not having an effect due to low perceptions of the chances of being caught. Thus, it follows that even more severe penalties would also be ineffective.

Question 40: C

The key to this answer lies in the passage's claim that "the **only fair** solution" is to take a levy from the pay of top athletes, to foster the development of up-and-coming athletes. At no point is it stated that the general taxpayer subsidising development of young athletes is **not** fair, and if this is not true, then suddenly we are presented with another **fair** option, and thus the argument is no longer valid. Thus, the argument relies on the assumption stated in C).

Answers A) and D) are incorrect because the passage simply claims that some athletes will fail due to lack of money if we do not take a levy from top athletes. How many will fail is irrelevant to the validity of this statement, so A) is incorrect, whilst D) is incorrect as the passage has *stated* that some will fail so we must accept this as true, and thus possible solutions for up-and-coming athletes are not relevant.

Statements B) and E) are irrelevant as the passage does not refer the notion of athletes becoming winners (it simply states that we should help not to fail due to money issues) or whether top athletes deserve their pay (it merely states they expect it as a reward). Thus, neither of these answers affects the **argument's reasoning or its conclusion.**

Question 41: D

The passage discusses how children whose parents act aggressively towards them often grow up to be violent, and concludes that if this were stopped we could eliminate a lot of violence from society.

The passage refers to what would happen *if* we could stop aggression towards children, so any comments on how difficult/impossible this is are irrelevant. Thus A) is incorrect.

C) and E) are irrelevant. What the distinction is between reasonable discipline and aggression, and the causes of aggression are irrelevant to the effects that aggression produces, so neither of these answers affect the argument.

B) does not weaken the argument because it makes no reference to the effects of aggression towards children. The fact that children of aggressive parents are not themselves aggressive does not affect how aggression in the first instance produces violence in people. Thus, B) does not affect the argument's conclusion.

D) does weaken the arguments as it states that other factors are *the major* causes of aggressive behaviour in both adults and children. If this is true, then it suggests prevent aggression from parents will not affect the major reasons behind aggression/violent tendencies in children, thus weakening the conclusion that this would eliminate *a significant proportion* of violence.

Question 42: E

There are 16 multiples of 3 between 1 and 49 inclusive (3, 6, 9, 12, 15, 18, 21, 24, 27, 30, 33, 36, 39, 42, 45, 48).

There are 9 further numbers which contain a 3 (13, 23, 31, 32, 34, 35, 37, 38, 43)

There are 3 further numbers which contain a 6 (16, 26, 46)

There are 3 further numbers which contain a 9 (19, 29, 49)

Hence the total amount of numbers that fit one or more of the criteria is $16 + 9 + 3 + 3 = 31$

Question 43: B

Oliver will be leaving on the 10th anniversary of beginning to work for the company. Thus, this will be at the end of his 10th year of working for the company. The allocation for this year is 25 days holiday. Thus, this will be the amount granted when Oliver hands in his notice, in order to stave off bad publicity.

We can see that in his 9th Year, Oliver took 20 days holiday time, which is 5 days less than the entitlement for the year, 25 days. Thus, 5 days will be carried forward to the 10th year.

Thus, a grand total of 30 days holiday will be allowed. Subtracting the 5 days of holiday already taken, we can see that this will result in 25 days *more* being allowed before he leaves.

Question 44: C

Over a wide area, the pattern can be considered a repeat of the section below.

This pattern contains 1 hexagon and 12 triangles.

Hence the answer is C.

Question 45: A

The passage discusses how agriculture and conservation have conflicting interests in wetland areas, with agriculture wanting to drain the wetland, and conservation wanting to not drain the wetland areas. The passage then acknowledges the conflict here, and says that because of this, an independent body should regulate wetland areas to achieve a balance.

We can readily see that the different intentions (draining and not draining) are mutually exclusive, so are irreconcilable. Thus, C) is a valid conclusion from the passage. B) and A) are also valid conclusions from the passage, and we can see that B) and C) both go on to support the statement in A). Thus, A) is the main conclusion, and B) and C) are *intermediate conclusions* in this passage.

D) is actually an assumption in the passage. At no point has it been stated that wetland *needs* to cater for both interests, and if this is not true we can no longer conclude that a balance must be struck – we could simply ignore one of the two opinions. Thus, D) is an assumption, and not a conclusion.

E) is an irrelevant statement, which is not a conclusion and is not *required* for the argument to be valid, so is not an assumption either.

Question 46: A

Time spent travelling can be viewed as the direct result of speed of travel and distance travelled. We can see here that if either of these two factors changes, it will directly affect time spent travelling. Thus the passage's reasoning describes a circumstance where one factor (Factor Z) is a direct result of 2 others, and that Factor Z is remaining constant. We are then told that if one of the factors contributing to factor Z is changed, the other factor must also change accordingly, such that Factor Z remains constant.

Only answer A) follows this pattern. Here, Factor Z is the mortgage as a proportion of annual income. This will obviously be directly affected by the size of the mortgage and the annual income in question. Since Mortgage as a proportion of Annual income is remaining around the same level, if annual incomes change, the size of the mortgage must change accordingly. Thus A) is the answer.

B) is not the same reasoning because there are many other factors in "total expenditure per household" than food. Thus, if food becomes more expensive, it *does not* mean that total expenditure will increase, so we cannot conclude that mortgage repayments will also increase.

C) is incorrect because inflation is not dependent on the rate of a mortgage repayment. Thus, we cannot include the fixed rate mortgage repayments in a calculation of how inflation will change.

D) is incorrect because there is a distinction between the number of homes present and the number of homes *owned*. Thus we cannot draw conclusions about things which are linked to home ownership from the building of new houses.

E) is incorrect because the number of old houses being renovated is not necessarily linked to the number of old houses on the market. More old houses could be put on the market without renovation, so E)'s conclusion is not valid.

Question 47: A

The passage refers to a situation where there is a *small* risk of a negative consequence occurring. However, *nothing can be done* about the risk, and informing people would cause unnecessary distress.

Only Answer A) follows this principle, where the risk of damage is small and nothing can be done about it, and informing people of the possible risk would cause worry and distress.

B) is different because in this instance, there is already a confirmed negative consequence, not a small risk of one. This is different from the principle in the question. C) follows a similar pattern, the train *is* delayed, so the negative consequence has already been confirmed, which is different from there being a small risk of a negative consequence.

D) seems to be correct; as the child may or may not be distressed by finding they are adopted. However, this is different from the principle in the question. In D), the event of adoption has already occurred, whilst the risk is causing distress. This is different from *definitely* causing distress by informing about *the risk* of an event occurring.

E) is different from the question because something *can* be done about this negative event. The child could implement new working strategies etc, so this is not the same as a situation where nothing can be done about a possible negative consequence.

Question 48: C

We can picture that in order for a driver to return to X during the shortest possible journey, some of the towns must be in directly opposite directions from X. Thus, it would be quickest to return to X, between visiting these 2 towns.

We can also see that this can only be the shortest journey if the third town is located on the opposite side of X from one of these two towns, such that a straight line drawn from X would go through both these towns. (Otherwise it would be quicker to head from the town on the opposite side of X straight through to this third town). If this is the case, then the quickest route is to visit the town opposite X from these two, then return to X, then visit the second town, then the third town, *then visit the second town again* on the way back to X.

We can see that route C must have this setup of towns, but does not visit B again after visiting C. Thus, C) cannot possibly be the shortest route.

Question 49: B

First we must calculate how much rainwater actually falls on the roof. We are told that 160 litres falls on every meter squared of roof, and that there are $25m^2$ of roof in total. Thus, a total of 4000 litres of water fall on the roof (160 times 25 is 4000). We are told that half of this is collected, so a grand total of 2000 litres of rainwater is collected. We are also told that there is never enough rainwater to overfill the butt, so we can assume that all of this 2000 litres is used to refill the pond.

Now we need to calculate how much water Joan uses. This is straightforward. She uses 100 litres a week, for 25 weeks, giving a grand total of 2500 litres of water used. Thus, Joan has collected 2000 litres and used 2500. Thus, there is a 500 litre deficit between the rainwater collected and the rainwater used.

However, we must also factor in the 200 litres of water that was present in the butt at the beginning. When this is included, we get a grand total of 2200 litres of water from the butt used to fill the Pond. 2500 litres was actually used, so Joan will need to use 300 litres of mains water. Hence, the answer is B).

Question 50: E

The view shown in E) is not a possible view because the Red and Yellow sides are in the wrong positions.

We can see from the view given, that when Blue and Yellow are folded round, they will be positioned such that if we are still looking at Red Face-on, the blue will be on the *left* behind the red, and the yellow will be on the *right* behind the red. When we rotate this round to get a top view, we see that if blue is on the bottom, then Yellow must be on the *right*, and red must be on the *left*. Thus, View E) is not a possible view. All other views are possible.

END OF SECTION

Section 2

Albert Einstein wrote that "The whole of science is nothing more than the refinement of everyday thinking." Do you agree?

The essay is easy to structure well; clearly define the rather loose terms 'science' and 'everyday thinking', then begin with the arguments for the case you want to make (that is, in favour of or against Einstein's sentiment). This should naturally be followed with counterarguments these points, and any additional arguments for or against (whichever you have not chosen to support), and then counter-counterarguments to these, and a reaffirmation of your position, which can be made in the conclusion.

Introduction:

Explore what Einstein meant by this quote:

➢ What constitutes 'everyday thinking'? This could be described as the way in which people navigate the world in their general lives – their reasons for believing what they believe and acting as they do.

➢ What constitutes 'science'? You may wish to define this in terms of an active investigation into truth, or an application of the scientific method which answers questions by making observations and drawing conclusions consistent with all that has been observed.

➢ 'Refinement' is also an interesting word – if you argue that there are differences between everyday thinking and scientific thinking, is 'refinement' the right word to describe it?

➢ Einstein is asserting that the way you think in a scientific investigation is an extension of the same logic you already use in your thinking – consider whether you think this is true, or if there are elements of a scientific investigation that are counter to our usual way of thinking.

➢ Clearly state whether you agree or disagree with Einstein and outline your reasons, as in the form "I believe X, because Y; although one could argue Z, this is not the case because W". Though of course this exact formula need not be used, you should make your position similarly clear.

Potential arguments for:

1. The logic used in the scientific method is much the same as the logic used in everyday life. For example, we generally do not accept that an assertion should be considered true unless there is some kind of evidence to support it.

2. *As a response to the second argument against, listed below*: the methods used in scientific research are not equivalent to the 'thinking' that Einstein meant. The 'thinking' constitutes the reasoning and conclusions we draw from evidence, not the evidence itself or our method of acquiring it.

3. The answers we seek to answer in scientific investigations are largely the same questions we have in daily life – why does X behave as it does? Why does Y happens? How do I get Z to happen? People are naturally curious about the answers to these questions from childhood; science is the 'refinement' of this thinking in that it provides a structure and method to the investigation.

Potential arguments against:

1. *As a response to the first argument for*: though it is true that we generally need a reason to believe something, what constitutes an *adequate* reason according to the mainstream scientific method is, or can be, vastly different from what a layperson considers an adequate justification for some other belief.
   a. Counterargument: this is why Einstein has used the term 'refinement'; we accept in everyday life that people should have reasons for believing what they do, but in a scientific investigation we define the terms of what constitutes a good reason.
2. The methods used in scientific research are far removed from the way in which we draw conclusions in everyday life; the use of carefully controlled experiments carried out with the aim of producing evidence for or against a given thesis cannot be considered 'everyday thinking'.
3. Some branches of science require thinking that is highly counterintuitive. Physics concerning very small particles, for instance, is like nothing we encounter in everyday life.
   a. A counterargument to this is that this is not concerned with the thinking about it. While we typically wouldn't think of objects interacting in the way that very small particles do, this is not the 'thinking' that Einstein meant; he meant our thinking is naturally investigative and rational, and these two qualities still apply when we are launching scientific investigations into not very everyday things. We still investigate and use our observations to draw conclusions, even if these conclusions seem bizarre at first.

Conclusion:

➢ Restate your position and summarise your main arguments.
➢ Be sure to closely link your conclusion to the original quote, mentioning scientific methods and everyday thinking.

If 'Humanitarian Intervention' is acceptable, why shouldn't Europe invade the USA to stop it using the death penalty?

This question can be read as asking two things – if 'humanitarian intervention' is acceptable, and, if it is, whether it is acceptable in this situation. As such, you should be sure to engage with both questions, asserting your position clearly in the introduction and summarising it in the conclusion. This essay can focus in depth on either the ethical or political considerations posed by the question, or can deal with both approaches slightly more superficially.

Introduction:
➢ Clearly your opinion in the introduction, and outline your reasons for holding it, as well as the counterarguments you will present and your reasons for dismissing them.
➢ Define 'humanitarian intervention' – a state's use of "military force against another state when the chief publicly declared aim of that military action is ending human-rights violations being perpetrated by the state against which it is directed."
➢ Consider whether humanitarian intervention is *ever* acceptable. If you are going to argue that Europe shouldn't intervene in the USA, you should make it clear whether this is because humanitarian intervention isn't ever acceptable, or it isn't acceptable in this case.

Potential arguments for intervention:
1. The death penalty is immoral and a human rights violation. Arguments for this include:
   a. Every person has the fundamental right to life
   b. European countries have outlawed the death penalty and declared life to be a fundamental right, show they must be of the opinion that the death penalty is a breach of rights
   c. Death is not an acceptable punishment for crime because the justice system is fallible, and this sanction is irreversible.
2. It is our duty to prevent the loss of life and human rights violations where possible.
3. It is unfair to apply foreign policy inconsistently; that we do not intervene when we see injustice in the USA is a result of Britain's desire to maintain our 'special relationship' with the USA, rather than a sound ethical judgement.
4. Intervention in the USA would set an example by showing the world that human rights violations are not acceptable. Additionally, the USA is equally as invested as Europe in keeping our relationship as peaceful as possible, so it is more likely they would be prepared to use methods other than

indiscriminate violent military action in response. Our mutual need means intervention in the USA is more likely to be productive that intervention elsewhere.

Potential arguments against:

1. The political and military unrest that an attack from Europe on the USA would cause would have consequences far more devastating and lethal than the death penalty is currently having.

2. Military intervention is not an acceptable way in which to address grievances with another country's conduct, or should be used only as a last resort in order to minimise violent conflict. Instead, European governments could petition the USA to reconsider its policy, or use our mutual dependence as leverage by threatening economic sanctions if the death penalty is not revoked.

3. The death penalty is not a human rights violation and is acceptable. Arguments for this include:
    ➢ Some crimes are so horrific and damaging to society that they cannot be forgiven, nor can there be any attempt at rehabilitation.
    ➢ The death penalty acts as a deterrent and prevents reoffending, and so decreases violent crime overall.

4. The USA is a democracy, meaning the laws that uphold the death penalty were instated by politicians given power by the electorate; as foreigners, for us to launch an intervention is to undermine democracy and their right to self-determination as a nation.
    a. A counterargument to this is that democracies are vulnerable to a tyranny of the majority. If there are not adequate safeguards to protect a vulnerable minority, it is our moral duty to aid them.

5. The use of the death penalty in the USA is relatively rare and used only in response to violent crimes; we should focus our efforts in countries where it is more common and used as punishment for 'crimes' such as civil disobedience or homosexuality.

Conclusion:

➢ Restate your position and your main arguments for it, as well as why you've not agreed with your counterarguments.
➢ Link it back to the question by specifying whether humanitarian intervention is in fact acceptable in any case, and then whether it is acceptable in this situation.

If you can give reasons for your actions, does that mean that your actions are rational?

The major argument in this essay is over the definition of 'rational' and whether it should include a criteria for a good or correct reason for acting; it is around this argument that it is most advisable you structure your essay.

Introduction:

➢ Give a broad outline of the definition of 'rationality' that you are going to be arguing for and give a broad outline of your reasons for doing so. Also introduce the counterarguments to your view, and your reasons for dismissing them.

➢ It is worth giving a brief explanation of how you will be using the word 'reason'. You will probably want to establish that the 'reason' must be true, it cannot simply follow the formula "I performed X action because Y", but rather the agent must truly have acted because of the fact of Y, or because they believed the fact of Y (and this distinction, as we will see, may be important later in the essay).

Potential arguments for:

➢ Rational action consists of actively pursuing a goal by acting in the way you think will enable you to achieve it. For example, if my goal is to quench my thirst, I drink water because I believe this will stop me being thirsty. Further, this follows even if my belief is false; for example, if my goal is to quench my thirst, and I brush my hair *because I believe this will stop me being thirsty*, I was rational even though I was wrong.

➢ Rationality means doing the most advisable thing given the resources you have – this includes information, mental faculties, and potential courses of action. If, from the resources available to you, you have drawn, say, the conclusion that brushing your hair will quench your thirst, then it makes sense to perform this action.

➢ The example used is deliberately absurd to demonstrate that the way of thinking, rather than how correct the belief is, is what is important to rationality. You may demonstrate that, in fact, this follows from how we view more typical cases of rationality in situations of false beliefs.

- For example: I want to catch the train at 4:30. I think it will take me an hour to get to the station, and I want to leave some time spare in case of a delay, so I leave at 3:00. A major accident happens while I am on my way to the station, delaying me by over an hour, and so I miss my train. In this situation, did I act rationally in leaving at 3:00? Most people would say yes, on the basis that although it later transpired that I had not left adequately early in order to catch my train, I chose the leaving time most recommended according to the information available to me – my beliefs regarding how long it would take me to get to the station and my beliefs regarding how much extra time I should leave in case of an emergency. Once we have established this as the definition of rationality, we can extend it to demonstrate that even in the more absurd scenarios, it follows that giving a reason for your action is all that constitutes rationality.

Potential arguments against:

The criteria for rationality is more stringent than in the argument given above – you must be able to justify that your *reason* was rational, not just that you *have* a reason.

➤ If you reason must be rational, there is the possibility of starting an infinitely regressing chain of explanations. When I say I perform X action to achieve Y goal, I must ask why I believe X will achieve Y. I give the answer Z. Why, then, do I believe Z means that X will help me achieve Y? The question here is whether these subsequent questions constitute an element of X action's rationality, or whether they are questions regarding a completely different rationalisation.

➤ If you take the former side – that they are necessary questions for establishing the rationality of X – then you may use this as an argument for answering 'no' to the essay question, but you are left with a further question you must answer: how far back in this chain do you have to go to establish rationality? Since this is a very obvious counterargument, if you make this argument you must be prepared to address it.

➤ You may give an answer to this counterargument along the lines of "you must rationalise your reason for X by one step, anything further than that is irrelevant", but this is weak to two further counterarguments:

- The line you draw between what is relevant and what is not is arbitrary.
- You may respond to this counterargument by reasserting that we are asking whether X action is rational, and giving Y reason. To ask whether Y reason is rational is a different question. This is why there are two

levels of justification – the reason for performing the action, and the reason the reason is a good one – and not any further levels.

- However, this argument is vulnerable to counterexamples such as: "I drink water to quench my thirst. I believe drinking water will quench my thirst because some dogs are brown." Since you are not required to justify the rationality of your reason for X, this would have to be considered valid. This is the case for any arbitrarily drawn line – you do not have to justify the rationality of your final reason, and so it can be utterly nonsensical and still be acceptable.

➤ A 'reason' alone is not enough to establish rationality; there are qualifications on what this reason must be in order to be sufficient. One condition is that you must be correct in thinking that Y action will cause X desire to be fulfilled. E.g.: the drink water because you are thirsty is rational because you are correct in thinking that drinking water will quench your thirst. You are not rational in brushing your hair because you are thirsty because brushing your hair will not quench your thirst.

- If you argue this case, you can give a subtle answer to the question in your conclusion – yes, but additionally the reason must be adequate, with X being the conditions for adequacy. Having a reason is a necessary condition for rationality – meaning you need one in order for your action to be rational – but it is not a sufficient condition – meaning it is not by itself enough to make an action rational.

➤ There are lots of things we do that we don't consciously justify or even choose to do, that we might still want to describe as rational. We might say something like being scared of heights is rational because it is a subconscious fear developed through the process of natural selection that stops us going near dangerous high cliffs, for instance, where we might fall and die. Though we can give an *explanation* of why are scared of heights, this isn't a *reason* because a reason is something you have for an action you choose to do. There are lots of examples of this – breathing, being around other people, sleeping.

Conclusion:

➤ Reassert your point of view and summarise the main arguments from your essay.

➤ Since most of this essay was concerned with definitions, restate your definition of reason and rationality, and summarise why that means a reason does or does not make your actions rational.

What changes in society will follow from increased life expectancy?

This question is very vague and leaves a lot of scope for you to decide exactly what you want to write about. Since the question does not specify things like by how much life expectancy will increase, or over what time frame this increase will occur, you should be sure to always fully justify and qualify your answer with under what conditions you believe these changes will occur – unless you believe they will occur under any conditions of increased life expectancy, in which case this, too, should be stated and justified. In terms of structuring the essay, you may wish to group your changes into categories – for example, legal changes, philosophical changes, lifestyle changes – in order to prevent your essay seeming like a list as you deal with each potential change.

Alternately, you could focus on the most significant changes that will occur, and explore the reasons for and against thinking they will happen in greater depth. In either case, be sure to explain the reasons one might have for believing these changes will not happen as well, and your reasons for dismissing these arguments.

Introduction:
➤ You should consider exactly what is meant by 'increased life expectancy'; presumably it amounts to an increase in the average age at which citizens die. There are two points to consider in relation to this:
  • Does it increase evenly across all demographics, or do the lives of the rich increase in length dramatically, while the lives of the poor not at all, or only by a relatively small margin?
  • How does your health fare as life continues?
➤ Doing this allows you structure your essay in the form "under X conditions, Y will occur, but under Z conditions, W will occur, for each condition to 'increased life expectancy' you consider relevant.
➤ You may wish to decide on one or a few of what you believe will be the major changes, and outline them here. Smaller points that will take up only a sentence or two later in the essay need not be mentioned in the introduction if you are covering a lot of changes, but be sure to outline your main points.

Potential changes:
➤ If health is still (in most of the population) good for the majority of one's lifespan, the ages at which people are expected (rightly or wrongly) to meet certain milestones will likely increase – this includes marriage, having children, and retiring.
➤ If health still declines severely after what we now consider to be middle-aged, healthcare services will have to expand rapidly to cover the rising demand.

We will also need to cover production of this, and other needs (including food production), with a proportionally smaller workforce, since less of the population will be of what is now considered 'working age'; our work will therefore have to become more efficient, and there may be a need to increase taxes to fund the necessary work.

➢ If access to the increased life expectancy is determined by, say, wealth, this may cause more fractioning and conflict in society, as those able to afford the healthy lifestyle that lends itself to longevity see even more tangible results.

Changes in the way we experience life:

➢ With more life, it is possible to argue either we will gain both in terms of quantity and quality of our experiences. As well as having more time in which to experience life, the extra time will lead to an increase mastery of skills by individuals (this will also depend on how healthy people are after a certain age). We may therefore see rapid development of technology or the arts as the masters in these fields have more time to work before passing.

➢ Alternately, with more life on our times, we may experience a decrease in a sense of urgency and motivation and so become complacent, and no such developments will be made, but instead development will slow as people no longer need to rush their cultivation of skills due to more limited time.

➢ We could also become bored with growing lifespans; this is especially the case if health still declines after middle age. With an aging population in ill health, society will have to develop ways in which to keep the population happy and entertained.

➢ People sticking around for longer could have two potential effects:

• With more time to learn and gain experience, people gain emotional and moral maturity. Society will benefit from the increase in a number of people with much more life experience; we will be able to take guidance from them in more wisely writing laws, etc.

• People's emotional and moral maturity will not increase as a result of longer lives because people stay the same after they have been socialised as a young person (after the age of about 25, say), and so increased life expectancy will have negative impacts on the moral growth of society as a whole; with slower turnover rates between generations, we will be 'stuck in our ways' longer, which will prevent positive social change.

• Further to both these points, an increase in the elderly proportion of the population gives them more voting power, so whichever effect occurs, it will be amplified.

> Retirement is a major point that spans many of those above: with life expectancies increasing, provided they are in good health, people will be expected for longer. This may cause resentment amongst younger generations towards people born before themselves who benefitted from the younger retirement age. It may also cause conflict between classes, as the working class is forced to work for longer whereas those who can afford to retire early simply enjoy a longer retirement as a result of increasing lifespans.

Conclusion:

> Summarise the most important changes, and the most important variables in determining how society will change.

> It is fine to acknowledge that predicting such effects is difficult, and so not argue too strongly that any particular changes will definitely happen; acknowledge that the future is not certain, and make it clear which changes you think are more likely.

END OF PAPER

2010

Section 1

Question 1: E

The passage describes how most plastic bottles in the USA are PET, and how there are health risks associated with PET recycling. It then goes on to describe how PET does not take up much space in landfill, and how it is not harmful to the environment. At no point is it claimed that PET *cannot* be recycled safely, and this does not necessarily follow on from the passage, as there may be ways to evade the health risks. Thus A) is not a valid conclusion. D) is not claimed by the argument, and is not required for its conclusion to be valid, so D) is an irrelevant point, and is not a conclusion.

E) correctly identifies the main conclusion of the argument, as if all the reasons given in the passage are true, they give us good cause to believe the statement in E). B) and C) are both reasons given in the passage to support this conclusion, and are not conclusions in themselves.

Question 2: D

First we need to work out the ordinary cost for 2 adults and 4 children to go swimming 40 times:
- The 2 adults pay £2 each per session. This is a total price of £80 each, so £160 in total
- The 4 children pay £1 each per session. This is a total price of £40 each, so £160 in total

Thus, the total price without the swimcard would be £320.

The swimcard costs £50 for the year, and allows unlimited swimming for 2 adults and 3 children. The 4th child is charged at half the normal rate. This is 50p per session, so £20 in total for 40 sessions. Thus, with the swimcard the family paid £70 for their 40 swimming sessions.

£320-£70=£250. Thus the family saved £250 with their swimcard.

Question 3: C

The passage discusses how there are many golf accidents, but not many golfers have insurance. It then concludes that insurance could reduce accidents. C) correctly points out that lack of insurance does not *cause* golf accidents, so the argument's conclusion is not valid.

E) is a completely irrelevant statement, so is not a flaw.

A) and C) are not flaws, because the argument is only claiming that insurance would *reduce* the number of accidents. Thus, the statements in A) and C) are irrelevant.

B) is also irrelevant for this reason. If some insurers did not provide adequate cover, this does not mean there would be no reduction in cases thanks to the other insurance policies.

Question 4: D

The argument states that owning handguns was banned in 1997, and that there has been an increase in crimes involving firearms since this action was taken. This does **not** mean that the law has *caused* the increase in crimes involving firearms, so A) is incorrect.

The passage also says that crimes involving legally owned firearms has increased by 0.1%, whilst the total increase has been 5%. However, none of this provides enough information to reliably conclude the statements in B), C) and E). We do not have any information on the number of legally owned firearms, so B) cannot be concluded. We have not been told anything about the number of crimes involving handguns, so C) cannot be concluded.

Equally, the fact that there are clearly now more cases involving illegally owned firearms does **not** mean it has become easier to acquire them (more people could have decided to go to the effort involved, or the number owned may not have changed, and there simply could be more *usage* of illegally owned firearms in crimes).

We can, however, reliably conclude that the law of 1997 has failed to reduce gun crime levels. Thus, D) is the answer.

Question 5: A

The passage concludes that we should not introduce payment schemes where people pay based on time spent on the roads. The reasons given to support this are based on studies done with driving simulators. At no point is it stated that driving simulators are a reliable guide to real life driving, and if this is not true, the argument's conclusion no longer follow on from its reasoning. Thus, A) correctly identifies an assumption.

D) and E) are irrelevant as the argument does not refer to whether these schemes would effectively solve congestion or whether other schemes may have success. It simply says the dangers involved in these schemes mean we should not use them.
C) is also irrelevant, whilst B) actually weakens the argument's conclusion. Thus, neither of these are assumptions.

Question 6: D

The best way to answer this question is to simply find the lowest common multiple (LCM) of 6, 8 and 18. This will be the number of months in which the companies will all make a payment in the same month.
The LCM of these numbers is 72: $(6 \times 12 = 9 \times 8 = 4 \times 18)$
72 months is exactly 6 years. Thus, the companies will all make a payment in the same month in 6 years time, which will be January 1996.
Thus, the answer is D)

Question 7: E

We know the woman is not more than 12 hours late, so the latest time the clock can show is 19:00. This means the first digit on the clock must be either a 1 or a 2. The first digit on the clock cannot be a 1 as the top horizontal line would not be present. Thus, the time must be earlier than 10:00am.
Thus, we know the time must be between 07:00 and 09:59. Thus, the latest time can possibly be is 09:59, meaning the latest the woman can possibly be from examining the first 2 digits of the clock is 2hr 59 minutes.
Now we look at the other two digits and see if a time of 09:59 is possible. The third digit could be a 5, so a time of 09:5X is possible (where X is an unknown number).
The fourth digit could be a 9. Thus, a time of 09:59 is possible. Thus, the latest the woman can be is 2hr 59 minutes.
Hence, the answer is E)

Question 8: B

We are told that an increase of 1 Unit on the Scale represents a ten-fold increase in the strength of the quake. Thus, we know that:
➢ Y is 10 times the strength of X
➢ Z is 10 times the strength of Y
➢ Thus, Z is 100 times the strength of X
➢ Thus, X is 1 hundredth the strength of Z
We can see that only statement B) fits in with these criteria.

Question 9: C

The passage describes how demand for elephant tusks has fallen sharply. It then goes on to describe how *because of this*, there will soon be a decline in elephant poaching. This is the crucial point. Both B) and C) weaken the argument's conclusion, suggesting that high numbers of elephants may be killed. However, B) is not relevant to the argument's reasoning, as the killing methods do not affect how a decrease in demand will affect elephant poaching.

C), however, directly affects how a decrease in demand will affect poaching. It suggests that the decrease in demand *will not* cause a decrease in poaching, because poachers will stockpile for future rises in demand. This directly weakens how the argument's reasons lead on to its conclusion, so C) most weakens the answer. Hence, the answer is C).

A), D) and E) all strengthen the idea that elephant poaching is decreasing/will soon decrease. Thus, none of these weaken the argument.

Question 10: B

The argument describes how breast cancer cases, and average consumption of alcohol by women have both risen in the same time period. It concludes that this means the increased alcohol consumption is responsible for the increase in breast cancer cases. B) correctly points out the readily apparent flaw in this reasoning, namely that it has confused cause and correlation.

D) is not claimed by the argument at any point, whilst E) is incorrect as the argument is only presenting an explanation for an increase, so the size of the increase is irrelevant.

A) and C) are not flaws, because the argument specifically refers to an increase in the *average amount* of alcohol consumed by women in this time period, and the study referred to a number of regional hospitals, so is not overly-localised.

Question 11: C

The argument discusses how in the 18th century there was no way of killing weeds, and close-cutting lawnmowers did not exist. It the finishes with the statement: "given this, lawns must have been like flowery meadows". We can see that this last statement clearly identifies the main conclusion of the passage, which is the statement given in C).

D) identifies an assumption in the passage, claiming that a lawn will more readily exist in a state like a flowery meadow. This must be true in order for the conclusion to be valid, as if it is not, the fact that lawnmowers and weed-killers were not around *does not* necessarily mean that 18th century lawns must have been like flowery meadows.

B) and E) are completely irrelevant statements, whilst A) is an incorrect statement that cannot be concluded from the passage (the fact that without these technologies, the lawns were like flowery meadows does not mean that these are the *only* things keeping modern lawns smooth).

Question 12: D

First, we must calculate the cost of items costing £96, with the reduction.

➢ The reduction is 33%, of the total price.
➢ A third of £90 is £30. 33% is 1 hundredth less than 1 third. 1 hundredth of £30 is £0.30. Thus the total reduction of £90 is £30-£0.30, which is £29.70
➢ A third of £6 is £2. Again, 33% is 1 hundredth less than 1 third. 1 hundredth of £2 is £0.02. Thus, the total reduction of £6 is £2-£0.02, which is £1.98
➢ Thus, the total reduction would be £1.98+£29.70, which is £31.68. Thus, the price after the reduction would be £64.32.

Next we calculate the cost, with a reduction, if extra items are added to £6:

➢ £96+£6=£102. The total cost is now £102.
➢ 50% of £102 is £51. Thus, there is a £51 reduction.
➢ Thus the price after the reduction is £51.

£64.32-£51=£13.32

Hence, the answer to the nearest pound is £13. Thus, D) is the answer.

Question 13: E

The table appears confusing, but to answer this question we actually only need to consider the prices the house holder pair for standard and off peak electricity. We do not need to consider the total number of units *or* the price per unit.

First, we calculate the price she expects to pay for standard electricity for the next quarter:

➢ Last quarter she was charged £168.15 for standard electrical units used.
➢ We are told she has reduced her standard consumption by half. Thus, we expect the charge for this in the next quarter to be half of £168.15, which is £84.075 (or £84.08 to the nearest whole pence)

Then, we can calculate how much she expects to pay for off-peak electricity.

➢ Last quarter she was charged £10.06 for off-peak electricity.
➢ We are told she has increased her off peak consumption by around a factor of 10. Thus, we expect the new charge for off-peak electricity for the next quarter to be 10 x £10.06, which is £100.60

Thus, we expect her to be charged £84.08 + £100.60 for electricity consumed in the next quarter, which is £184.68. We then need to add on the fixed charges described in the last bill (£12.30 + £5.45), which will also be present. Thus, we expect a total bill of £202.43. Thus, we expect a bill of *around* £200.

Question 14: A

We can readily see that if shape B) is used to fill the window, we would need to use 2 of the, one vertical and one horizontal, and that they would overlap in the middle, so B) cannot be used.

If shape C) were to be used, there would be a square shaped gap in the centre of the star shape, and shape C) would only fill in the points of the star. The same problem is encountered with Shape D).

Shape E) would cover this gap, but then each shape would overlap with the shapes either side of it, and thus E) cannot be used.

Shape B) would readily fill the window with no gaps left and no overlap. Thus, A) is the answer.

Question 15: B

A) cannot be confirmed or refuted as we have no information on the tolerance of smoking of young people as a whole. We do not know what percentages of young people approve of smoking, as we have only been given information on those that *do* smoke. D) similarly cannot be refuted or confirmed, as we have no information on how smoking affects a young person's relationship with their parents.

We can see from the table that 63% of parents of young smokers don't like the fact their children smoke, so C) can be dismissed as incorrect.

B) we can reliably conclude as correct. We know that only 19% of young smokers believe their parents do not like the fact they smoke, when in fact 63% of parents do not like it. Thus, B) can be reliably concluded.

E) cannot be concluded because we do not have information on other habits, or how likely parents of non-smokers would be to express strong disapproval of their children smoking. We can conclude that many parents of young people who smoke do not express their strong disapproval, but this does not necessarily mean that E) is true.

Question 16: E

The argument describes how RFR emissions of mobile phone masts have been frequently monitored for masts located near schools and hospitals, and that the levels have consistently been found to be below guideline levels.

The argument then concludes that there is no danger from Mobile phone masts. At no point has it been stated that RFR emissions are the only health risk from mobile phone masts, and we can see that if this is not true then the argument's conclusion no longer necessarily follows on from its reasoning. Thus, E) correctly identifies an assumption in the passage.

B) and D) are irrelevant as they do not affect the argument's conclusion that mobile phone masts do not pose any health threat. A) is also irrelevant as the fact that RFR emissions are more injurious to young people is irrelevant to the fact that the levels being below guideline levels means the mobile phone masts do not pose a health threat.

C) is also irrelevant, and would actually weaken the argument's conclusion, if true, so is not an assumption (an assumption must be needed for the argument's conclusion to be valid, and so cannot weaken an argument's conclusion if true).

Question 17: B

The passage describes how advertising raises costs involved in making products, and thus raises prices for the consumer. It concludes that this means that advertising disadvantages the consumer. If we accept the statement in B) as true, then this suggests that advertising actually benefits the consumer by resulting in a higher quality of goods, thus weakening the argument's conclusion.

A) does not affect the conclusion as the manufacturers' beliefs may be different from the truth, whilst D) is irrelevant as the passage is describing harm to the consumer, so a benefit to the unemployed is irrelevant.

C) and E) both reinforce the argument's conclusion by suggesting there is little benefit to the consumer from advertising, reinforcing the notion that advertising's effects may be negative on the whole.

Question 18: D

The person in the question weighs 80kg. Thus, in each journey in the lift, they can take 320kg of weight in boxes with them.
There are boxes weighing 25kg and boxes weighing 20kg. 12X25=300, thus they can take 12 boxes weighing 25kg on one journey. This leaves an extra 20kg of space, so they can carry one box weighing 20kg on each of these journeys as well. 120/12=10. Thus, in 10 journeys the person can transport all of the boxes weighing 25kg and 10 of the boxes weighing 20kg.

Now we need to account for the remaining 80 boxes weighing 20kg. 320/20=16, so 16 boxes weighing 20kg can be carried on a single journey. 80/16=5. Thus, 5 journeys can transport the remaining boxes weighing 20kg.
5+10=15. Thus, the minimum number of journeys is 15. Thus, the answer is D)

Question 19: B

The meeting is due to last at least 3.5 hours, thus this is the minimum length of parking required. The question has told us that the person cannot leave any later than 5:30, so 5.5 hours is the maximum length of parking required. Thus, we are looking for the car park which offers the cheapest parking for between 3.5 and 5.5 hours:

➢ Grove Street will cost £6.00 for this time range, thanks to the flat rate
➢ Victoria Square will cost between £4 (for 3.5 hours) and £6 (for 5.5 hours)
➢ Central Park will cost between £4 (for 3.5 hours) and £8 (for 5.5 hours)
➢ Bonningtons will cost between £4.50 (for 3.5 hours) and £7.50 (for 5.5 hours)
➢ Grange Road will cost between £4 (for 3.5 hours) and £7.50 (for 5.5 hours)

Thus, the cheapest option is Victoria Square. We can see that no car park has a cheaper charge than Victoria Square for 3.5 hours, and no car park has a cheaper charge for 5.5 hours than Victoria Square. Thus, the cheapest option overall is Victoria Square.

Question 20: D

The taxi charges at a rate of £70 plus £10 per passenger after the first. Thus, the prices are as follows:

1 person = £70.   4 people = £100
2 people = £80   5 people = £110
3 people = £90   6 people = £120

Per person, these prices work out as:

1 person = £70 per person.   4 people = £25 per person
2 people = £40 per person   5 people = £22 per person
3 people = £30 per person   6 people = £20 per person

Only Bar Graph D) follows this pattern.

Question 21: C

The question is describing how more people are choosing to use private healthcare, and how in the same time period, the NHS has suffered a decline. The argument then concludes that this means that people choosing private healthcare has caused the decline in the NHS. Answer C) correctly points out the flaw in this reasoning, that it could be the other way round. It may be people are choosing private healthcare *because* of the NHS' decline, not that people choosing private healthcare is *causing* the decline in the NHS.

E) is not a flaw in the argument because the argument has made no reference to funds being diverted to private healthcare, so this is not relevant to the argument's conclusion.

A) is an irrelevant statement. B) and D) are simply alternative arguments that counteract the one given in the question, and are not flaws in the presented argument.

Question 22: C

The argument's reasoning can be summarised as "A cannot happen because C is so high. C is even higher for B, so B cannot happen either". In this instance, "C" is the cost, and "A" and "B" are Amrik purchasing the 2 software packages.

Only argument C) follows this pattern of reasoning. Here, "C" is the caffeine content of the drinks, and "A" and "B" are Amrik drinking the 2 drinks after 9pm.

A) is different, because in this instance, the garlic is simply *present* in the foods. This is not the same as the garlic content being *even higher* than in a food we know Amrik does not like.

B) is summarised as "A cannot happen because C is too high", but then differs, because "C" (the distance) is lower for the option "B" which is given, so "B" can happen.

D) can be summarised as "A cannot happen because C is too high" (with A being finishing the jigsaw puzzle and C being the patience required), but then incorrectly states that because "C" also factors in "B", this cannot happen either. This is incorrect, and different from the question, because the crossword may require *less* patience than the puzzle.

E) is summarised as "A is less than C, B is greater than C, so A is less than B". This is not the same as the reasoning in the question.

Hence, the answer is C)

Question 23: D

The principle in the argument is that those who use a service more should pay more than those who use it less, such that those who use it less do not subsidise those who use it more. D) illustrates the same principle, with the toll system ensuring that those who use the road more are charged more than those who use it less.

B) is the opposite to this principle, with everybody paying the same regardless of how much they consumed at the restaurant.

C) and E) relate to situations where services are provided to, or charges are adjusted for, different people based on need, not how much of a given service is used. Thus, they do not follow the principle described in the question.

A) is a completely irrelevant statement. Thus, the answer is D)

Question 24: B

It is easy to calculate the possible distributions of letters in this instance. Let the three intended letter recipients be termed X, Y and Z:

➤ If the letter intended for person X is sent to person Y, then the letter for person Y must be sent to person Z, and the letter for person Z be sent to person X.

➤ If the letter intended for person X is sent to person Z, then the letter for person Y must be sent to person X, and the letter for person X be sent to person Y.

This accounts for all possible ways of ensuring everybody receives a letter intended for someone else.

Question 25: B

We are told that a serious claim costs 10 times as much as a slight claim, and that a write-off costs 10 times as much as a serious claim. Thus, a write-off must cost 100 times as much as a slight claim. Thus, to calculate relative costs, we should ignore the grant total of claims. Instead, we should treat each slight claim as 1 unit, each serious claim as 10 units, and each write-off as 100 units. Then, the total number of units will determine the relative cost of the month.

To avoid the need to calculate costs for all 12 months, we should simply calculate the months provided as possible answers, in the interests of time:

➤ January has 2891 slight claims, 539 serious claims and 30 write-offs. Under our system, this gives a total of 11281 units.

➤ March has 2972 slight claims, 550 serious claims and 31 write-offs. Under the system, this gives a total of 11572 units.

➤ June has 3230 slight claims, 509 serious claims and 24 write-offs. Under our system, this gives a total of 10720 units.

➤ October has 3236 slight claims, 474 serious claims and 30 write-offs. Under our system, this gives a total of 10976 units.

➤ Finally, November has 2895 slight claims, 578 serious claims and 21 write-offs. Under our system, this gives a total of 10775 units.

Thus, we can see that March has the most units under our system.
Thus, June is the most expensive month and the answer is B)

Question 26: D

The exact figures are mostly difficult to read on this graph, so the best we can do is to examine the bank balance over the course of the year and deduce the pattern in which the bank balance goes up and down. Doing this, we put together a list of whether each change is positive, negative, or no change, and we see that the order is:

- Negative, Positive, Negative, Negative, Positive, No change, No change, Positive, Negative, Positive, Negative, Positive.

Thus we are looking for a graph that reflects these changes. An important thing to note is that we must remember to look for the change in bank balance in the correct month. For example, a positive change between February and March would result in the correct graph showing a "positive change" *in* the month of March, not in February. We can see that this means whatever change is shown for the month of January (the first month shown) is irrelevant, as we have no information on whether this balance has raised or lowered from the previous month (which we cannot see).

We see that only Graph D) accurately reflects the order of changes on the account.

Question 27: C

The passage describes how all supermarkets now possess loyalty cards, and thus they are no longer an incentive to shop at a single supermarket. It then states supermarkets should abandon these cards, and describes them as costly. It then backs up this conclusion by stating that they cannot be the main reason people shop at a supermarket.

All these reasons, if accepted as true, together provide good cause for us to believe the statement given in C), which thus correctly identifies the main conclusion of the passage.

A) and E) are both simply facts stated in the argument, and are not conclusions.
B) and D) are both valid conclusions that can be drawn from the argument, backed up by reasoning within the argument. However, they both go on to support the statement in C), which is also a valid conclusion from the argument. Thus, B) and D) are intermediate conclusions in this argument, which go on to support the main conclusion, given in C).

Question 28: E

The passage describes how the demand for blood donors is growing much faster than the population of 18-65 year olds which can provide blood donors. At no point does the argument provide reasons why the demand for blood donors is growing, so D) is incorrect. It also makes no reference to changes in the supply of blood donors, or changes in the rate of growth of the relevant populations that can supply blood donors. Thus A) and B) are incorrect.

The argument does describe how there is no medical substitute for human blood, but *does not* say there would be no need for such a substitute if we could find more blood donors. There may be other reasons why it would be desirable to find a substitute, so D) is incorrect.

We can only conclude the statement provided in answer E). If the demand is growing faster than the supply, and a huge research effort has not found a substitute, then we can conclude that there are *no signs* of the problem of increased demand disappearing (we cannot conclude that it will not disappear, but we can conclude there are *no signs* of it disappearing). Thus, E) is the answer.

Question 29: A

The passage describes how there is no evidence that rhinoceros horn has an effect on the nervous system. It then describes how in a clinical trial of people taking powdered rice and people taking rhinoceros horn, more people taking rice had an increase in sexual arousal.

The argument then concludes that Rhinoceros horn is not an aphrodisiac. However, it could be that Rhinoceros horn actually does have aphrodisiac properties, and that Rice simply has stronger aphrodisiac properties, which would explain the results of the clinical trial. If this is true, the argument's conclusion is no longer valid. At no point has it been stated that rice is not an aphrodisiac, so this is a valid assumption in the argument. Thus, the answer is A).

B) and E) are irrelevant to the argument, so are not assumptions.
D) would actually strengthen the argument, adding further reasons why the claims of aphrodisiac properties may be false, so D) is not an assumption.

C) is not an assumption because it is not *required* to be true for the argument's conclusion to be valid. Powdered rice could have non-aphrodisiac effects on the nervous system, and the argument's conclusion would still be valid

Question 30: B

The simplest way to solve this question is to group the men into pairings, and see how much is owed by each person to each of the others.

Thus:
- Bill *owes* £200 to Fred, and *is owed* £300 *by* Fred.
- Fred *owes* £100 to Joe, and *is owed* £150 *by* Joe.
- Joe *owes* £200 to Bill, and *is owed* £250 *by* Bill.

By finding the differences in these amounts we can work out how much each person owes in total.

We see that:
- Bill is owed £100 by Fred.
- Fred is owed £50 by Joe.
- Joe is owed £50 by Bill.

Thus, Fred needs to give £100 to Bill. Bill needs to give £50 to Joe, and Joe needs to give £50 to Fred.

We see here that if Fred gives £50 to Bill, all the debts are cancelled. This is because Fred now owes Bill, Bill owes Joe, and Joe owes Fred, all by the same amount (£50). This is a pointless transaction, as this £50 will simply move around the group, back to Fred.

Question 31: C

We are looking for the cheapest way to purchase aftershave, Talc, body spray and 2 lots of shower gel. We can see that purchasing any pack offers a saving over purchasing all these items separately, so we should purchase as many items in packs as possible without spending extra money on unnecessary items.

We can see that the shower gel and body spray offers a discount for 2 of these products, without purchasing any unnecessary items, and that there are no other combinations which account for both lots of shower gel required without acquiring unnecessary items. Thus, we should purchase the shower gel and Body spray pack, costing £2.99

Now we have accounted for the body spray and one of the shower gels. Thus we can ignore the body spray double pack + free talc, as this purchases unnecessary items, which unnecessarily increases the cost.

There is now a choice to make. Either the Aftershave and Talc pack can be purchased, and then the other shower gel purchased separately, or the Aftershave and shower gel pack can be purchased, and the talc purchased separately:
➢ The aftershave and talc pack costs £4.49, and the shower gel costs £1.49. Thus, these purchases will cost a total of £5.98
➢ The aftershave and shower gel pack costs £3.49, and the talc costs £1.99. Thus, these purchases will cost a total of £5.48. Thus, this is the cheapest option.

Therefore, the cheapest option will cost £5.48, plus the £2.99 for the shower gel and body spray pack. This will cost a total of £8.47.

Thus the answer is C)

Question 32: C

We can see that in 1990, 40% of the adult population smoked, and in 1991, 30% of the adult population smoked. Thus, 10% of the adult population have stopped smoking between 1990 and 1991.

10% is 25% of 40%. Thus, there has been a 25% drop in the number of people who smoke if the number of people who have stopped is expressed *as a percentage of the number of smokers in 1990*. Thus, this is how the campaign organisers have expressed the drop.

Thus, the answer is C)

Question 33: D

The argument discusses how attempts to stop the supply of illegal drugs have not stopped drugs being readily available. It then goes on to say the USA should switch focus and instead attempt to reduce the usage of drugs, and suggests giving treatment to heavy drug users in prisons. If heavy drug users are in fact responsible for the majority of drug offences, then this supports the notion that this action will be effective in reducing the number of people using drugs. Thus, D) readily strengthens the argument.

A) and E) are irrelevant as they do not affect the argument's reasoning or its conclusion.

B) and C), meanwhile, actually weaken the argument. B) suggests that efforts to reduce drug supply are being successful, whilst C) suggests that the suggested action to reduce usage will not be successful, as the users do not wish to receive treatment.

Question 34: D

The passage describes how athletes/those with high levels of fitness are highly susceptible to disease, including cancer, placing them at risk of early death. It then concludes that in order to have a better chance of long-life, strenuous exercise should be avoided. D) correctly identifies the flaw in this reasoning. A high level of fitness may save more lives than the early cancer in this group kills. This would suggest that a high level of fitness *increases* your chances of a long life, thus making the passage's conclusion invalid.

B) is not a flaw because the fact that other reasons may contribute does not necessarily mean that a high level of fitness does not contribute, so the argument's conclusion may still be valid.

C) is incorrect because the passage describes the *chances* of a long life, so the fact that it might not work out that way is irrelevant to the conclusion.

E) is a completely irrelevant statement, whilst A) is incorrect because the argument has stated that studies have shown strenuous exercise damages the immune system, so there *is* evidence.

Question 35: D

The passage describes how road bumps should be abolished in residential areas. It backs this up with reasoning about how road bumps delay emergency services, and cause deaths from heart failures. It states how electronic speed signs and more effective speed limit signings would be just as effective at preventing road traffic accidents.

All of this, if treated as true, supports the notion that road bumps should be abolished in residential areas, which is the main conclusion of the passage.

E) and C) are reasons given in the passage to support this conclusion, whilst A) and B) are simply statements explaining why road bumps are there, a position which the argument goes on to suggest be abolished. Thus, none of these answers are conclusions from this passage. Hence, the answer is D).

Question 36: B

First we need to work out Ted's fuel consumption:

➤ 20km is travelled at 90km/h, as seen in the question. We can see from the table that travelling at 90km/h consumes 6 litres per 100km. 20km is 1/5 of 100, so this will consume 1/5 of 6 litres. Thus, this will consume 1.2 litres.

➤ 40km is travelled at 110km/h. Using similar calculations, we can see that this will consume 2.6 litres of fuel.

➤ 20km is travelled at 50km/h. Again using similar calculations, we can see that this will consume 1.5 litres of fuel.

Thus a total of 5.3 litres of fuel have been consumed. Fuel costs 80c per litre, so this will cost a grand total of 424c, which is $4.24. Thus, B) is the answer.

Question 37: B

First we must calculate how many sheets of paper each pack will use:

➤ The basic information sheet uses 1 sheet of paper, with both sides printed, giving 2 sides.

➤ The prices sheet also involves printing on both sides of 1 A4 sheet of paper, giving a further 2 sides.

➤ The information about local amenities involves 1 side of A4.

Thus, a total of 5 sides of A4 need to be printed for each pack (the colour brochure is provided for free by the local angling association so need not be considered).

With 300 packs to be printed, a grand total of 1200 (5X300) sides of A4 need to be printed at the local printer.

Since the cost of printing is 2p per side, this means the total cost will be 2400p, which is £24.

Question 38: E

If the shapes are examined, we see that they all correspond to the orientations of the different symbols as shown in the 3 views in the question, apart from the die in E).

The Die in E) shows arrow pointing away from the X, which is the correct orientation, as seen in the left-hand view of the question. However, the crescent in Die E) is in the wrong orientation. We can see in the question that the Arrow points toward the face with the two parallel lines, which both lie perpendicular to the direction of the arrow. We can also see that one end of the 2 parallel lines point towards the face with the crescent on, such that they point towards the *concave* side of the crescent.

Thus, we can see that one of the tips of the crescent must point towards the face with the arrow on. In Die E), it is the concave side of the crescent that faces toward the arrow. Thus, Die E) is not the same as the one in the question. Hence, the answer is E).

Question 39: B

The passage describes how when speed cameras are painted yellow, drivers drive quickly between them, braking when they see one. The argument claims this is a dangerous practice. It then describes how if the cameras were almost invisible, drivers would have to stick to the speed limit all the time, for fear of being caught unawares. This does *not* mean that speed cameras were difficult to see, drivers would be *likely* to keep within speed limits. The drivers may simply disregard the risk of being caught by a speed camera, so this conclusion does not necessarily follow on from the passage. Thus, E) is incorrect.

However, the reasons given *do* suggest that making speed cameras visible is not a sensible policy, as it claims the response to obvious cameras is dangerous, which readily gives this conclusion. Thus, B) is the answer.

A) is incorrect as at no point does the argument *refute* the suggestion that obvious cameras act as a deterrent to speeding motorists. It merely claims that this notion is the opposite of what should be followed.

D) is a summary of the reasons in the passage leading onto the conclusion in B), whilst C) could be described as an assumption in the passage, which invalidates the conclusion if it is untrue. Thus, neither of these are conclusions from the passage.

Question 40: E

The passage describes how success in America is measured by possessions, and that those with few possessions are *judged* to be unsuccessful. It then concludes that those with few possessions must feel a strong sense of failure.

For this conclusion to be valid, we are required to accept as true the idea that those with few possessions *wish to be seen* as successful. If this is not true, then the fact that others judge them to be unsuccessful is irrelevant, and does not necessarily lead on to the notion that they will feel a sense of failure. At no point is this idea stated, it is simply assumed. Thus, E) correctly identifies an assumption in the passage. None of the other answers are relevant to the argument's conclusion, so none are assumptions.

Question 41: C

The passage describes how different countries in Eastern Europe (such as Greece, Cyprus, Russia and Ukraine) are consistently voting for one another. It then discusses how as more eastern European countries enter the competition; Western nations will find it difficult to win, before concluding that the result is now decided by geo-politics, not music.

However, if it is true that Eastern European countries have similar tastes in music, this suggests that the Easter European countries' habit of voting for each other *is* based on music, not geo-politics. Thus, C) weakens the argument's conclusion.
B) is a completely irrelevant statement, whilst both D) and E) refer to *past* competitions, so bear no effect on conclusion, which refers to the result *now* being decided by politics, in the present tense. Thus, both D) and E) are irrelevant

A) actually strengthens the argument by implying that western powers have their own, geo-politically decided voting blocks, strengthening the conclusion that geo-politics, and not music, decides the competition.

Question 42: D

Firstly we see that there are 2 possible coffee varieties, caffeinated or de-caffeinated.

Next, we see that each of these 2 possible varieties allows black, or 3 sorts of milk, giving a total of 4 options. Thus we now have a total of 8 options (2X4=8).

Next, we see that for each of these 8 options, we have a total of 5 options relating to sweetener (those being no sugar/sweetener, 1 spoonful of sugar, 2 spoonfuls of sugar, 1 sweetener or 2 sweetener).

Thus, this gives a total of 40 possible options (8X5=40).

Question 43: A

As the question explains, each team carries through half their points from the first round to the next. At the end of this round, the winner subtracts the points carried through from their first round from their total score, to work out their "new" points. This number is then halved, and the resultant number carried through to the next round.

Thus to answer this question, we must track each team from the first round, applying these calculations as described in the question, to see how many points each team will enter the final with.

First we shall assess the Indigo Iguanas:
➢ The team earned 82 points in the first round, so would have carried through 41 for the Quarter Finals.
➢ They finished the quarter finals with 125 points. 125-41=84, so the team earned 84 new points in the Quarter finals. Thus, they carried through 42 to the semi-finals
➢ They finished the semi-finals with 118. 118-42=76, so the team earned 76 points in the Semi-Finals. Thus, they will carry through 38 points to the final.

Now we assess the Orange Ocelots:
➢ The team earned 76 points in the first round, so carried through 38 points through to the Quarter-Finals.
➢ They finished the quarter-finals with 130 points. 130-38=92, so the team earned 92 new points in the quarter-finals. Thus, they carried through 46 points to the Semi-Finals.
➢ They finished the semi-finals with 128. 128-46=82, so the team will carry through 41 points into the final.

Thus, the Indigo Iguanas will begin the final on 38 points, and the Orange Ocelots will begin on 41. Thus, the Indigo Iguanas must earn 4 more points than the Orange Ocelots in the final in order to be victorious.

Thus, the Answer is A)

Question 44: C

There are 5 starred points identified. One of these occupies a central location where 6 paths converge on one point. 3 of the other starred locations are to the left of this point, whilst one is to the right of this central point. Let the 3 starred locations to the left be termed A, B and C, the central point be termed X, and the starred point to the right be termed Z.

We can quickly see that to go from *any* of points A, B or C to point Z, or vice versa, will *always* require going past point X. We can see that X is the *only* point which will *always* have to be passed to make a certain journey. Thus, we can identify X as the Bandstand, which *always* must be passed to move from the statue to the fountain. Hence, we can also see that the Fountain and the statue must be on opposite sides of the bandstand, otherwise you would not *always* have to pass the Bandstand to move between them.

Thus, we now know that the one out of the Fountain and the Statue is Z, and the other is one of A, B or C.

We are then told that to move from the lake to the bowling green, the fountain is *never* passed unless the bandstand is passed twice. This means that the Bowling Green and Lake must both be located on one side of the Bandstand, and the Fountain on the other (otherwise the bandstand would not *always* be passed twice whenever the fountain is passed). Since there is only one point on the right-hand side of the Bandstand, the Bowling Green and the Lake cannot *both* be located there. Thus, the fountain *must* be point Z in our labelling.

Thus, we can identify Z as the fountain, and X as the Bandstand. We know that A, B and C must be the other 3 monuments, but we cannot determine which ones they are.

Thus, 2 points can be identified from this information.

Question 45: B

The passage discusses how people take care of passports better when they are a book-style document which cannot be easily slipped into a pocket, and then easily lost. Ordinarily, we would not assume that this necessarily gives a conclusion that the proposal to replace book-style passports with small plastic cards should be rejected.

However, the passage has stated that the proposal should be rejected, near the start. This means that the passage has identified this notion as its conclusion, and is providing reasons to back up the conclusion. Thus, B) correctly identifies the main conclusion of the passage.

A), C) and D) are all intermediate conclusions from this passage, which all go on to support the main conclusion given in B). Thus, none of these are in themselves the main conclusion.

E) is not a valid conclusion from the passage. The passage actually states that the proposal should be rejected outright. This is different to suggesting that the proposal be examined more carefully, so E) is incorrect. Hence, the answer is B)

Question 46: D

The passage's reasoning can be summarised as "A must happen for B to happen. A will not happen, so B cannot happen". Here, "A" is Nusra accepting a lower salary, and "B" is her finding an interesting job. Answer D) follows this same reasoning, where "A" is Paul and Lisa talking to each other more, and "B" is them having a happy marriage.

B) and C) both identify that "A must happen for B to happen", and point out that "A" is not currently happening. However, they both then go on to suggest ways in which "A" can be achieved (e.g. by Julie and Mike working hard at stability, or by Myra borrowing the rest of the money), which is not the same as simply concluding that "B" cannot happen.

A) also follows different reasoning, and can be summarised as "A must happen for B to happen. We want B to happen, so A must happen". This is different from the reasoning given in the passage.

E) can be summarised as "A must happen for B to happen. B is identified as the only option, so trying to stop A is pointless". This is not the same as the passage's reasoning.

Question 47: C

The passage discusses a principle in which rather than educating people about the dangers of something which can hurt them, we should simply ban the hurtful thing.

➤ C) follows the same principle, arguing that rather than educate about the dangers of alcohol, we should simply ban alcohol.

➤ A) follows an opposite principle, whereby rather than banning a hurtful thing, we should educate people about the dangers of it.

➤ B), D) and E) all discuss the effectiveness of different methods employed to attempt to educate people about the dangers of a certain thing. Thus, none of them have any reference to banning the hurtful thing, and thus none follow the principle in the question.

Question 48: B

The Hovercraft takes 45 minutes to travel between ports, and stays in berth for 15 minutes at each Port before travelling to the other. Thus, if the Hovercraft leaves at 8:00am, it will arrive at the next port at 8:45am, and depart at 9am. It will then arrive at the other Port at 9:45am, and depart at 10:00am.

We can see here that the Hovercraft will always be in Berth between 45 minutes past an hour, and the start of the next hour. It will be in each of the 2 ports as follows:

➤ 08:45-9:00 – Selmar
➤ 09:45-10:00 – Harport
➤ 10:45-11:00 – Selmar
➤ 11:45-12:00 – Harport
➤ 12:45-13:00 – Selmar
➤ 13:45-14:00 – Harport
➤ 14:45-15:00 – Selmar

We now need to calculate the berthing times for the Ferry, and see when they match up with the Hovercraft. The ferry takes 75 minutes to complete its first journey to Selmar, thus arriving at 9:15. It then waits 30 minutes before departing for Harport at 9:45.

Thus it will arrive at Harport at 11:00. It will then depart Harport at 11:30, and arrive at Selmar at 12:45. We can see from the list above that the Hovercraft will also be at Selmar at 12:45.

Question 49: D

We know that the telephone numbers are all 6 digits long and that they all start with "58". The first thing to notice about the 4 digits given in the paper is that they all look the same upside down. Thus, this piece of paper could read "8011" or it could read "1108".

Thus, we have 3 possibilities about what these numbers can represent.

➢ One possibility is that the first 2 digits have been ripped off, and that these 4 digits read "8011", and represent the last 4 digits of the phone number. This gives us 1 possibility for what the phone number could be, as we would therefore know all the digits

➢ Another possibility is that the first 2 digits have been ripped off, and that these 4 digits read "1108", and represent the last 4 digits of the phone number. This gives us 1 more possibility for what the phone number could be, as we would therefore know all the digits.

➢ The other possibility is that the first and the last digits have been torn off, and that these digits read "8011" and represent digits number 2, 3, 4 and 5 of the phone number (thus the "8" would be part of the "58" that we know the number starts with). If this is the case, we know what the first digit must be (a 5), but we do not know the last digit. Thus, this would allow 10 different possibilities for what the number could be.

We know that the 4 digits cannot be the first 4 digits, because the number has to start with 58. Because of this, we can also see that the numbers cannot read "1108" and represent digits 2-5, as this would also mean the phone number didn't start with 58.

Thus, there are 12 different possibilities for what the phone number could be.

Question 50: A

We can see from the right-hand view that the face with 6 dots is adjacent to the face with 1 dot, such that the lines of 3 dots run *towards* the face with 1 dot on, not perpendicular to it. Thus, in the second-left view, the face with 1 dot on could be to the right or the left of the face with 3 dots on. This means that the face with 1 dot on must also be adjacent to the face with 5 dots on.

We can also see from the left-hand and second-right views that the face with 3 dots on is adjacent to *both* the face with 1 dot on *and* the face with 4 dots on. We are looking at the face with 3 dots from the same direction, and can see that in these 2 pictures it has either been rotated 90° or 270°, depending on which direction we consider the rotation in. Thus, we know the face with 1 dot on must also be adjacent to the face with 4 dots which.

Thus, returning to the second-left view, we now know that 3 of the faces we cannot see are the faces with 3, 1 and 4 dots on. All of these faces are adjacent to each other. This means they must occupy the face at the rear side of the die (i.e. opposite the 5 dots), the bottom of the die (i.e. opposite the 6 dots) and *1* of the sides (i.e. to the left or to the right of the 5 dots).

This means that the other unseen side in the second-left view must be the face that we have not seen in any view, with 2 dots. Since we know that the face with 1 dot is on one of the sides in the second-left view, this means that this face *must* be opposite the face with 2 dots.

Thus the face opposite the face with 2 dots has 1 dot.

Thus, the answer is A)

END OF SECTION

Section 2

'Printing and the telephone were truly revolutionary inventions. All the internet brings is a difference in scale.' Is that true?

This essay can be structured well by doing so simply – begin by defining the terms of the argument (what constitutes a 'revolutionary' invention?), then laying out your side of the argument. Follow this, or follow each individual argument, with the counterargument another person might use, then your reasons for considering them incorrect. Conclude simply and concisely by restating your position and summarising your overall argument.

Introduction:

➤ Establish what you consider to be a 'revolutionary' invention; you may wish to define it as an invention that significantly changes the way in which we act in whatever field it is concerned with (in this case, information and communication).

➤ Outline the reasons that printing and the telephone were revolutionary inventions, then state your position on the internet, and outline the main arguments you will be using.

➤ If you have an overall theme to your arguments – for example, you might have argued that the internet has subsumed the functions of printing and the telephone, and so could be mistaken for a simple expansion in scale, but is still revolutionary due to the additional functions it provides – this should be stated clearly in the introduction.

Potential arguments for:

➤ It is worth first establishing that printing and the telephone were revolutionary inventions (it is unlikely you will want to argue against this, but you can do if you have sufficient justification for doing so). Both technologies vastly expanded our potential to communicate, reproduce, store, and transport information. They also represented large technological leaps.

➤ A lot of the functions the internet provides are the same as printing and the telephone, kicked up a notch. The two major groups into which these functions can be placed are communication and information storage. The telephone allowed us to communicate with people across the world, while the invention of printing allowed us to reproduce (at a much faster pace and with much less labour intensive work) and store information so that it can be accessed by anyone at a later time. The internet provides both of these services, but faster, and on a much larger scale; we can make information public so anyone with internet access can find it (for free, if we so choose), not only those to whom we send the printed word, or those we call up.

➤ The internet made the functions provided by printing and the telephone cheaper and accessible to many more people; nearly everyone in the developed world has access to the internet (whether in their home or in, say, a nearby public library), which allows far more people to publish work (online) than physical printing, an expensive process only accessible to a few through publishers, etc., ever did.

> The internet has taken over the functions of the telephone and printing – more and more people are using the internet to stay in touch with people close to them (email, Facebook, etc.), and to otherwise contact people (emailing employers with job applications rather than sending them letters or phoning them, for instance), and more work is being published online all the time (e-books, online newspapers, blogs).

Potential arguments against:

> Printing, the telephone, and the internet all have very different functions; while the internet combines some of the functions of the previous two, it is a technology that has not subsumed them and has functions they never provided. These functions include communicating instantly with potentially any number of people, providing a platform to share videos and audio media, searching through vast amounts of information to find what you need, and entertainment in various forms.

> That the internet has not subsumed the telephone or printing is demonstrated by the simple fact that both technologies are still widely in use.

  o **Counterargument:** but the roles of both are fulfilled by the internet (most mobile phones, for example, now allow you to access the internet, which is widely used for instant communication), and the use of telephones and printing is in decline; that they are still in use at all may just be indicative of old habits dying hard, but society as a whole is still moving away from them, and will eventually stop using them all together.

  o However, this does not necessarily mean that the internet is not revolutionary – it still provides functions that neither of the previous technologies did.

> You could argue that the difference in scale is itself revolutionary; giving the public at large access to the means of publishing their own work, finding information for free, and communicating with everyone from family members to their local politicians instantly vastly changes the way we interact with information and communicate with each other; this is a revolutionary change.

> This is especially the case for communication with individuals, not simply with stored information. Historically, communication between the powerful and other people ('powerful' including politically powerful people, celebrities, experts in various fields of study, etc.) has been very one directional; the powerful publish papers or give press releases, and the general public read it. For the first time in history, this is becoming more two directional – and the internet is to thank. People can do everything from send emails to MPs to tweeting Obama to sending reviews of published work straight to the creator, all at no cost to themselves, and quite often to recognition and response from the people they are contacting.

Conclusion:

> Restate your position and summarise the arguments you've presented above.

> Link your conclusion back to the question by referring to the concept of revolutionary inventions, and why the internet does or does not qualify.

> If you have a more nuanced argument, such as the example given in the introduction, this should be restated here with the arguments that justify it.

Is it justified to insist on facial visibility in public spaces?

This question is easy to structure well. In your introduction, clearly state your view and outline the arguments you will use to support it, as well as potential counterarguments and your reasons for dismissing them. It is important to note the vague wording of the question; the interpretation of 'public space' is left open, and it is particularly important to give a clear definition of what a public space is. Regardless of the definition you give, it will most likely be a broad category, so it is fine to give a nuanced answer that outlines the criteria for in which public spaces it is justified to insist on facial visibility, and in which it is not.

Introduction:

➤ It is important here to establish what you take 'facial visibility' and 'public spaces' to mean. Facial visibility might be defined as having your face recognizable as you; this means no clothing covering it, and not so much makeup that you become unrecognizable. 'Public spaces' is trickier to define, but we might do so by saying it encompasses spaces which are free for anyone (or anyone of certain demographics, for example, bars which only admit adults) to enter – this includes shared public land, e.g.: streets and parks, and private land that has been opened to public entry, e.g.: shops.

➤ Once you've defined the terms of the question, clearly state your position and outline your main arguments, the counterarguments to these, and your reasons for dismissing them.

Potential arguments for:

➤ Most crimes which could be caught on CCTV occur in public places; insisting on facial visibility would improve our chances of identifying criminals after the fact, and discouraging people from committing these crimes in the first place.

➤ Further to the above point, the only people who would object to this reasoning and insist on covering their face are those who intend on committing crimes – only the guilty have something to hide!

➤ It's fine if people don't want to be seen or recognised – but if that's the case, then they should stay home; having unidentifiable people out in the street is a potential danger.

➤ A more nuanced view might argue that facial visibility need not be insisted upon in all public places (and so is not acceptable, since it would only be acceptable to violate a person's right to self-expression and privacy if it were necessary for some greater good), but it is in some e.g. where it's *necessary* to verify someone's identity like at airport security or court.

    ○ **Counterargument:** this misses the very crux of the argument – the question does not ask whether there are some places where insisting on facial visibility is necessary and are some of these places, coincidentally, public places, but rather is asking whether there is something about the nature of public places that makes insisting on facial visibility acceptable; this says nothing to support the view that it does.

➤ Given the above counterargument, we might want to consider which public spaces our previous arguments regarding crime and identifying criminals apply to. Crime that could be discouraged or sanctioned by insisting on facial visibility might be prevalent in shops, but not by students in schools (where they would be identifiable by their clothing, mannerisms, etc. to the teachers who know them, if any misdeed were to occur at all). If we are insisting on facial visibility on this basis, it should only apply to those public places where it is beneficial.

   ○   **Counterargument:** this is ridiculous; crime and other misdeeds occur everywhere at one time or another, but even if we were to narrow our insistence on visibility to those places where it is most prevalent, it would be deeply unfair to effectively ban people who wish to cover their face from these spaces, and to treat them as a criminal for this simple desire for privacy.

Potential arguments against:

➤ Insisting on facial visibility is discriminatory against people of some religions and cultures in which the face is traditionally covered.

➤ Facial visibility is only considered acceptable to insist upon in the UK because facial visibility is generally viewed as the norm. Disallowing baggy clothing that conceals the shape of one's bodies would also aid in, for example, recognition of criminals, but would be considered a ridiculous ban because of cultural norms. This is further exemplified when we look specifically at facial visibility – large sunglasses might be considered acceptable because they are not particularly unusual in dominant British culture, whereas a cloth face covering which does no less or more to obscure personal identity might not. Although facial visibility is considered the norm, or even better and more polite, by much of the UK, this is not an adequate justification for insisting on it at the expense of other people.

➤ People have a right to privacy, which includes privacy over their body.

➤ People can wish to avoid detection and recognition for reasons other than criminal activities – for example, avoiding someone who has been abusive towards them. It is important that people be able to avoid those who pose a threat to their safety.

   ○   **Counterargument**: if someone poses a threat to another person's safety, our police force ought to be dealing with that; if they are not, the response is to improve our protection services and justice system, not to allow members of the public to hide from dangerous people better.

   ○   **Counterargument**: additionally, allowing people to cover their faces also allows the dangerous person to conceal themselves, so we are no better off.

Conclusion

➤ Restate your position and summarise the arguments you have used to support it.

➤ Link your conclusion back to the question by referring to your definition of 'public space' and what about that, specifically, makes insisting on facial visibility acceptable.

Why do we need banks?

This question implies an assumption that we *do* need banks; it is perfectly fine to challenge this assumption and instead argue that we do not, as long as this position is well justified. In either case, you should provide some reasons that we don't need banks (either supported or refuted), and attempt to challenge the reasons you give for us needing banks (again, either supported or refuted).

Introduction:
> Give an outline of the functions banks perform, then clearly state your position on whether these functions are needed (or *which* of these functions are needed).
> Outline the arguments you will be using to support your position, and the counterarguments you will present and your reasons for dismissing them.

Reasons we need banks:
> Banks enable the flow of currency by providing a space in which to store it, and then transfer it instantly.
> In a globalised economy, dealing only with physical currency is completely unfeasible; everything from individual online purchases to dealings between massive multinational corporations would either be impossible or deeply impractical. Securely sending that amount of money between people could take days or even weeks in some cases, and would be simply not worth the effort and expenditure for most people.
> It is necessary to be able to safely store savings; though robberies (both physical burglaries and digital crime) of banks do occur, money is much safer than if people were keeping it in their homes, given that most people do not have the means to invest in a secure safe, whereas a bank account is not only free, but often comes with monetary rewards.
> Banks provide loans, which are necessary for investing in the future, for everything from buying a house that could otherwise only be afforded in retirement after a lifetime of saving, to starting up businesses before they begin to turn a profit. Banks make commodities and investments (in one's own business, education, etc.) accessible to more people.
> Banks are ingrained into our economy and provide basic services such as currency exchange, organising money into different accounts (savings accounts, current accounts, accounts for organisations managed by an individual, etc.), making online purchase, etc. Even if we once could conceive of an economy without banks, they are now far too integrated to ever consider doing away with them.

Reasons we don't need banks:

➢ While it is true that banks provide the function of storing and transferring money (which may well be necessary in today's economy), that is not their primary purpose; they exist to invest money and make a profit and this, as we have seen (think of the recent 2008 economic crisis) makes them dangerous and unstable. If it is storing and transferring money that is essential, we should be building more institutions like building societies, which are owned by their members and don't invest the money stored in them.

➢ This is similarly the case for loans; loans provided by banks are done for the sake of the bank wishing to make a profit from interest payments, not because they are interested in providing a start for small businesses. Their ultimate concern in profits means any positive economic outcomes are an accidental by-product, whereas they should be the focus of investment by our government and community.

➢ Loans are dangerous to the individual if they fail to succeed in repaying according to the agreed terms, and do little to combat inequality in opportunity, since they put those who cannot afford what they need out of their own pocket at the mercy of banks, while those who can do so can invest as they wish. We consequently ought to move towards more stable and community-orientated means of investing in small businesses, such as crowd funding.

➢ Though it's true that banks are heavily integrated into our economy, this doesn't mean we can't ever move away from relying on them, it just means it will have to be done slowly, and carefully until they are no longer necessary; if we believe banks are ultimately harmful and destabilising, then this needs to be done.

Conclusion:

➢ Restate your position and summarise the arguments you have used to defend it.

➢ Be sure to link your conclusion back to the question by referring to the roles of banks viewed as necessary (and whether you believe they actually are).

If two reasonable people claim the same fact as evidence for opposing conclusions, does it follow that it can't actually be evidence for either?

This is an interesting question with lots of room for debate on both sides, hinging on what we take the precise definition of 'evidence' to be. Given that it rests on giving quite a precise definition of quite a complex concept – evidence – it is good to make a comment on the complexity of the argument, and that is it unlikely we will be able to find an answer which *any* two reasonable people would themselves agree with. That said, it is fine to have a very strong opinion one way or the other, though of course be prepared to justify it, and give your reasons for dismissing other definitions.

Introduction:

➢ It is first important to establish what you mean by 'evidence'; "the available body of facts or information indicating whether a belief or proposition is true or valid" is one available definition.

➤ We should also note the use of the phrase 'reasonable people', and establish that we take this to mean that the conclusions drawn are logically consistent with the evidence, and are sound conclusions to draw on the basis of the piece of evidence under dispute alone.

➤ Clearly state your position, linking it to what you take to be the criteria for a fact being 'evidence' and outline the arguments you will use to defend it, as well as opposing views and your reasons for rejecting them.

Potential arguments for:

➤ If evidence is a fact that can be used to draw a reasonable conclusion, then the fact that an observation can be used to draw two reasonable conclusions shows it is useless for conclusion drawing. While it may be consistent with both conclusions, and be a relevant consideration (rather than, the observation "some dogs are brown" being *consistent* with the conclusions "the bus will arrive at 3:00" and "the bus will arrive at 4:00", but not *relevant* to them), it cannot be said to be 'evidence' because it doesn't help us draw a reasonable conclusion.

➤ Suppose that two facts, X and Y observed in isolation, both allow you to reasonably draw conclusions A and B but, when observed together, allow you to reasonably draw only conclusion B. You may argue that X and Y must both alone be evidence of B but this is not true; since they can be used to definitively establish B as the reasonable conclusion only when observed together, it is the conjunction of X & Y that is evidence of B. A and B alone are not evidence of X or Y- they are merely consistent with them.

➤ If two reasonable people can take a fact to be evidence of opposing conclusions, this is indicative of insufficient data to draw a conclusion at all – so we cannot say we have evidence either way. The conclusions drawn are most likely a result of bias from previously held opinions.

Potential arguments against:

➤ Since evidence is nothing more than a true observation that is indicative of some fact about the world, any true observation that is made as a result of some fact about the world is evidence of it. Take evolution, for example: if we rightly observe that giraffe's necks have lengthened over generations, we can take this as evidence of natural selection breeding giraffe's with longer necks, or we can take it as evidence of Lamarckism, which would say a giraffe's neck stretches during its life in order to, say, reach high leaves in trees; and this change is passed down genetically. Though without further information, a reasonable person could take this as evidence of either theory, it can only *actually* be evidence of a true theory; being taken as evidence of both does not negate that it is evidence of one.

➤ Alternately, taking the definition "the available body of facts or information indicating whether a belief or proposition is true or valid" we can argue that if an observation is consistent with some conclusion then it is evidence for it; if we have a set of observations used to justify two opposing conclusions, this is simply indicative of us having insufficient evidence to draw a reliable conclusion, but does not mean it is not evidence.

➢ We could further suppose that what is and is not evidence of a conclusion are not fixed categories, into which all facts definitively fall. In the case of the above example, could we say that the fact that giraffe's necks have elongated generationally is, alone, evidence of both natural selection and Lamarckism but, when combined with other observations, which are incompatible with Lamarckism, it is actually evidence of natural selection. Since 'evidence' is a function of human reasoning (being defined as that which we can use to draw a supported conclusion), rather than a category of thing that naturally exists, we can define it in terms of whether it *is* used to draw a conclusion, or whether it is *reasonably* used to draw a conclusion. In these situations, a fact was at one point evidence for both, and then evidence for only one.

➢ The way in which people use very difficult to accurately define terms such as 'evidence' is context dependent; what is 'evidence' in one situation may not be so in another. To make sweeping statements such as "if two reasonable people claim the same fact as evidence for opposing conclusions, it follows that it can't actually be evidence for either" is to ignore the nuance of language and communication.

➢ Being a 'reasonable person' does not necessarily mean your reasoning will always be flawless, and that you will always draw correct conclusions from a piece of evidence. Further, it seems absurd to suggest that the status of a fact as evidence for a conclusion is at least in part dependent on no one misinterpreting it. For example, let us say reasonable person A sees that things tend to fall to the ground when released and takes this as evidence of a force pulling us towards the earth. We would probably quite reasonably say their observation of facts were evidence of this force (let us also suppose it is true that gravity exists and was correctly observed here). Later, reasonable person B also observes this fact, and incorrectly concludes that this is evidence of a force pushing us down, away from the earth's atmosphere. Supposing this conclusion is correct, and opposing person A's correct conclusion – does the fact suddenly *stop* being evidence, where previously it was? This seems ridiculous, and yet is what the question is proposing.

Conclusion:

➢ Link your conclusion back to the question by referring to the definition of 'evidence', what does it mean for something to be 'evidence'?

➢ This is the sort of question where it is nice to make some concluding remark about the debate itself – does the precise definition of 'evidence' *matter*, so long as each person in a particular conversation is clear on what is meant by it? Does the definition of 'evidence' rigid and the same across all conversations and usages? Can something that is said to be evidence of a belief at one point stop being evidence of that belief when combined with other observations? Use this to show the examiner you are really thinking about and engaging with the implications of the question and wider field of study itself, not merely answering one question within it.

END OF PAPER

2011

Section 1

Question 1: A

C) is simply a stated reason stated in the passage, so is not a conclusion.

B) and A) are both valid conclusions from the passage, but only A) is the main conclusion. We can see that the statement in B) actually goes on to support the statement in A). Therefore, A) is the main conclusion and B) is an intermediate conclusion, supporting the main conclusion.

D) and E) are both statements which would weaken the argument, if true. Therefore, they are not conclusions. E) also appears to be incorrect, as it seems to have incorrectly concluded that because 39% of nurses working alternating shift patterns want to leave, the other 61% prefer alternating shift patterns. This is not a valid deduction.

Question 2: C

The simplest way to answer this question is to go through the answers and see if each one can be achieved from the possible scores for 4 matches:

➤ 8.5. points can be achieved through 2 draws, an away win and a home win (3+3+1+1.5=8.5), so A) is a possible score.
➤ 9 points can be achieved through 2 draws and 2 away wines (3+3+1.5+1.5=9), so B) is a possible score.
➤ 9.5 points cannot be achieved, so C) is not a possible score.
➤ 10 points can be achieved through 3 draws and a home win (3+3+3+1=10) so D) is a possible score.
➤ 10.5 points can be achieved through 3 draws and an away win (3+3+3+1.5=10.5) so E) is a possible score.

Question 3: C

The argument has described how many low-budget films are very popular, and how many high-budget films are not successful. However, it does not follow that this is *always* the case, so the argument's conclusion is not valid. C) correctly points out the flaw in the argument's reasoning that it need not be cost that determines a film's popularity.

The rest of the possible answers are all irrelevant in that they do not affect how the argument's conclusion follows on from the given reasons. Therefore, the rest of the answers are not flaws in this argument.

Question 4: E

The argument describes how the only thing that can slow down global warming is an immediate switch to green technologies. It then discusses how if global warming continues *at this rate*, many species will not be able to reproduce. Thus it can be concluded that if we do not switch to green technologies, some species will not survive. Therefore E) is the main conclusion. It does *not* follow from this that the species *will* survive if we do switch to green technologies, it can only be said that they *won't* survive if we don't. Therefore C) is not a valid conclusion.

B) and D) both contradict statements in the passage, so are not conclusions.

A), meanwhile, is irrelevant, as nothing has been claimed about whether species cannot breed in warmer climates. It has only been said they cannot *survive*. Also, it has only been said that *some* species cannot survive, not *most*. Thus, A) is an irrelevant statement, and not a conclusion.

Question 5: B

The argument concludes that we should legalise Cannabis in order to reduce its use. It backs this up with reasoning describing how the dangers of Cannabis need to be more widely known if its usage is to decrease. At no point has it been stated that the dangers will not be widely known without legalising cannabis, and if this is not true the argument's conclusion is no longer valid. Therefore, B) is an assumption in this argument.

D) is irrelevant because the argument has stated that it is more dangerous than people realise, so we accept this as true. C) and A) are both irrelevant to the idea that legalising cannabis would allow the dangers to become more widely known. Thus, none of these three answers affect the argument's conclusion, so none are assumptions.

E) would strengthen the argument, if true, but is not required for the argument's reasons to lead on to its conclusion. Therefore, E) is not an assumption.

Question 6: E
The £50 goes to who has lost the most weight after 4 weeks. Thus we need to calculate the difference in weight at the start, and after 4 weeks for each person. Weeks 1, 2 and 3 are irrelevant.

➢ Alma started at 71kg, and weighed 64kg after 4 weeks, so has lost 7 kg.
➢ Brigit started at 67kg and weighed 62kg after 4 weeks, so has lost 5kg.
➢ Cara started at 63.5kg and weighed 57.5kg after 4 weeks, so has lost 6kg
➢ Danni started at 66.5kg and weighed 60kg after 4 weeks, so has lost 6.5kg
➢ Evelyn started at 69kg and weighed 61kg after 4 weeks, so has lost 8kg.

Thus, Evelyn has lost the most weight after 4 weeks, and thus Evelyn get the £50.

Question 7: E
First, we need to calculate the total length of the reign of each King, from the dates given in the table:

➢ Henry II reigned for 35 Years
➢ Richard I reigned for 13 years
➢ John reigned for 17 years
➢ Henry III reigned for 56 years
➢ Edward I reigned for 35 years
➢ Edward II reigned for 20 years
➢ Edward III reigned for 50 years
➢ Richard II reigned for 22 year

We can see that all the possible answers have the same groupings when grouping kings according to length of reign. Therefore, we can take these groupings and see how many kings fit into each category. We see that:

➢ 1 King reigned between 0-15 years (Richard I)
➢ 3 Kings reigned between 16-30 years (John, Edward II and Richard II)
➢ 2 Kings reigned between 31-45 years (Henry II and Edward I)
➢ 2 Kings reigned for longer than 45 years (Henry III and Edward III)
➢ We see that only Graph E) shows this distribution.

Question 8: D
To answer this question we should break apart each section of the journey described in the question, and see what we would expect the graph to do at this point:

➢ First, the driver drives *away* from home at a *constant speed*. Therefore, we should expect a straight line (because of the constant speed), heading up and to the right (because both time and distance from home are *increasing)*

➢ Next, the driver *increases* his speed to a *new constant speed*. Thus, we expect the next section of graph to have a line with a steeper gradient than the last (because the new speed is higher than the last). The line should still be going upwards because the driver is going *away* from home.

➢ Next, the driver meets a hill, which slows him down to a new constant speed. Thus, we expect the next section of the graph to have a line with a *decreased* gradient (due to the lower constant speed). The line should still be straight, and going upwards and to the right, because the time and distance from home are both increasing.

➢ Next, the driver stops for several minutes. At this point we expect a *flat* line because there is no movement either away from or towards home. The line continues to the right because time continues to progress whilst the driver is stopped.

➢ Finally, driver heads back down his route. Thus, we expect the next section of graph to have a line going *down* and to the right, because the driver is now becoming *closer* to home as time progresses.

Only graph D) follows the expected pattern.

➢ Graph A) does not have a line heading downwards after the flat section, so does not show the driver's return hum.

➢ Graph B) shows a decrease in speed rather than an increase in speed on the 2nd section of the graph, so does not show the driver's increase in speed.

➢ Graph C) starts with a flat line, so does not show the driver's initial constant speed.

➢ Graph E) does not have a flat section, so does not show the several minutes of the driver being stopped.

Question 9: E
C) actually weakens the argument by suggesting that work can be better done with children sitting in groups at tables. B) also weakens the argument by suggesting there is less importance whether children sit in groups or rows, as children may be distracted either way. A) is an irrelevant statement. D) is also irrelevant as the fact that traditionalists favour this arrangement does not affect the conclusion that it is better to do so.

E) strengthens the argument, as if children can see visual aids more clearly this strengthens the idea that they can concentrate more on their work.

Question 10: C

The argument describes an increase in police officer numbers, and then concludes that this is why crime is down. C) correctly points out the flaw in this reasoning – crime may have fallen anyway, and may thus not be down to this factor.

B) is not a valid flaw because the question states that crime is down. Thus we must accept this as true for the purposes of a critical thinking assessment, and thus different ways of measuring crime are irrelevant.

A), D) and E) are all irrelevant statements that do not affect the argument's conclusion (D) is incorrect because the question refers to crime *last week*, so any future rises/falls are irrelevant).

Question 11: C

E) is a completely irrelevant statement, whilst B) is also irrelevant as the argument does not say anything about whether risk-taking humans are atypical. It simply mentions variation.

A) is simply a stated reason in the passage, and thus is not a conclusion. D) is also a stated fact in the passage. It can be seen as a conclusion, but it is an intermediate conclusion, which goes on to support the main conclusion from the passage. It is not the main conclusion in itself.

C) readily follows on from the reasoning given in the passage, as a whole. If the reasoning in the passage as true, we have good reason to believe the statement in C). Thus, C) is the main conclusion of the passage.

Question 12: A

To solve this question, we need to work out the prices for a kilogram of coffee from each supermarket:

➢ Kostless normally charges £2.50. With the offer of 80p off, this will now be £1.70. 5 X 200 jars will make 1 kg of coffee. Thus, the price for 1kg of coffee is 5 X £1.70, which is £8.50

➢ Savemore usually charges £2.50 for 200g. With the offer, we now get an extra 25% extra for the same price. Thus, for £2.50 we will now get 250g of coffee. Thus, 1kg of coffee will cost 4X£2.50, which is £10.00

Therefore, a kg of coffee costs £8.50 from Kostless, and £10.00 from Savemore. Thus, a kg of coffee is £1.50 cheaper at Kostless.

Thus the answer is A)

Question 13: A

In answering this question, we can safely ignore the actual area of each country, and the population density of each country. The % of EU area accounted for by each country is sufficient information, meaning we only need to consider the middle column of the table. This simplifies the question.

To get the minimum number of countries required to account for 50% of total area, we should simply add up countries in size order, beginning with the largest, until we reach 50% of total area:

➢   The largest country in the table is France, accounting for 14.6% of total area.
➢   The next largest country is Spain, accounting for 11.4% of total area (we have now accounted for 26% of total area)
➢   The next largest country is Sweden, accounting for 10.2% of total area (we have now accounted for 36.2% of total area)
➢   The next largest country is Germany, accounting for 8.1% of total area (we have now accounted for 44.3% of total area)
➢   The next largest country is Finland, accounting for 7.6% of total area (we have now accounted for 51.9% of total area)

Thus, these 5 countries together account for over 50% of the total area of the EU. Thus, the answer is A).

Question 14: C

This question is simpler than it appears at first glance. Let the books be numbered 1-7, starting on the left (i.e. the left-most book will be Book 1, the second left-most book will be Book 2 and so forth, such that the right-most book will be Book 7).

If we look at Books 1, 2 and 3 under this system, we find that Book 1 is the shortest, Book 2 is taller than Book 1, and Book 3 is the tallest of these 3 books. Thus, we know that any possible view from the left-most side (the direction of the arrow) must show a short book at the front, with a slightly taller book *immediately behind it*, and a taller yet book *immediately behind* this book.

We can see that in the view shown in C), there is a short book, followed by a much taller book immediately behind, and then a book which is between those 2 in height behind this one. Thus, these books cannot be Books 1, 2 and 3 as we observed in the front-view. Thus C) is not a possible view of the books, and C) is therefore the answer.

Question 15: B

A) and C) are both incorrect as the argument states that the universe resembles a vegetable *just as closely* as it resembles a house. It does not say it resembles a statement more, or that it does not resemble a house.

D) and E) are also incorrect as the argument makes no claim as to which is the most likely origin of the universe, and it does not state that any possibility is definitely incorrect. It simply states that we cannot conclude that it was the result of intelligent design.

B) correctly points out the argument's conclusion. The argument is explaining how this particular conclusion of the universe's origin is not justified.

Question 16: A

The argument claims that fanciful claims of aliens causing crop circles can be dismissed on the basis that a more mundane, ordinary explanation exists. A) correctly points out that this assumes that where 2 explanations exist, we should accept the more ordinary one. The argument provides no reasons why we should accept the more ordinary one. Thus, if the statement in A) is incorrect, the argument's conclusion is no longer valid.

B), C) and D) all provide further reasons to believe that aliens have not produced crop circles, and why they are simply a form of rural graffiti. Thus they all strengthen the argument, but are not essential for its conclusion to be valid, and so are not assumptions.

E) is a completely irrelevant statement.

Question 17: C

A) and B) actually strengthen the argument's conclusion, suggesting that houses with burglar alarms are less at risk from burglary because of this, whilst houses/people without alarms are at higher risk.

D) is a completely irrelevant statement, whilst E) is not relevant to the argument's conclusion as it does not say anything about how a visible burglar alarm box affects the risks of a house being burgled.

C) implies that burglars will be more likely to burgle houses with visible burglar alarm boxes, due to the implied value of items in the house. Thus, C) weakens the argument's conclusion. Thus, the answer is C).

Question 18: D

First we need to assess what possible digits the month and the date can have.

- The Month can be any number from 01 to 12. Thus, the Month *must* contain either a "0" or a "1".

- The Day can be any number from 01 to 31. Thus, the day *must* contain either a "0", a "1", a "2" or a "3".

- All the possible years have a "2" in, so the day *cannot* include a "2". Thus, it *must* either contain a "0", a "1" or a "3".

- We can see that if the day contains a "3", it must be either "30" or "31". This means that the month must either *not* contain a "1", or not contain a "0".

Now we can assess the years, and see if the numbers taken up leave a possible combination of day and month, without repeating any digits.

- If 2013 is the year, then "2", "0", "1" and "3" are already taken up. This means this year is not a possible answer, as the month has to contain either "0" or "1".

- If 2134 is the Year, then "2", "1", "3" and "4" are already taken up. This means this year is not a possible answer. In order not to share a digit, both the Month and the Day would have to contain a "0", which means they would share a digit with each other.

- If 2145 is the year, then "2", "1", "4" and "5" are already taken up. Thus, the Month will have to contain a "0", as "1" has been used. This means the day cannot contain "0", "1" or "2", so it must contain a "3". This means the day has to be either "30" or "31", both of which already include a digit already used in the date. Thus this year is not a possible answer.

- If the year is 2345, then "2", "3", "4" and "5" have already been taken up. Thus, the Month can contain either a "0" or a "1", as neither of these have been taken up. The day can also contain either "0" or "1". Thus, the Month can be any of (06, 07, 08, 09) without sharing any digits with the year or using up both a 0 and a 1. Once one of these is selected, the day can then be selected from of (16, 17, 18 and 19) without sharing any digits with the Year or Month. Thus, 2345 is a possible answer.

Thus, we can see that 2345 is the *next* possible year in which a date will occur which can be written using 8 different digits. This means that D) is the answer. The Year given in E) is now irrelevant, as we have found a year *earlier* than it that is possible, so it cannot be the *next* year in which such a date will occur.

Question 19: B

A) is the view looking at the logo from the right-hand side. We can see the 3 points of the "E" in the Logo, which are on the left, middle and right in this view.

C) is the view looking at the logo from the bottom. We can see the bottom point of the "T" in the centre, with gaps either side, as expected. On the left and right are the wide bases of the "J" and "E".

D) is the view from the top. On the right-hand side we see the upward flick from the "J", with the gap next to it, as expected. The rest of this view comprises the wide top of the sculpture.

E) is the view from the left-hand side. We can see the side of the "J", with the upward flick on the right-hand side of the image.

No viewpoint would give the view seen in B). Therefore, the answer is B.

Question 20: B

This question appears to require some complex calculations of compound interest, but on closer inspection we can see that all the information we require is provided in the table.

Raul's savings are rising at a rate of 6% per year. Thus we can calculate how much they will be worth in years by looking at how much an item will cost in 8 years, and treating Raul's savings as rising in exactly the same manner as 6% inflation. We can see that in 8 years, what was worth $1000 will be worth $1594. Thus, Raul's $10,000 of savings will be worth $15940

We now calculate the cost of the car in 8 years, based on an 8% inflation rate. Raul will buy an equivalent model, so at present it would cost $10,000. In 8 years, with an 8% inflation rate, we can see that an item currently costing $1000 will cost $1851. Thus, an item currently costing $10,000 will cost $18510. Thus, the car will cost $18510.

Thus Raul's savings will cover $15940, of a total expense of $18510.

18510 − 15940 = 2570. Thus, Raul will need an extra $2570 to purchase the next car.

Question 21: A

B) is incorrect as the argument does not assume that police do not protect criminals or protect the public. It simply argues for a "proper focus" to be put on this. This does require us to accept there is not currently a proper focus on this, but it does *not* require us to accept that this job is not currently carried out. Thus, B) is not an assumption.

C) and E) are both irrelevant to the argument's conclusion and are not flaws. D) is incorrect as the argument states that a proper focus could be put on catching criminals *and* protecting the public. It does not claim that catching criminals equates to protecting the public, these jobs could be carried out independently.

A) is a flaw, because the argument is implying that focus on road offences currently detracts from catching criminals and protecting the public. If road incidents are criminal and dangerous, then this conclusion is no longer valid,

Question 22: B

The argument's reasoning can be summarised as "If A happens, B will happen. A hasn't happened, so neither has B. If we want B to happen, A must happen". In the question, "A" is practicing an instrument, and "B" is becoming better at playing it. Only answer B) follows this reasoning, with "A" being working hard at trampolining, and "B" being getting better at it.

In A), "A" does not happen, but "B" still happens, so this is different from the question. In C), "A" does happen, so "B" does happen.

D) follows a different style of reasoning, claiming "If A happens, B will happen. Therefore all who have achieved B must have done A". This is not the same reasoning as the question. E) also follows a different style of reasoning, claiming that "A causes B. A has happened, so we expect B to happen". Again, this is not the same as the question's reasoning.

Question 23: D

The question refers to a situation of people not being penalised for things over which they have no control. D) illustrates this payment, saying Jamuna's payment was delayed by something she had no control over (postal strikes), so she should not be penalised.

A) is claiming that Kelly did have control over her accounts, even though her mistake was not deliberate, so she should be fined. C) is saying that Phillip did have control over his losses so he should not be helped. Neither of these answers follows the principle outlined in the passage.

E), meanwhile, is referring to those responsible for a problem (the financial advisors) being punished (by losing their licenses). B), meanwhile is discussing a situation where those responsible for helping people in a give situation should be left to do so, and others should not intervene. These are both vastly removed from the principle described in the passage.

Question 24: C

To answer this question we must calculate how long each section would take by each road:

- Each part of the journey (Bowbridge to Clatterton and Clatterton to Downland) is 35 miles long. Since the average speed on the motorway is 60mph, each section will take 35 minutes if travelling by motorway.
- From Bowbridge to Clatterton is 30 miles on Buttercup Way. Since we are travelling at 40mph (average), this will take 45 minutes.
- From Clatterton to Downland is 20 miles on Buttercup Way. Since we are travelling at 40mph (average) this will take 30 minutes.

Thus, the fastest route is to travel by Motorway from Bowbridge to Clatterton, and by Buttercup way from Clatterton to Downland. This will take (35+30) minutes, which is 65 minutes.

The slowest route is to travel by Buttercup way from Bowbridge to Clatterton, and then by Motorway from Clatterton to Downland. This will take (45+35) minutes, which is 80 minutes.

Thus, the fastest route will take 15 minutes less than the slowest route.

Thus, the answer is C)

Question 25: B

The secret to this answer lies in examining the sides and angles of the parallelogram in B). In squares, all adjacent sides lie at 90° to each other. Thus, the slanted sides in B) and the horizontal sides cannot be from the same square, as the angles at which they meet are not 90°.

The other way of forming this shape would be to have one square making the horizontal lines, and another on top of it, rotated slightly, to give the slanted lines. As we can see, this would not produce a parallelogram of this shape, because in this instance the width of the square would have to be smaller than its length. This means it would not be a square, whose width and length are equal by definition.
The only way shape B) can be formed is with a square and a *rectangle*. It cannot be formed with 2 squares.

Question 26: D

This question asks us to calculate the change in the *percentage* of households with fewer than 3 children. In calculating this, the total number of households and the average are not necessary. The % figures give us enough information. This simplifies the question as we need only consider a small section of the table.
First we calculate the total % of households with < 3 people in 1971:
- 18% of households had 1 person in 1971
- 32% of households had 2 people in 1971
- Thus, a total of 50% of households had fewer than 3 people in 1971
Next, we calculate the total % of households with < 3 people in 1991:
- 27% of households had 1 person in 1991
- 34% of households had 2 people in 1991
- Thus a total of 61% of households had fewer than 3 people in 1971
The difference between 50 and 61 is 11, so we can see that the change in percentage is 11%. Thus the answer is D)

Question 27: E

E) correctly identifies the main conclusion to the passage.
B) is not a conclusion, and simply a fact stated in the passage, which the arguer then questions and refutes.
All the other possible answers are reasons which go on to support the main conclusion. If we accept answers A), C) and D) as true, they give us good cause to believe that we should see the fall in house prices as a good thing. Thus, E) is the main conclusion.

Question 28: C

The argument discusses how working class areas of London drank tea regularly during the first half of the 20th century, and enjoyed a longer life expectancy than other areas.

E) is an irrelevant statement, which has no relevance to the reasoning of the argument. D) is also irrelevant, the argument says nothing about whether tea replaced other parts of a normal working class diet.

A) and B) both assume too much. From the reasons given in the paragraph, we cannot conclude that Tea *definitely* increases life expectancy, as correlation does not necessarily mean causation. Therefore A) is incurred. Similarly, we cannot conclude that everyone should drink tea, so B) is incorrect.

However, from the reasons in the paragraph, we do have cause to believe that tea *may* be beneficial to health. Thus, the conclusion in C) is valid, and C) correctly identifies the main conclusion of this passage.

Question 29: C

The argument discusses how different areas of the country spend different amounts per head of the population over 65 on a certain treatment for Alzheimer's, and then concludes that this means that different areas of the country will have differing levels of treatment for Alzheimer's. At no point is it stated that different areas of the country experience the same incidence of Alzheimer's per head of the population over 65. If this does differ in different areas, then it may well be that different areas spend the same amount *per case of Alzheimer's* on the treatment, making the argument's conclusion invalid. Thus, C) correctly identifies an assumption in the argument.

A) is incorrect as the argument states that the pills are the most effective treatment available. Thus, how they are used is a significant factor in how effective treatment can be. Whether or not they are significantly effective is irrelevant, and thus A) is not an assumption. B) is a completely irrelevant point, which does not affect the argument's conclusion.

D) is irrelevant because the argument refers to the expenditure on the treatment *per head* of the population over-65, so has already taken into account regional variations in numbers of people over 65. E) is not an assumption because it is not needed to be true for the argument's conclusion to be valid.

Question 30: A

To answer this question we must work out what we can tell from the table, and then deduce other results as we move along.

Immediately, we can tell several things:

- Rovers have won all their games, and United and County have both only lost one game each. Thus, both teams have lost to United.
- United have won 2 games, and have only scored two goals. Thus, both those games must have been won 1-0 by United.
- Similarly, United have lost one game, and have only conceded 1 goal. Thus, they must have lost that game 1-0.
- This accounts for all of United's scored and conceded goals. Thus, we know United's other game must have been a 0-0 draw.

Thus, at this point we know the following:

- Neither team can have lost the game, as each team has only lost 1 game each, both against Rovers.
- The score must be either 1-0 or 0-0, because these are the only scores which have occurred in any of United's games.

The only possibility is thus that the game between United and County ended 0-0.

Question 31: C

An important point to remember is that each player can play an X **or** an O for their go, thus deviating from the normal rules for Naughts and Crosses.

Thus we need to assess each board and see whether a victory can be guaranteed next turn:

- In A), we can see that if the next player puts a Cross in the bottom-right space, there is no possible victory on the next turn. Thus A) is incorrect
- In situation B) we can see that unless the next player puts a cross in the Top-left, Bottom-left or Top right spaces, no victory can be achieved next turn. Thus, B) is incorrect.
- In Situation C) we can see that wherever an X or an O is placed by the next player, a victory can be achieved on the next turn. Thus, C) is how the current player can guarantee herself victory next turn.
- In situation D) we can see that the next player can prevent a victory on the next turn by placing an O anywhere on the board, thus D) is incorrect.
- In situation E), we can see that if the next player places an O in the left-most two columns, or places a cross in the bottom-right corner, no victory can be achieved next turn. Thus E) is incorrect.

Thus, the answer is C)

Question 32: B

We are trying to calculate how many more people have quit smoking thanks to the nicotine patches than would be expected if they had just been given placebo.

We can see from the table that 24 out of 120 smokers given placebo have quit successfully.

We are told that the researchers predict the *same proportion* of people would have quit without using Nicotine patches as did whilst using the placebo. Since there are 120 people given placebo, and 120 people given nicotine, this means that we would expect 24 people to quit successfully without using the nicotine patches.

In fact, we can see from the table that 56 smokers have successfully quit whilst using the nicotine patches. 56−24=32. Thus, 32 more smokers have quit using nicotine patches than would be expected without the nicotine patches.

Question 33: C

A) and B) are irrelevant. The issue of drivers losing control of the vehicle is irrelevant to which turns they will take whilst what happens in TV car chases may not necessarily be what happens in real-life car chases. Thus, both A) and B) are incorrect.

D) is also irrelevant as further assistance is irrelevant to what direction the drivers being pursued will go.

E) appears relevant, but does not affect how the argument's reasoning leads on to its conclusion. The argument describes how pursued drivers will frequently wish to turn, and how left turns are easier and quicker, and then describes how this means police taking left turns will soon catch up to the criminals. The idea of criminals turning left because that leads to their destination is a separate point from this reasoning.

C) strengthens the argument. C) relates to the idea that even if police follow the path of a criminal, if they wish to catch up they must surely travel at a faster speed. Thus, if C) is true, the argument's conclusion is much more solid.
Therefore, the answer is C)

Question 34: C

The argument describes how the money spent on a new entrance hall is a waste, and how the money should instead be spent on better conditions for scholars who already come to study. However, the argument also states that scholars currently using the museum will continue to do so regardless of how artistic the displays are, and that all scholars who wish to use the museum already do so. This implies that the number of scholars using the museum will not really change much regardless of how the money is spent, so surely spending the money on better conditions for scholars is also a waste? C) correctly points out this flaw in the argument's reasoning.

A) and B) actually strengthen the argument, adding reasons that spending money on the entrance hall may not produce significant results, so contributing to the argument that this expenditure is wasteful. E) also collaborates with the argument, arguing that the money should be spent on current visitors, not attracting new ones.

D) is an irrelevant statement, not relevant to the argument's conclusion.

Question 35: A

The argument discusses the effects of population growth from unrestricted immigration policy, and then concludes that this will cause Extremist political parties to gain political ground. Answer A) correctly identifies this main conclusion.

E) is irrelevant to the argument's conclusion. The fact that opposition parties believe immigration is responsible for population growth does not affect how extremist parties will benefit from the rise in population.

B) and C) are a mixture of facts and opinions stated in the passage, whilst D) is an intermediate conclusion that goes on to support the main conclusion in A).

Question 36: E

Each Pizza has a fixed charge. Let the fixed charge be termed X.

Each pizza also has a variable charge, proportional to the amount of ingredients used. Let the variable charge for a small pizza be termed Y.

➢ A small Pizza will have 1Y as its variable charge.

➢ A regular pizza will have 2Y as its variable charge, as it uses twice the ingredients of a small pizza.

➢ A large pizza will have 4Y as its variable charge, as it uses twice the ingredients of a regular pizza.

Thus we are looking for a set of prices which can be described as $(X+Y)$, $(X+2Y)$ and $(X+4Y)$, where X and Y are constants. Only the prices in E) follow this pattern, with X and Y both being £1.

Question 37: A

Without the extra item, the total price would have been £74.60. We can see from the question that for an order of this price, there would be a £12.00 charge for postage and packing (for orders between £50.00 and £74.99). Thus the total price would be £86.60.

With the extra item, the total price for the order is now £75.85. We can see from the question that the normal charge for postage and packing for such an order would be £15.00. However, since we now have 8 items, the postage and packing charge is halved. Thus, a £7.50 charge is levied for postage and packing. Thus the total price is £83.35

86.60-83.35=3.25. Thus, the extra item took £3.25 off the total price.
Hence the answer is A).

Question 38: A

Let the number of brochures be X. We can now describe the price of each structure as follows:
- ➤ Price structure 1) cost simply equals X (Y), where Y is the cost per brochure.
- ➤ Price structure 2) cost equals W + X(Z), where W is the fixed price and Z is the cost per brochure. We know that Z is smaller than Y.

Thus we can see that:
- ➤ Price structure 2 will start out as the most expensive, due to W.
- ➤ However, because Y is larger than Z, as the number of brochures increases, the price of Price structure 1) will increase at a larger rate than the price of price structure 2).
- ➤ Thus, as the number of brochures increases, Price structure 2) will be comparatively less expensive when compared to Price Structure 1), until we reach a point where they are the same (let this number be termed Equiv).
- ➤ Above point Equiv, Price Structure 2 will be cheaper.

Thus, knowing point Equiv (the number of brochures for which each price structure is the same) is sufficient to know which price structure will be cheaper. If Point Equiv is greater than 500, price structure 1) will be cheaper. If Point Equiv is less than 500, Price Structure 2) will be cheaper.

Thus A) is the answer.

Question 39: E

The passage describes how both mobile phones and masts emit radiation, and describes how mobile phones emit much more. The passage then discusses how these levels are both below what the guidelines say is dangerous, but that we cannot be sure if these guidelines are accurate. From this, we cannot conclude that mobile phones put people's health at risk, we can only conclude that we can't be certain they don't. Thus, A) is incorrect. Neither can we conclude that the guidelines are incorrect, or those living close to a mast over-estimate the risk. Thus, B) and D) are incorrect.

C) is mistaken. The passage has said that there is less radiation emitted from a mobile phone than a mast, and described how much lower the radiation level is.

However, occasional/infrequent mobile phone use may result in less radiation than living near a mast. Thus, C) is not a valid conclusion.

However, E) identifies a valid conclusion. Since the radiation levels are lower from a mast, if *extensive* mobile phone use poses no threat, it is *unlikely* that living near a mast does.

Question 40: D

The passage describes 2 purposes of University education, and then mentions there are others. It does not claim that any of these is the primary purpose, so A) and B) are incorrect.

C) and E) are not relevant to the argument's conclusion (which is that University should not simply consist of forcing through as many graduates as possible at minimum cost), thus neither are assumptions.

D) correctly identifies an assumption. The argument discusses how we should not simply force through graduates at minimum cost. However, it is not stated that cost-cutting policies will stop Universities achieving their overall purpose. If this is not true, the argument's conclusion is no longer valid. Thus, D) is a valid assumption in the passage.

Question 41: B

The passage is giving reasons that the maintenance of a First Class section on trains is detrimental to the service enjoyed by *most* passengers (those travelling in standard class). We can quickly see that if B) is true, then the opposite is actually true, and First Class is of benefit to the rest of the rail service, thanks to the revenue it produces. Thus, B) weakens the argument.

A) and E) do not affect how the maintenance of a First Class service affects the facilities in Standard class, so neither of these affect the argument's conclusion.
D) is an irrelevant statement as the passage has said that First Class is not indefensible because of the expense.
C) actually strengthens the argument, as it reinforces the idea that the majority of people are travelling in standard class, thus contributing to the conclusion that *most* passengers suffer from the First Class provision.

Question 42: E

If the piece of card is folded up, then we can see that the triangle extension on the bottom-right of the net will align with the top section (with the diagonal line separating shaded and non-shaded), such that the tip of the non-shaded section of the triangle is touching the tip of the *shaded* section of the top section. Thus, A) will be a possible view from the right-hand side of the shape once it is made.
We can readily see that B) will be a possible view, because we can see that the triangle extension on the bottom right is already attached to the bottom section (with a horizontal line separating shaded from non-shaded), as seen in B).

C) is also possible, because the bottom-right triangle extension will align with the middle section (with a vertical line separating shaded from non-shaded), such that a non-shaded edge of the triangle is aligned with the shaded section of the middle section, as seen in C).

D) is a possible view because the middle-left triangle extension will align with the top section (with the diagonal line separating shaded from non-shaded), such that a non-shaded edge of the triangle is aligned with the *shaded* side of the top section, as seen in D).
E) is not a possible view. We can see that the bottom-right triangle is aligned with the bottom section in the opposite way to that seen in E) (i.e. the shaded and non-shaded sections are reversed compared to how they appear in E). Meanwhile, the left triangle extension will align with this section such that a non-shaded edge aligns with the bottom section, which is not what is seen in E). Thus, E) is not a possible view.

Question 43: C

First we must calculate the number of students studying Spanish. We can see that Spanish features twice in this table, in the Second row from the top, and in the right-hand column.

Thus, we simply add up the numbers in the second row from the top, and in the right-hand column. This gives us a total of 40 (14+9+13+4=40).
Now we see how many students are studying Spanish *and* French. We see from the left-hand column of the table that there are 14 students studying Spanish and French.

Thus we simply calculate 14 as a percentage of 40: $\left(\frac{14}{40}\right) X 100 = 35$

Thus 35% of Students studying Spanish are also studying French.
Hence, the answer is C)

Question 44: D

We can see that the different lines readily produce 5 triangles, immediately apparent. Thus, this accounts for 5 possible routes. The other routes are as follows:

➤ Start at the central intersection, proceed to the top left corner, then proceed to the bottom-most corner, then proceed back to the intersection. A mirror image route is also possible using the top-right corner. Thus, this accounts for 2 more possible routes.

➤ Start at the central intersection, proceed to the Top-left corner, then proceed to the bottom-most corner. At this point we then proceed in the direction of the top-right corner, but stop where there is an intersection with a path leading to the central intersection. We then head back to the starting point, along the path to the central intersection. Again, an opposite route is possible, beginning by heading to the top-right corner. Thus this accounts for 2 more possible routes.

➤ Start at the central intersection, and proceed to the top-left corner, then head to the top-right corner. At this point, we proceed in the direction of the bottom-most corner, but stop at the same intersection described in the last possible route, and head back to the central intersection. Again, there is an opposite possible route, beginning be heading to the top-right corner, then to the top-left corner. Thus, this accounts for two more possible routes.

Thus, we have accounted for 11 possible routes.
Thus, D) is the answer.

Question 45: D

The argument discusses how study leave, whilst benefitting hardworking students, does not produce the best results. It then finishes by saying "it is time to ditch study leave". This last sentence is crucial. Without this last sentence, C) would probably be the main conclusion, as there would be no suggestion in the argument that study leave should be abandoned, simply that it is not the best way to attain high results. However, the last sentence means that the argument *does* conclude that study leave should be abandoned. Thus, D) is the main conclusion. This means that C) is now an intermediate conclusion, going on to support the conclusion given in D).

A) is a reason given to support C), and thus contributing towards supporting D). Thus A) is not a conclusion in itself. E), meanwhile, adds further strength to the argument but is not a direct conclusion from it, as the argument has not claimed that traditional methods need to be updated.

B) actually weakens the argument by picking up on the fact that some students do very well from study leave, thanks to their own hard work and organisation.

Question 46: E

The argument is discussing how these lands were not obtained through just means, and so should be redistributed. The claim that they should be confiscated *directly leads on* from the fact that they have not been voluntarily redistributed, *because* of this fact.

Thus B) is incorrect, as B) implies that a different set of reasons is behind why they should be confiscated. D) is also incorrect, as the argument does not make any *legal* claims about why they should be confiscated, the argument is talking about social justice, and therefore referring to moral reasons, not legal reasons. A) is also irrelevant as the argument gives no economic reasons why they should be redistributed.

C) and E) both pose the issue of confiscation as leading on from the fact that the lands have not been voluntarily redistributed. However, only E) states that the confiscation should happen *because* they have not (*since* they have not). Thus, E) logically follows completes the argument.

Question 47: A

The argument's reasoning can be summarised as "All things that are A have/do/are B. This item is A, so must have B". Here, "A" is being a tree, and "B" is having leaves.

A) most closely follows this reasoning. Here "A" is all leaves growing, and "B" is those leaves being on trees. Thus, we conclude that where there are leaves, they must be on a tree. Thus, if a plant has leaves, it must be a tree.

B) reasons that "All of A has B", and the incorrectly concludes that if something has B, it must be A. This is not valid, as there may be other things apart from "A" that also have "B". D) also follows this incorrect reasoning, but with "oak" replaced by "tree" and "tree" replaced by "plant".

C) reasons that "All of A has B", then observes "This instance of B is C", and then incorrectly concludes that "All of A must be C". This is completely invalid, as there is no suggestion that everything that only C gives rise to B.

E) is also incorrect, claiming that "All of A has B, and that this example is not A", before incorrectly concluding that it does not have B. This follows the same flaw as B) and D). There may be other things apart from A that have B.

Question 48: B

First we calculate how much the charge would be for the detailed information on the 5 companies:

➢ Each request would be charged at 50c
➢ Thus, a total of $2.50 would be charged for detailed information on 5 companies

Then, Megan has used the other services 42 times. Each other service costs 10c, so it is irrelevant which services she has used. Thus the total charge for all other services would be $4.20

The question states that Probe's charges do not include the cost of phone calls, and then asks how much Megan will be billed by *probe*. Thus, the call charge need not be considered, as this will not be included in her Probe bill. The phone company will bill her for the call charges.

Thus, Megan will be charged $2.50 + $4.20, which is $6.70.
Thus, the answer is B)

Question 49: C

We are asked how many different possible combinations of course there are for a student taking Drainage. Since there is now one of the options filled, we can quickly work how many combinations would be possible without the restrictions given in the question:

➤ There are 6 other courses. Thus, multiplying 6X5 gives us the total number of ways in which each option could be listed with each of the other options. This gives us 30 possibilities.

➤ When we are thinking of possible course combinations, this number needs to be halved, as it will count each possible course twice (e.g. this number will include "Bricklaying and Damp-proofing" AND "Damp-proofing and Bricklaying" as possible course combinations. We can quickly see that both of these would result in the same combination of courses).

➤ Thus, without the restrictions given in the passage, there would be 15 possible combinations.

Now we can work out how many possible course combinations are made not possible by the restrictions given in the passage:

➤ Drainage and Damp-proofing may not be taken together with Bricklaying or Plastering. This removes 2 possible course combinations (Drainage/Damp-proofing/Bricklaying and Drainage/Damp-proofing/Plastering)

➤ If Joinery is taken, Flooring must also be taken. This removes 4 possible course combinations (The combinations which now cannot be taken are Drainage/Joinery/Bricklaying,   Drainage/Joinery/Damp-proofing, Drainage/Joinery/Plastering and Drainage/Joinery/Roofing)

Thus, 6 possible combinations are removed by the restrictions given in the question. Thus the number of possible combinations is 15-6, which is 9.

Hence, the answer is C)

Question 50: C

Let the fixed postal charge be termed "Y".

There is a £2.00 discount per book versus shop prices. Thus, the total savings in £ versus shop prices can be described as: 2(Number of Books)-Y.

We can see from this equation that as the number of books increases, the savings will increase *in multiples of 2*, as each book adds another £2.00 saving (and we cannot add a fraction of a book to the order, we can only add whole numbers of books). Thus, graph B) cannot be correct, as in this graph the saving increases by more than £2 for each book that is added.

We can also see that thanks to the fixed postal charge, the saving for 1 book **cannot** be higher than £2, as there will be a £2 saving *minus* the postal charge. Graphs A) and E) both show the saving for 1 book being £2 or higher, thus both of these graphs cannot be correct. We can also see that in Graph A) the saving increases in increments of less than £2 per book, adding further reasons why this cannot be correct.

Additionally, we can readily see that answer D) is incorrect, because this shows the saving being higher for 1 book than it is for 2, 3 or 4 books. This cannot be possible, as we can see from our equation that the saving will increase as the number of books does.

Graph C) is the only graph which fulfils all these criteria, with a saving of less than £2 for 1 book, and the saving increasing at a rate of £2 per additional book.

END OF SECTION

Section 2

Is the general understanding of science damaged by the way it is presented in the media?

When answering this question you should be careful to define your terms. Specify which forms of media you will be discussing (these should be the ones you think most relevant to the question) and what you consider to be 'damage' to general understanding – is any kind of misunderstanding damaging, or only that which causes actual harm to an individual or the general public? Be wary of generalising 'media' as a whole also; consider whether some forms of media have been more damaging than others, or whether it's a case of good science and bad science, both of which can occurs in any form of media.

Introduction:
➢ You should use your introduction to give an overview of how you believe the media presents science, and what media you will be referring to. Since the 'general understanding' of science through media is mostly through popular media such as pop science books and documentaries, you will most likely want to start there and give a few examples of the kind of media you will be discussing.
➢ You may wish to describe the way science is presented in media as any number of: accurate, inaccurate, sensationalised, biased, unbiased, varied.
➢ Once you have established what you here mean by 'media' and how you think it presents science, clearly state your opinion on whether the general understanding of science is damaged by this, and the arguments you will use to defend this view, as well as the counterarguments to these and your reasons for dismissing them.

Potential arguments for:
➢ Popular media often simplifies scientific concepts so they can be understood by more people, but as a result the concept is twisted and misunderstood.
➢ The media is sensationalistic and presents scientific breakthroughs or a discovery of some new piece of evidence as more significant and conclusive than they actually are. Where a researched might say "study Y has found evidence consistent with conclusion X", a newspaper may print that "scientists prove theory X!"
➢ Some presentation of 'science' in popular media may be misleading or downright inaccurate – think of the arguments against vaccinating children that point to the tiny, harmless mercury content in vaccines, or use fear

mongering and hyperbole. Although we can dismiss this as 'bad science', the extent to which the public has been taught to believe representations of science presented on TV or in books uncritically is damaging, and a result of a lack of emphasis on transparent sourcing of information in these mediums.

Potential arguments against:

➤ Any moderately accurate representation of science in media accessible to the public (popular science books, documentaries, etc., as opposed to scientific journals) aids a general understanding. Although the concepts may be simplified to make them accessible and understandable, this is still preferable to no understanding at all, and people generally know they do not derive a completely accurate understanding of the subject from these sources alone.

➤ It is fine for the general public's understanding to be slightly inaccurate, or communicated primarily through, say, analogy rather than a more precise explanation. There are certain things the public needs to have some understanding of – how vaccines work, for example, and why they're important – so they can make an informed decision, and this understanding should be communicated in a way that is accessible to someone without a biology degree.

➤ The simplification of scientific concepts that occurs in popular media is no worse than the simplification that occurs at various levels of education. For example, until a certain point, school children are taught that light always travels in straight lines, because this is usually true, and is all the information they need to understand things like how we see colour, reflection, and so on. If they pursue physics to higher levels, they will learn that light bends near sources of very strong gravity – but this is not something you need to know if your physics education doesn't go beyond more simplistic concepts.

➤ It is impossible to say that all media presentation of science is damaging because it is such a vast and varied industry. While there are undoubtedly some inaccurate, overly simplistic, or sensationalist representations of science in the media, there are just as many representations that are highly beneficial to the general public. To say that the media in general is damaging is overly simplistic itself.

Conclusion:

➤ Summarise what constitutes media, and how it generally presents science.

➤ If you have given a more nuanced view – that some presentations are damaging while others are not – be sure to make that perfectly clear in the conclusion, and outline what makes the difference between a damaging and beneficial presentation of science.

Do patent laws encourage or hinder development?

This essay is easy to structure well. Begin by clearly presenting the case for your side, then explain the potential counterarguments to your points, and your reasons for dismissing them. It is worthwhile to note that the question assumes patent laws have either a positive or negative effect on development; it is perfectly valid to question this assumption by asserting that they have no impact on development. If you wish to take this route, make this point in your introduction, then present the case for them encouraging development, then the case for them hindering development (or the other way round; the order is unimportant if you take this route), and refute each side. Patents are a controversial topic with many arguments on both side; be careful not to get off topic, and limit your argument to that which concerns development specifically.

Introduction:
➢ Begin by outlining what you believe 'development' to be. One potential definition is "the process of growing and becoming more mature, advanced, or elaborate". Given that this question applies the concept to patents, the development will be in technology, including electronics, manufacturing processes, recipes, medication, etc. – in short, anything that can be sold.
➢ It is worth also giving a (very) brief explanation of what a patent is – "a government authority or licence conferring a right or title for a set period, especially the sole right to exclude others from making, using, or selling an invention" – or some other explicit indication that you know what it is.
➢ Clearly state your position and outline the main arguments you will be using to defend it, as well as counterarguments to these and why you feel they should be dismissed.

Potential arguments for encouraging development:
➢ Patents give an individual sole possession over their intellectual work. This motivates people not only before they have developed a piece of technology (since they know they will get the recognition for and ownership of the product they deserve), but after they have developed it, they will be motivated to keep working on it, as they are the only ones who can.
➢ Patents of technology encourages the competition to develop their own. Without patents, everyone would simply use the technology developed by other people, with no motivation to create new, better products.
➢ Patents allow developers of new technology to ensure they can make a profit, by being the sole producer of a certain product. Without this guarantee, people wouldn't be as motivated to develop new technology.

> Patent holders can license their technology to other developers, so there is no risk of completely limiting development if the patent holder decides to go no further with their technology, or if other developers have the potential to improve it.

  o **Counterargument**: this may be the case, but licenses can be very expensive, and represent a cost that at least some, if not many, developers will not be able to afford, and so naturally limits development – and this is if the patent holder is willing to license their patented technology at all.

Potential arguments for hindering development:

> Patents disallow the possibility of new developers either improving on existing designs, or using small pieces of technology as component parts in new products; patents prevent these products being developed at all.

> Patents allow one company to hold a monopoly over a certain industry. This is not only bad for consumers in everyday industries (as monopoly holders can set prices according to what will maximise their individual profits, rather than at competitive rates), but can be fatal when applied to the healthcare industry. Medication patented and monopolised by one company can be vastly too expensive for some people to afford; consider the millions of poor people who die from HIV every year because they can't afford the patented medication that could save them. This many people dying preventable deaths as a result of patents naturally hinders development.

> The development of new technology rarely happens by developing completely new products. Rather, people tend to modify and improve on existing products, but this is too similar to the old technology to be legal if it is patented, so patents prevent this kind of development.

> People don't develop new technology for the sake of profit alone, they do so because of natural human inventiveness and drive, and a desire to fill a need or want not currently being fulfilled. They would continue to do this even without a guarantee of profit as a result of patents and, indeed, they already do – even with patents, there is no guarantee their efforts to develop new products will be fruitful, or successful in the market, and yet they continue to develop.

> The cost of developing new technology – requiring intellectual labour, manufacturing of various designs, testing, etc. – is very high, but the cost of reproducing technology once we know how to make it is relatively very low. If technology is all patented, the overall cost of production in any given industry is very high, since each producer must develop and produce their own technology. This is particularly concerning in fields such as medication,

for the reasons discussed above, but hinders development in all fields by raising the costs of production.

➤ These higher costs of production further hinder development by preventing *new*, potentially very good, producers from entering the industry – the costs of entry are too high. If they could use the technology already available to them, they could work on developing only their one or two particular areas of interest, and progress would be made there. As it is, in order to enter an industry developing new technology, they would need to develop new forms of all the technology they need.

Conclusion:

➤ Restate your position and summarise the main arguments you have used to defend it.

➤ Be sure to link your conclusion back to the question by referring to the concept of development, and the impact patents have on it.

Do coalitions necessarily adopt policies which unite party leaders but alienate party followers?

The two most important words to note in this question are 'alienate' and 'necessarily'. The concept of alienation is a tricky one, so be sure to give a clear definition of how you will be using the term in the introduction, and refer to a concrete concept of alienation (rather than some other 'bad' outcome for party followers) throughout your essay. 'Necessarily' is important because the question is asking whether this will *always* be the case, whether alienation of party follows *must* follow from coalitions which will *always* adopt policies which unite party leaders. It is possible to answer this question, for instance, by arguing that coalitions *tend* to have this result, and *usually* will, but it is not *necessarily* the case. This essay can be structured simply by presenting your case, considering the counterarguments, and giving your reasons to dismiss them.

Introduction:
➢ The term to give a clear definition of here is 'alienate' – one potential definition of alienate is "to make someone feel isolated or estranged".
➢ It is also important to give a clear indication that you know what a coalition is. This need not be a precise definition, and should be implicit throughout your whole essay, but be sure to make sure this is clearly conveyed to the reader.
➢ Clearly state your viewpoint and outline the arguments you will use to defend it, and your reasons for dismissing counterarguments.

Potential arguments for:
➢ In a coalition, there usually needs to be some form of agreement between party leaders on any legislation; this means there will naturally have to be compromise on party policy, and the party followers, presumably broadly in support of their party's original policy promises, will naturally feel alienated by the leaders' move away from the party's principles.
➢ Having voted for their party on the understanding that, if they get into power, they will enact their policies, party members will feel alienated when seeing their party leaders agree to policy not in line with their principles.
➢ Coalitions will adopt policy that unites party leaders because this is the *only* policy they are able to agree on: where party leaders' are too opposed to changing their established policy to compromise, no policy will be able to be enacted. Where this occurs, in the UK at least, legislation is often left to an open vote in the House of Commons (rather than members of both parties being whipped into voting one way or another); this is not the coalition adopting a policy, but rather legislation emerges from the components of the Commons and their say on proposed Government policy.

Potential arguments against:
➢ Though we may observe any number of coalitions that have done this, this is not even close to establishing that they *necessarily* do.
➢ It is not the case that there needs to be some form of agreement between party leaders on legislation. In coalitions where there is a dominant member (i.e.: a coalition in which one party has a large plurality, and the other a minority) and there is a clear leader of the coalition, they are able to dominate policy and adopt ones consistent with their followers' preferences. An example of this is the 2010 UK coalition between the Conservatives and the Liberal Democrats.
➢ Compromise on policy is not likely to make party members feel alienated. They will understand that their party does not have the power to enact policy without the approval of their coalition partner(s); so long as their party leaders continue to attempt to enact party policy, they may be frustrated and disappointed with the result, but will not feel alienated.
➢ Coalitions do not necessarily adopt policies that unite party leaders. In Germany, for example, coalition governments are the norm, rather than single party governments as in the UK, and so open disagreement between coalition members is considered usual.
➢ Further to this, where coalitions are more frequent than they are in the UK, party members are perhaps less likely to feel alienated by leaders compromising on policy, as it is expected even when the electorate votes for their preferred party.
➢ Parties tend to enter into coalitions with other parties at a similar position on the political spectrum as themselves. Their policies may therefore not be too dissimilar, and compromise on some or many issues may not be severe enough to cause feelings of alienation (which includes isolation and estrangement from) the party among members.

Conclusion:
➢ Link your conclusion back to the question by referring to the nature of coalitions, and whether they can have a fracturing impact on party members.
➢ When answering questions of this nature, it can be nice to, at the end of your essay, make a short concluding comment (only a sentence or two) on the debate itself – for example, a comment on how significant alienating party members may be to the party, to democracy, etc.

Should we have a right to choose when and how we die?

This question is highly controversial, and as such provides a great many points to make on both sides of the argument. Be sure to note the interesting concept of a 'right', which implies that anyone should have this freedom, not only those to whom the term 'euthanasia' would apply, as many people would otherwise assume. This essay is easy to structure well: lay out the outline of the argument in your introduction, then make the case for your view point. Follow this with counterarguments, and give your reason for opposing each of them.

Introduction:
> ➤ Define the concept of a 'right' – one such definition is "a moral or legal entitlement to have or do something". If someone has the right to choose when and how they die, then it is something they *prima facie* should be allowed to do.
> ➤ Clearly state your position and outline the arguments you will use to defend it, as well as the counterarguments to these and your reasons for dismissing them.
> ➤ If you are going to argue that people do have a right to choose when and how they die, you may want to use your introduction to quickly outline any limitations on this – for example, if there are limitations on exactly how they may do it (suicide in public spaces, for example, being prohibited). If you like, you may expand on this in greater detail later in the essay, but given the limited time it is also fine to focus on arguments surrounding whether we have any right to choose to die at all.

Potential arguments for:
> ➤ Many people who want to make the choice to die are terminally ill and/or in a lot of pain that cannot be prevented. Allowing them to die is the kindest thing to do, so they may do so as painlessly and with as much dignity as possible.
> ➤ The choice between a lot of pain for a short amount of time and then death, and immediate death, is not a choice anyone but those in the situation can relate to, so it is not up to anyone but them to weigh in on the decision.
>> • **Counterargument**: is this tantamount to a generic 'right to die'? Surely a '*right*' to choose how and when you die must be applicable to anyone, not only the terminally ill or those in a great deal of pain. This argument does not concern a right to choose how and when you die, it concerns a right to euthanasia, which is a related, though different, debate.
> ➤ People should have completely bodily autonomy; they know what is best for themselves better than anyone else, and should be able to carry this out.

Indeed, even if they *don't* know what is best for themselves, they ought to be able to make choices about their bodies, which are wholly their own.

- **Counterargument:** what about people who can't make even good decisions for themselves? We do not allow, for instance, small children to decide their own medical care; are there are cases of adults who are in an inferior position to someone else to make medical decisions?

➤ We already allow, and mostly agree with allowing, people to decide in advance when they would like to stop being assisted in living ("do not resuscitate" orders, for instance), and to make the choice to stop receiving treatment if they decide the effort of continuing to get better outweighs the benefits. Allowing people to make the active choice to die is no morally different from this, but does save them the pain of having to die slowly without medication, or wait until their condition is severe enough that simply not being resuscitated will kill them.

Potential arguments against:

➤ Giving people the right to choose when they die is open to abuse by, say, people who no longer want the responsibility of looking after elderly or sick family members, or who want their inheritance; they could bully or manipulate these family members into 'choosing' euthanasia. This is especially relevant given that a disproportionate amount of the people who would choose to die would be very old or sick, and so vulnerable to such manipulation.

- **Counterargument:** isn't this just an argument for restricting how one may enact that choice to die? Perhaps they must sign a waiver and discuss their choice with a doctor or psychiatrist (perhaps one specially trained in such matters) before going through with it, to ensure such coercion does not occur. This is not an actual argument against the right to die.

➤ People who would choose to die are not in their right minds, since no one in their right mind would choose to die; they ought to be protected from themselves and prevented from acting rashly.

- **Counterargument:** this argument is circular and unfounded. True, the choice to die seems farfetched to a lot of people, but that is because most people do not have a desire to die. This desire does not come only from being of unsound mind, but also from being in extreme, unpreventable pain, or facing inevitable and imminent death anyway – both of which are scenarios the average people cannot relate to. To label this as evidence of insanity from which the person needs to be protected is judgemental and condescending.

- **Counterargument:** further, who are we to say that, say, a depressed person is not 'in their right mind' or this is not 'what they really want'? They are still capable of rational thought and making the best decision for themselves; if their mental pain is so severe they decide they would like to die, how is this different from the patient in an extreme amount of physical pain who would like to die?

➢ People should only have the right to die in certain situations – for example, if they are terminally ill and want to avoid the pain of wasting away slowly. Allowing it at any time has too much potential to be exploited by dangerous, manipulative individuals, and for death to occur as a result of neglect – not taking into account someone's severe depression when they 'choose' to die, for instance.

- **Counterargument:** is it really a 'right' if it's only allowed in some circumstances? No other person has the right to choose when another is in a severe enough situation to warrant control over their own life.

➢ Giving people the right to choose how and when they die has implications for people who are not able to kill themselves; this 'right' will effectively mean they have the right to assisted suicide, i.e.: they have the right to insist that someone else kill them. This is not a right to which anyone is entitled.

➢ Dying doesn't only affect the individual who dies; family, friends, involved medical professionals, all deal with hurt, loss, grief, and guilt, among other emotions; is it right for the dying person to inflict this on them?

- **Counterargument:** a great many choices we make over our own bodies may cause distress to another person (e.g.: people who have abortions distress those who oppose abortions; transgender people who seek gender confirming surgery distress transphobes; people who get tattoos may upset their parents), this is not a reason to undermine their fundamental right to bodily autonomy.

Conclusion:

➢ If you have taken a nuanced view – for example, if you have argued that people have the right to choose when and how they die only in certain situations, e.g.: in the case of a terminally ill patient – be sure to make that explicit in your conclusion, and outline what constitutes an appropriate situation for this right to be made available.

END OF PAPER

2012

Section 1

Question 1: D

D) correctly identifies the main conclusion of the argument. If we accept the reasons given in the passage as true, they support this conclusion.

A), B) and C) are all reasons given in the passage which support this conclusion. E), meanwhile, is neither a reason nor a conclusion from the passage. The passage makes no reference to whether speaking a foreign language is easier or harder than sign language

Question 2: A

Stewart and Michael live 8 kilometres apart so to meet they will need to travel a total of 8 kilometres in total. It only matters who travels each distance in terms of the time it will take; as long as the total is 8km as they can meet anywhere between the two houses. Michael can cycle 5/3 as quickly as Stewart can run so Michael can travel 5/3 the distance as Stewart in the same time.

Therefore when they meet, Michael should travel 5/3 as far. Hence Michael should travel 5 kilometres and Stewart should travel 3 kilometres. It takes Stewart an hour to run 12 kilometres so it will take him quarter of an hour, or 15 minutes, to run 3 kilometres (we can verify this by checking how long it takes Michael to cycle 20 kilometres). Hence the answer is A.

Question 3: E

E) correctly identifies a flaw in the argument's reasoning. If we accept E) as true, then the argument's conclusion no longer logically follows from its reasoning, and thus E) is a valid flaw from the argument.

D) is not a flaw, as possible methods to solve the issues created by a lack of demand for meat and dairy do not detract from the fact that government advice to eat more fruit has been a cause of this. A), meanwhile, is a matter of opinion, and does not directly affect whether the argument's reasoning lead on to its conclusion. B) and C) are irrelevant to the argument's conclusion.

Question 4: D
The argument says nothing about whether the risk outweighs the benefit, and for the purposes of a critical thinking assessment like the TSA, we should accept the reasons given in the argument as true. Therefore B) and C) are incorrect. E) is also incorrect as the argument makes no claims about whether government should take a role in regulating piercings.

A), meanwhile, is incorrect as the fact that specialist piercers account for few hospitalisations does not necessarily lead on to the conclusion that they give good advice about caring for piercings.

D), however, can be reliably concluded, as it does readily follow on that people would be well advised to go to a reputable piercer if these account for few hospitalisations.

Question 5: D
At no point is it stated that women are as likely as men to possess the skills required for senior working positions. However, if this is not true, the argument's reasons do not logically lead on to its conclusion. Therefore, D) is a valid assumption in the passage.

B) and E) do not affect the argument's conclusion and are thus incorrect, whilst C) is not required to be true for the argument's conclusion to be valid, so is not an assumption.

A), meanwhile, actually weakens the argument, if true, so is not an assumption.

Question 6: B
When the daughter is not at home, they spend £120. 70% of this is the food bill, which is £84. 20% is household goods, which is £24. 10% is store cupboard essentials, which is £12.

When the daughter returns, the weekly food bill increases by 20%. 20% of £84 is £16.80, so the food bill is now £100.80. Spending on household goods goes up by 5%. 5% of £24 is £1.20, so the household goods bill is now £25.20. They still spend £12 on store cupboard essentials.

Hence the total food bill is £100.80+£25.20+£12.00 = £138.00. Hence the answer is B.

Question 7: C

On Wednesday afternoon, there must be an English teacher and a Spanish teacher invigilating. All of the English teachers are female, so Marjorie or Jenny must invigilate with a male Spanish teacher. The only male Spanish teacher is Keith, so he must invigilate on Wednesday afternoon.

We also know that each person can only invigilate once a day. In the morning, there is a Maths exam, and Marjorie is the only Maths teacher. Therefore she must have invigilated in the morning, which means she cannot invigilate in the afternoon.

Hence Jenny must invigilate in the afternoon. Hence the invigilators are Keith and Jenny.

Question 8: C

Cutting the cylinder lengthways down the middle allows the views seen in A) and D). Cutting widthways across the middle of the cylinder allows the view seen in B). Cutting diagonally across the length allows the view seen in E). There is no cut which produces 2 equal halves which allows the view seen in C).

Question 9: C

C) would weaken the argument, as it suggests that the risk present to endangered animals is small and not significant, since endangered bear populations have not been affected by the growth in hunting clubs. B) does not necessarily weaken the argument, because the fact that few people take part in the activities does not definitely mean that they will not have an effect on the populations of endangered animals.

D) and E) actually strengthen the argument, suggesting that the clubs are not necessary and that they have a larger effect on wildlife by killing more animals than their targets. A) is an irrelevant statement.

Question 10: E

E) correctly identifies a flaw in the argument, pointing out that even if laptops run out, they will still be of some use to passengers, and therefore the argument they take up a "disproportional" amount of space may be invalid.

C) and D) are completely irrelevant to whether the laptops take up a disproportional amount of space, whilst A) does not affect the conclusion because the argument has stated this should happen "regardless" of whether the laptops are used for personal or business use.

B) meanwhile actually strengthens the argument by providing reasons for laptops being carried in the hold rather than as carry-on items.

Question 11: A

A) correctly identifies the main conclusion of the argument. All the reasons provided come together to support the idea that parents should to more to regulate what their children watch on TV.

C) and D) both contradict points of the argument, and so are not conclusions.
B) and E), meanwhile, both serve to reinforce the main conclusion. If parents are not concerned by what their children watch on TV, and some do not believe it is causing their children to behave badly, then this helps support the idea that parents are not doing enough to control what their children watch on TV, and should "do more"

Question 12: B

45 people had neither maths or economics as part of their degree, so 230-45 = 185 people must have had either maths or economics, or both, as part of their degree. 127+89 = 216 so there is an overlap of 216 − 185 = 31 people. Hence 31 people must have had both maths and economics as part of their degree. Hence the answer is B.

Question 13: A

1 playing board is needed for each box, so 8 are needed for a carton. There are 98, so this makes 12 cartons.50 question cards are needed for each box, so 400 are needed for a carton. There are 5000 question cards, so this makes 12 cartons.

6 playing pieces are needed for each box, so 48 are needed for a carton. There are 1000 playing pieces, so this makes 20 cartons.

40 money tokens are needed for each box, so 320 are needed for a carton. There are 5000 money tokens, so this makes 15 cartons. 12 bonus tokens are needed for each box, so 96 are needed for a carton. There are 1000 bonus tokens, so this makes 10 cartons.

2 dice are needed for each box, so 16 are needed for a carton. There are 300 dice, so this makes 18 cartons.

We only have enough bonus tokens to make up 10 cartons of the complete game, so only 10 cartons can be dispatched. Hence the answer is A.

Question 14: B

D) cannot be correct as there is no orientation in which it could have a hexagon-shape in the bottom-right corner, and a rectangle shape just below the top-left corner, thus it cannot be the same layout as the one in the question.

The other shapes can all be placed in an orientation where there is a hexagon-shape in the bottom right corner and a rectangle shape just below the top-left corner. We now look to see what other shapes these boards have.:

➢   If A) is placed in the same orientation as the image in the picture, we see that there would be a triangle shape 1 space above and 1 space to the left of the hexagon shape. We can see from the image in the question that this space is uncovered and that there is no triangle shape, so this cannot be the answer.

➢   In C) we see a triangle shape in the space immediately to the left of the top-right corner. In E) we see a rectangle shape in this space. In the image in the question, we see this space is uncovered and there is neither a triangle nor a rectangle shape in this space, so neither C) nor E) can be the answer.

➢   If B) is placed in the same orientation as the image in the picture (i.e. rotated 180 degrees), there are triangle shape in the bottom-left corner, and in the space above and to the right of the bottom-left corner. There is also a rectangle shape immediately above the bottom-right corner. In the image in the question, all of these spaces are covered by counters, so this could be the same board as in the question.

Question 15: C

C) correctly identifies a conclusion that readily and logically follows on from the reasoning given in this paragraph.

B) is irrelevant to the argument, whilst A) and E) actually contradict/weaken the argument.

D) is not completely irrelevant to the argument, but it is irrelevant to its conclusion. It offers more explanation of the purpose of punishing directors, but does not directly affect how the argument's reasons lead on to its conclusion.

Question 16: B

The argument's conclusion is that America has high levels of free debate. It's thread of reasons to support this refer to the amount of anti-administration debate in the country following 2004. Thus, if the statement is B) is not true, then it's conclusion is invalid. B) is not stated at any point, so it is therefore an assumption.

C), D) and E) are all completely irrelevant to the argument or its conclusion.

A), meanwhile, actually contradicts the argument, as the argument claims that there was ferocious support of the administration in 2004.

Question 17: C

The argument concludes that diet is responsible for higher cancer rates in Europe. If we accept C) as true, then this suggests something else is responsible, and weakens this conclusion.

B), D) and E) are completely irrelevant to the argument or its conclusions, whilst A) actually strengthens the argument. Suggesting that diet is not a contributing factor towards cancer in areas with low cancer rates reinforces the notion that it may be contributing towards cancer in areas with higher cancer rates (i.e. Europe in this instance).

Question 18: A

From the signal Gordon gets, the bird could be at (21,05), (22,05), (23,05), (20,06), (21,06), (23,06), (24,06), (21,07), (22,07), (23,07) or (22,08).
From the signal Helen gets, the bird could be at (22,05), (23,05), (24,05), (21,06), (22,06), (24,06), (25,06), (22,07), (23,07), (24,07) or (23,08)
From the signal Ingrid gets, the bird could be at (22,07), (24,07)
The coordinates that are possible for all 3 are: (22,07)
Hence the answer is A.

Question 19: D

(100-11) = 89% of men consume more than 6g of salt per day. (100-30) = 70% consume more than 6g of salt per day. If there are equal numbers of men and women then the percentage of the population that consumes more than 6g of salt per day is halfway between this, which is 79.5% or to the nearest percent, 80%. Hence the answer is D.

Question 20: B

The software programmer is organising the program in **descending** size order, and assigning them to the first disc which has enough room for it. In B), the plumber is doing the same thing, organising lengths in **descending** size order, and cutting from the first pipe which has enough length for it.

In E), the plumber is doing the opposite by arranging lengths in **ascending** size order. In D) he is deviating from the method by cutting alternate longest and shortest lengths. In C), he is deviating by simply taking them in the order listed, not organising at all.

In A) he is deviating from the method in the question by cutting the lengths which add up to 12 ft first, a feature which is not seen in the programmer's method.

Question 21: A

The passage concludes that pesticides are a waste of money and it would be better to let other insects control pests. However, if pesticides are more effective than letting the other insects control the pests, then pesticides are not a waste of money, and the argument's conclusion is invalid. Thus, A) is correct.

B), if true, would actually strengthen the argument, but is not essential for it to be valid, so B) is not a flaw. C) is not a flaw because it is not required for there to be a positive benefit associated with using insects to control pests in order for one to suggest it as a solution. Therefore, the fact that the argument does not establish this is not a logical flaw with the argument's reasoning.

D), if true, would also strengthen the argument, so is not a flaw, whilst E) is irrelevant. For a critical thinking assessment, we treat the stated reasons given as true, so it is not a flaw in this context that this fact is not explained or justified.

Question 22: C

The passage describes a situation where there are 2 courses of action, one of which must be followed. One of them cannot be followed, due to dire consequences, so the other must be followed regardless of the drawbacks. C) follows this reasoning. Aspirin or Paracetamol need to be taken, and aspirin cannot be taken due to allergy, so paracetamol must be taken.

A) presents a course of action that would ideally be followed but cannot be. B) presents 2 possible sources of a negative situation, one of which cannot be fixed, so we may as well implement a solution to the other. D) and E) present a 2 courses of action, one of which is simply *preferable*, and not *essential*. None of these alternative answers follow the reasoning in the passage.

Question 23: E

The question describes a principle where policies/initiatives which *help* a situation should not be dismissed because they do not fully solve the problem on their own. Only E) follows this reasoning.

A) contradicts the principle, suggesting a policy be abandoned because it has failed to solve a problem. B), C) and D) are completely irrelevant to the argument, and can be safely ignored.

Question 24: C

Alan bought the jug for £80 and then sold it again for £100 which is £20 profit. He then bought the jug again for £110 and sold it for £120, which is another £10 profit.

Hence the total profit is £10 + £20 = £30. Hence the answer is C.

Question 25: D

The crew take off from Rome at 09:05 and arrive in London at 09:55, then take off from London at 10:30 and arrive back in Rome at 13:45. They then depart Rome at 15:05 as that is the next flight and arrive in London 15:55, and then depart London at 16:30 and arrive back in Rome at 19:45.

Hence the total time from first take off to last landing is the time between 09:05 and 19:45, which is 10 hours 40 minutes.
Hence the answer is D.

Question 26: A

We can see that because the two holes in A) are mirror images of each other, and each would be a reflection of the other, if a mirror were placed along the dotted line. Thus, once the paper is folded along the dotted line, they will align onto each other, and the resultant shape will be the holes seen in A), not the hole seen in the picture.

All the other answers, when folded together, will overlap each other's edges, such that a new hole will be seen not resembling either of the holes as seen prior to folding. This will result in a new hole being seen, the same shape as that in the question.

Question 27: B

B) correctly identifies the main conclusion of the passage, which readily follows on from the reasoning given in the passage.
The passage makes no reference to what the result of a referendum would be, whether this would be a positive outcome, or whether the Scottish government receives sufficient funding. Therefore, A), E) and C) are all incorrect.
D), meanwhile, is a reason given in the passage that leads on to support the main conclusion given in B)

Question 28: D

The argument describes how everyone is exposed to asbestos in the environment, and how it is no cause for concern when exposed to it if it is in good condition. D) is the only answer which can be confidently concluded from these reasons.

A), B) and C) are incorrect, as they do not necessarily follow on from the reasons given in the passage. Equally, there is nothing in the passage to suggest that removing asbestos poses more of a threat than leaving it in place, so E) is incorrect.

Question 29: C

At no point does the argument state that law-breaking motorists are a significant cause of road accidents, yet it concludes that a substantial reduction in road accidents can be achieved by taking action to prevent law-breaking on the roads. Thus, C) correctly identifies a valid assumption, which is required to be true for the argument's conclusion to be valid.

E) is not an assumption because the passage states that many drivers break the law because the penalties do not act as a sufficient deterrent.

Meanwhile, A), B) and D) do not affect the argument's conclusion, so are not assumptions.

Question 30: B

For the first application, 12 litres is made up which is 1/16 Greatgrass. Hence 0.75 litres or 750ml of Greatgrass is used in the first application. For the second application, 12 litres is made up which is 1/25 Greatgrass. Hence 480ml of Greatgrass is used in the second application.

Hence the total amount of Greatgrass used is 750ml+480ml = 1230ml.

Hence the answer is B.

Question 31: E

There are 200 pupils altogether. 90 got A-C in their mock exams and then again in their actual exams, so this was correctly predicted. Another 60 got other grades in their mock exams and then again in their actual exams, so this was correctly predicted.

Hence for 150 of the 200 pupils, the mocks correctly predicted their GCSE results. This is equal to 75% of the pupils.

Hence the answer is E.

Question 32: A

The shape in A) can be used 4 times to make the trapezium. First, take 2 of the shapes. If we rotate one by 180 degrees, they can then fit together, with the slanted lines joined together, to form a rectangle shape. The other 2 shapes will then fit either side of this, to form the 2 sides of the trapezium.

Triangles can be used to form a trapezium, but 5 are required, so B) and C) are not correct. The shapes in D) and E) obviously do not readily form a trapezium without many being used, beyond the scope of what is expected in the timeframe of a test such as the TSA.

Question 33: A
The passage argues that over time, the intervention group will change their diet, and less strictly follow the healthy diet regime. This will cause their diet to become closer to that of the control group as time progresses. If the control group are also editing their diet according to health information released by the media, this will further narrow the gap in diet between the 2, strengthening the argument that the diets will be similar over time, and will differ less and less.

None of the other possible answers make reference to the notion of the 2 diets becoming more and more similar over time, therefore none of them are relevant to the conclusion of the argument.
Therefore the Answer is A)

Question 34: A
The argument discusses how the police have used excessive force and breached people's liberties, and then goes on to conclude that it would be better if this did not happen and drugs were simply allowed to be sold in nightclubs to keep dealers off the streets. A) correctly points out that the argument has assumed that these are the only options, and neglected to consider other possible ways of stopping drug dealers without such excessive force.

B) is incorrect as the question states that it was a worrying breach of civil liberties. Therefore for the purposes of a critical thinking test we assume that this does constitute a breach of civil liberties.

The other answers do point out flaws in how valid the argument's reasons are, but they do not affect how strongly the reasons support the conclusion. Since we assume that all reasons in a given argument are correct for an assessment such as this, we therefore do not consider these as flaws in the argument.

Question 35: D
D) is the main conclusion of the argument, whilst B) is a reason given in the argument which supports the main conclusion.

A) expresses an opinion which the argument explicitly contradicts, whilst C) and E) are simply facts stated in the passage. None of these 3 answers are valid conclusions from this passage.

Question 36: C

Anton's original salary was £29000. Hence his first annual salary increase was £3000 (£2900 rounded up to the nearest £500). Hence his new salary is £32000. Anton's second annual salary increase was £3500 (£3200 rounded up to the nearest £500). Hence his new salary is £35500

➢ Anton's third annual salary increase was £4000 (£3550 rounded up to the nearest £500). Hence his new salary is £39500.

➢ Anton's fourth annual salary increase was £4000 (£3950 rounded up to the nearest £500). Hence his new salary is £43500.

➢ Anton's fifth annual salary increase was £4500 (£4350 rounded up to the nearest £500). Hence his new salary is £48000

➢ Anton's sixth annual salary increase was £5000 (£4800 rounded up to the nearest £500). Hence his new salary is £53000.

➢ Anton's seventh annual salary increase was £5500 (£5300 rounded up to the nearest £500). Hence his new salary is £58500.

➢ Anton's eighth annual salary increase was £6000 (£5850 rounded up to the nearest £500). Hence his current salary is £64500.

➢ Hence the answer is C.

Question 37: C

In each race, the winner gets 10 points, and anybody not finishing receives 0 points. This means for each race left, a given driver can move 10 points closer to the people above him (i.e. the driver who is winning at that point). So if the number of races X 10 is greater than the difference between a given leader's points tally and the points tally of the leader with the most points, the driver who is trailing can still win the championship.

Thus, we look for a race after which there is a leader who is more points behind the leader in first place than the number of races X 10. After Billard, we see that the number of races X 10 is 40, and that no driver yet has 40 points. So at this point, any leader can win. After Menz, the number of races X 10 is 30. The leader in first place (Damon) has 47 points, whilst the leaders in last place have 24 points. Thus, they can still catch up with Damon.

However, after Fondra, we see the number of races X 10 is now 20, and that David, the leader in last place, is 23 points behind Damon, the leader in First place. Thus, after Fondra, David can no longer win the Championship.

Question 38: C

Since each room must be carpeted with a single piece of carpet, the offcut purchased must be big enough to cut 2 rectangles, one 2.6m by 4.2m, and one 1.8m by 2.2m. There are two ways this can be achieved:

➤ Firstly, an offcut could be purchased which is at least 2.6m wide, and at least 6m long (long enough for us to cut the rectangle for the smaller room, and still leave enough length to cover the larger room)

➤ Alternatively, an offcut could be purchased which is at least 4.2m long, and at least 4.2m wide (i.e. long enough to cut a rectangle of 1.8m wide for the smaller room, and still leave enough width to cover the larger room).

As we can see from the choices available, only C) (an offcut of 4.2m by 4.4m) satisfies these minimum criteria. Therefore, the answer is C

Question 39: C

We cannot determine from the passage that removal of these 2 heavy metals would mean the rest of the sludge is safe, so A) is incorrect. Equally, the passage does not say whether it is possible to make sewage sludge safe, or whether it is safer to dump it in the north sea, so D) and E) cannot be reliably concluded from the passage.

B), meanwhile, is in contradiction to the passage, which states that Zinc kills plants at lower concentrations than are needed to harm animals, so this is unlikely to pose a health threat.

The only answer we can reliably conclude from the passage is C)

Question 40: B

D) and E) are completely irrelevant to the argument's conclusions, so are not assumptions. C) is also irrelevant as the argument does not state that financial considerations should be a primary consideration, merely that it is an added bonus. Therefore, C) does not directly affect the argument's conclusions, and is incorrect. A) is not assumed, as the argument merely states that the chances have receded, not disappeared entirely. Therefore the argument does not rely on assuming that forensic evidence is a foolproof way of determining guilt.

Therefore by process of elimination the answer is B). At no point does the answer explicitly say the statement in B), and if this is not true the argument's conclusion that capital punishment would ensure real justice does not necessarily follow on from its reasoning.

Question 41: C

A) and B) are not assumptions as the argument does not claim that it would be suitable to plant trees in urban spaces, it merely claims that it would reduce asthma rates, so other problems with the notion are irrelevant.

E) is irrelevant as the argument does not assign the increase in asthma rates to a lack of trees, it merely claims that more trees would reduce the rates.

D) does not necessarily weaken the argument because we do not have sufficient information on the asthma rates in the question. If these asthma rates being described are relative to the local population, D) would not have any effect on the strength of the argument.

C) would weaken the argument by suggesting that other factors are responsible for the decrease in asthma rates in areas with trees, not the trees themselves. C) implies that the argument has confused cause and correlation, and this weakens the argument.

Question 42: D

If the minute hand travels 3 times as fast down to 6 as it does back up to 12, it must spend a quarter of the hour going down to 6 and then three quarters of the hour going back up to 12.

Hence it reaches the position for half past the hour at quarter past the hour. It then travels the distance which should be half an hour in 45 minutes, which means it takes 1.5 minutes to travel the distance which should be a minute.

Hence it will take 22.5 minutes for it to travel back up to "quarter to the hour" and there will be another 22.5 minutes left in the hour. Hence when the clock shows quarter to the hour, it will actually be 22.5 minutes to the hour.

Hence the answer is D.

Question 43: D

We can work out how long the sun and moon are in the sky together for each town then pick the shortest:

➢ Avonmouth: Between 16:25 and 19:09 = 2 hours 44 minutes
➢ Dun Laoghaire: Between 16:45 and 19:22 = 2 hours 37 minutes
➢ Greenock: Between 16:49 and 19:18 = 2 hours 29 minutes
➢ Hull: Between 16:22 and 18:59 = 2 hours 37 minutes
➢ Leith: Between 16:43 and 19:11 = 2 hours 28 minutes
➢ Liverpool: Between 16:32 and 19:10 = 2 hours 38 minutes
➢ London: Between 16:12 and 18:56 = 2 hours 44 minutes

The shortest of these is Leith at 2 hours 28 minutes. Hence the answer is D.

Question 44: C
This test is most easily answered by looking at each shape in turn, and seeing if it is the same shape as any of the others. If we find that this shape matches any of the others, we can immediately discount both of those shapes from our reasoning. Doing this, we quickly find that A) and D) can be easily identified as the same shape, and that B) and E) can also easily be identified as the same shape. This leaves us with C, which we find does not resemble any of the other shapes. Therefore, the answer is C)

Question 45: E
E) correctly identifies the main conclusion of the argument. This argument follows an unusual structure in that it states the main conclusion right at the start, then gives reasons to support it, rather than the more usual structure of giving the main conclusion at the end.

However, if we look through the other answers we find that B), C) and D) are all intermediate conclusions which if accepted as true, support the statement given in E), which thus serves as the *main* conclusion.

A), meanwhile, is part of the argument's reasoning, and is not a conclusion.

Question 46: C
The reasoning in the passage can be summarised as "A only happens because of B. B is stopping/has stopped happening, therefore A will stop happening". Only C) follows this style of reasoning.
  ➢   E) can be summarised as "A *always* happens if B happens. If B happens, A would happen".
  ➢   B) can be summarised as "A *may* have been caused by B. A started when B started, and stopped when B stopped".
  ➢   D) can be summarised as "If A happens and B did not happen, negative consequence C could happen. Therefore, B must happen".
  ➢   A) can be summarised as "A cannot happen if B happens. B happens, therefore A cannot happen".

None of these other answers follow the same reasoning as the passage.

Question 47: E
B) and C) are irrelevant statements, whilst A) is simply a reason stated in the argument, and is not a principle underlying the argument.

Both D) and E) are valid principles, but only the principle in E) is used in the passage. Since a vast majority of people are right-handed, the argument suggests that buttons be placed on the side which is easier to fasten for right-handed individuals, following the principle in E.

The argument makes no claims about a break with tradition being a reason for the relocation of buttons on women's clothing to the right-hand side.

Question 48: D
The required number of votes to be elected is 127, 50% of the total number of votes cast. Since no candidate has achieved this number, Reeta Marthur will be eliminated and the 2nd preference votes for this candidate re-allocated accordingly. This means there will be 17 votes re-allocated to the other candidates. We can see that no candidate is within 17 of 127, so no candidate can achieve 50% of the vote in the second count.

Therefore we will go to a third count. Even if Wayne Daniels receives all of the votes from Reeta Marthur, he will still be in last place at this point, as the maximum number of votes he can possibly have (if he gets all the re-allocated votes from Marthur) is 35. Therefore, he will be eliminated, and the votes for him re-allocated according to second preferences.

Once these 35 votes are re-allocated, however, the situation can no longer be reliably predicted. We know there will need to be at least one more round of counting, because no candidate is within 35 votes of 127, no candidate can have achieved this number after the reallocation of the 35 votes for Wayne Daniels and Reeta Marthur. However, we cannot predict who will be in last place for the next round of counting.

This is because if Ian McBride receives 10 of the 35 re-allocated votes, he will move above Pedro Gonzales. This would leave Pedro Gonzales in last place for the next round of counting, and he would therefore be eliminated, and his 45 votes re-allocated according to second preferences. This would be sufficient to elevate any remaining candidate into first place. Thus, beyond the elimination of Wayne Daniels, we cannot predict what will happen, and any of the top 4 candidates could win.

Question 49: C

A standard 100W bulb costs £9.60 less than a low power equivalent wattage bulb. Thus, we are calculating how long it will take for a low power equivalent wattage bulb to cost £9.60 less in electricity.

➢   A 100W will cost 15p of electricity per week if it is on for 20 hours as stated in the question (7.5p per 10 hours multiplied by 2)
➢   7.5p of electricity will run a low power equivalent wattage bulb for 50 hours. Thus, in 20 hours a low power bulb will us 3p of electricity per week.

Thus, the weekly saving in terms of electricity cost for 20 hours of run time is 12p. Thus we are looking to calculate how many weeks it will take for a 12p weekly saving to cancel out the £9.60 extra cost of the bulb. 960/12 = 80. Thus, it will take 80 weeks for me to recover the extra purchase cost.

Question 50: E

A) can be easily created by drawing a mirror image along the right-most edge of the shape in the question, then drawing a mirror image along the bottom of the resultant structure.

B) can be created by taking 2 copies of the shape in the image, rotating one by 180 degrees, and fitting them together to form a rectangle shape. Two more shapes can then be added to this, one on the top-right corner and one on the top-left corner, with the inside corner of the L shape on the corner of the rectangular centre, to give the shape in B).

C) is created by forming 2 rectangular shapes, as described for B). One of these is then rotated, as a whole, by 180 degrees, and placed below the other to give the shape in C).

D) is created by drawing a mirror image with a symmetry line going along the left-most edge of the shape in the question. Then a mirror image is drawn with a symmetry line going along the bottom of the shape in the question, to give the shape seen in D).

E) cannot be formed by 4 of the shape in the question.

END OF SECTION

Section 2

Should convicted criminals be allowed to vote?

Introduction

This question is easy to structure around the two elements of this question – criminals and voting. Both need to be explored and clearly defined to answer convincingly.

➢ A criminal can be defined as someone who's action or omission constitutes an offence and is punishable by law.

➢ Voting has two elements; it is both a right – in the sense that individuals within democratic society have a right to say who governs them, and a duty in that it is important that the person voting does so responsibility.

Ideas to explore

➢ One option could be to explore that while the idea of criminality is binary – either you are a criminal or not – the severity of those crimes is not (parking illegally is not as severe as mass murder), and therefore a convincing argument could be made to allow certain criminals – i.e. those who commit less bad crimes – to vote.

➢ A good approach would be to point out that while voting is a right, it is an alienable right in that it can be denied to some people within society. One option could be to look at other groups in society who are not allowed to vote – for example those under the age of 18 – and explore the rationale behind the decision. In this case those under 18 are deemed to not be sufficiently mature politically

Arguments against

➢ One potential argument is that criminals gave up their right to vote. If a person optionally chooses to commit a crime, they are branding themselves criminals. Criminals should not be allowed to vote. Why should the leaders of a democracy be partly chosen by those who would seek to ruin and harm those around them?

➢ A democracy does not function as a democracy when the troublemakers are making the decisions.

Arguments for

➤ One of the mains functions of prison is to rehabilitate prisoners who have done crimes in the past and to allow them to be functioning members of society. Not allowing them to vote would alienate these criminals from society and thus not allow them to become functioning members of society.

➤ A convicted criminal or not, criminals are still members of our society. To say they no longer deserve a voice is not only inconsiderate but selfish. Just because their opinion may not align with yours, does not mean that it should be stripped from them. Prisoners are put under the protection of the government and therefore have the full right to be able to have a say on who protects them.

Conclusion

➤ Restate your position and summarise the main arguments you have used to defend it.

➤ Link your conclusion back to the question by referring to the definition of 'criminal, what does it mean for someone to be a 'criminal' in regards to their place in society?

➤ The key thing in this question is the idea that voting is an important duty that cannot be given to just anybody - can society can trust someone who has violated the laws of society with having a say in who governs it?

Does a country's ideal political system depend on its level of economic development?

Introduction

➤ This question requires an answer that explores and defines different political systems and different levels of economic development. Unlike other questions, both the definition of political system and economic development are complex and would be very difficult to define in full within the time allocated. As a result, some simplifications must be made.

Arguments

➤ What is meant by ideal political system? 'ideal' is a very subjective term – ideal for who? Try to think of some examples of an ideal political system for different situations. A political system which results in an equal and fair income distribution would be ideal for the majority, whereas a system which allows for a militarised industrial complex and a large number of loyal soldiers would be ideal for a country engaged in a war.

> Is there anything unique to the level of a country's development which determines what is the ideal political system for it? It is possible to argue for that a country which is very undeveloped economically, a political system which aids development and an increase in wealth would be ideal in order to reach minimum levels in health, education and income. In this sense, it could be argued that the ideal political system could depend on economic development. However, once these minimums are reached, there is little to link an ideal political system to development.

Real life examples

Economic growth may be affected by a great deal of extraneous factors independent of a political system (international economic environment; industrial cycles; geopolitical factors, both permanent and temporal - including natural resources, navigable rivers, etc...). Use real life examples of economic development. For example:

> France was able to relatively well economically since WW2, but how much of that can be attributable to USA taking on the costs of allowing France to be safe from both an invasion by Germany AND by USSR, no matter what French thought of NATO?

> China's political system change had less to do with the economic growth than both the absolute zero level that the economy started with when Deng Xiaoping started; AND the fact that the western countries were at an economic point of wishing to outsource industrial production. If China was on its own, it would not have seen the same growth even remotely.

> Other examples: Democracies such as the United States is doing better financially than some Authoritarian countries such as North Korea. However some Authoritarian countries such as Libya (now a Democracy?) and Saudi Arabia have profited well due to natural resources. Since most Non-Democratic Republic countries are in the Middle East/ Africa, they have profited well from oil – what effect does this have on the question?

> If you consider that Authoritarian leaders can spend all the money they want to, it might make an Authoritarian government less economically secure. Also considering that leadership can't be changed even if they are destroying the country. Mainly though, economic growth depends on location and allies.

> Also, if an Authoritarian government is unstable and are at war with another country, or rebels due to their leadership, they might be spending the majority or their money on their army. In a democracy the budget is regulated by a congress, or parliament so that the right choices can be made

Conclusion

> This question is difficult due to the complex nature of the subjects covered. As a result, it is vital that candidates take extra effort to make their definitions, arguments and examples very clear throughout.

> Restate your position and summarise the arguments you have used to support it.

> Link your conclusion back to the question by referring to your definitions of a 'political system' and also 'level of development'. What, if anything links the two?

Should governments only fund scientific research if it is of direct benefit to society?

Introduction

Explore the ideas of government funding and scientific research:

> What is the idea behind government funding? It is plausible to define 'correct' government funding as that which directly benefits society.
> What is the nature of scientific research? What does it try to do?

Arguments for

Government funding and public funds

> Government funding comes from taxation, which itself comes from members of society. It is, therefore society's money and should be used for their benefit.
> Play with the question – should government spending as defined above be used to fund something which results in the benefit of an elite number of individuals? Clearly not – public money should be used for public benefit.

Scientific Research
- A key issue here is that scientific research is not predictable in terms of results due to its experimental nature.
- Some of the most beneficial scientific breakthrough occurred by accident – for example the discovery of penicillin happened purely because a scientist who was trying to discover something else left a Petri dish out by mistake. Equally, some research projects which had good intentions have resulted in discoveries that are detrimental to humanity – such as for example Alfred Nobel's discovery of TNT. These ideas can be extrapolated into arguments, as below.

Arguments against
- Research should not have to be economically justified, as academic research is often an issue of "what happens when…". The results are often not predictable, but they often have a huge beneficial impact.
- Computers, television, modern vehicles and modern building advances, have all been impacted by university (public) research. A world where research couldn't exist without a business justification would be without these amenities.

- More examples: the current hard drive in your computer probably benefited from research done in computer labs for NASA. NASA wanted high resolution cameras on a couple satellites, but had to have a hard drive that wrote quickly enough that the steady stream of data received wouldn't be lost. Was there a commercial value at the time? No, just a scientific one. But computer manufacturers and users now pay royalties for the research done 20 years ago. Indirect benefits to the scientific community can lead to direct benefits to society in the future. Using examples like this will help make your argument more convincing.

Conclusion
- While in theory the government should fund only that which is in the benefit of society, in the field of scientific research, it is impossible to know exactly which research projects will have positive (or negative) results. Therefore, in reality, the government should, as a general rule, fund projects which can reasonably expected to produce positive results for society, but, as per the reasons above, should not rule out funding those with less of a direct benefit.
- You may wish to come to a decision either way, or it is equally fine to sit somewhere in the middle, so long as this is fairly justified.
- One option could be to conclude with a normative policy guide in response to support whatever side you side on.

Could a robot ever think like a human?

Introduction

This argument centres on what you understand of the concept of humanity. Make sure that you clearly outline a definition and stick to it throughout the essay.

Real life application and examples make answers much more impressive. In this case, the Turing test is an example of a useful theory to base your argument around:

➢ The Turing test is a test of a machine's ability to exhibit intelligent behaviour equivalent to, or indistinguishable from, that of a human. Alan Turing proposed that a human evaluator would judge natural language conversations between a human and a machine that is designed to generate human-like responses. Think about the implications this test has for the question.

Argument for

➢ While the brain is incredibly complex, and is able to perform X million calculations per second, looking at the development of computer technology over the past 50 years, it is just a matter of time before a computer with a comparable computing ability is designed.

➢ In theory, any neural process can be reproduced digitally in a computer, even though the brain is mostly analogue.

Argument against

➢ What it is to be human goes beyond just the ability of our brains to make millions of calculations per second – there is an emotional and sensitive side to humanity that computers will never be able to replicate, no matter how complex computers become.

➢ While sensory feelings like heat, cold or pain could easily be felt from the environment if the machine is equipped with the appropriate sensors, this is not the case for other physiological feelings like thirst, hunger, and sleepiness. These feelings alert us of the state of our body and are normally triggered by hormones. Since machines do not have a digestive system or hormones, it would be downright nonsensical to try to emulate such feelings.

> Emotions are too complex for robots: emotions do not arise for any reason. They are either a reaction to an external stimulus, or a spontaneous expression of an internal thought process. For example, we can be happy or joyful because we received a present, got a promotion or won the lottery. These are external causes that trigger the emotions inside our brain. The same emotion can be achieved as the result of an internal thought process. If I manage to find a solution to a complicated mathematical problem, that could make me happy too, even if nobody asked me to solve it and it does not have any concrete application in my life. It is a purely intellectual problem with no external cause, but solving it confers satisfaction.

Counter Argument

> Is there anything inherently un-computable about the emotional side of humanity? Emotions are, after all, just another of one of the many computations that the brain makes – it is simply the receiving of data and acting accordingly.

Conclusion

> This question boils down to whether you agree with the idea that what it is to be human is merely having a complex piece of matter in your head – your brain - which is able to perform a large number of calculations.
> Restate your position and summarise the main arguments you have used to defend it.
> Link your conclusion back to the question by referring to your definitions of 'robotics' versus 'humanity', and what about them, specifically, makes them different or similar.

END OF PAPER

2013

Section 1

Question 1: D

The passage is talking about the fact that in Britain, horse meat is a heavily unpopular food substance, and arguing that this is not a logical view.

B) and C) are not valid conclusions from the passage. At no point does it imply that Britain should follow the example of France and Belgium, so C) is incorrect. B) is implied in the passage from the quote from the rival chef, but it is not a conclusion. The reasons given in the argument, if true, do not lead us to think that B) is true. Therefore, B) is not a conclusion.

A), D) and E) are all valid conclusions of this passage. However, the statements in A) and E) go on to support the statement given in D). Therefore, D) is the main conclusion of the argument, whilst A) and E) are intermediate conclusions from the passage.

Question 2: D

Each thermometer is accurate to within 2 degrees of the temperature stated. The lowest temperature given by any thermometer is 7 degrees, therefore the temperature cannot be any higher than 9 degrees, otherwise this thermometer would have to be stating a temperature more than 2 degrees away from the real temperature.
Similarly, the highest temperature given by any thermometer is 10 degrees, so the lowest that the true temperature could possibly be is 8 degrees. If it were any lower, this thermometer would be out by more than 2 degrees.

The middle thermometer is actually irrelevant in this instance, as the other two thermometers give sufficient information to work out the minimum temperature range.

Question 3: D

The passage has described how evidence confirms the predictions of this theory of how the moon was created, and has then incorrectly gone on to conclude that this means we should accept the theory as true. Answer D) correctly identifies the flaw in this reasoning – Just because the predictions of a theory are proven correct does not mean the theory is correct.

B), C) and E) are all irrelevant in this particular situation. The passage is describing how the evidence and facts available are consistent with the theory. However, these 3 answers all describe cases where the facts/evidence are *not* consistent with the theory. Therefore, these are not flaws of the argument, and can be ignored.

A) is completely irrelevant as the passage makes no references whatsoever about how a theory's popularity influences the truth. It simply states that this is the most popular theory.

Question 4: C

A) and E) are irrelevant and incorrect as the argument does not make reference to common sense. It claims that the system is flawed, and claims that the original name *Eohippus* was more sensible, but does not claim anything about whether common sense is, or should be, a part of scientific naming conventions. Meanwhile, D) is incorrect because whilst the argument has claimed that *Eohippus* was a more sensible name; it does not claim that the name should be changed back.

B) initially appears to be a valid answer, but on closer inspection we see that B) states that the system is *not the most appropriate*, a claim the passage does not support. The passage does claim that the system is flawed, but does not claim it is not the most appropriate system, so B) is incorrect. However, the passage does claim that a name produce by the current system (*Hyracotherium*) is not the most sensible. Therefore, the passage unarguably supports C) and is thus the correct answer.

Question 5: A
The spokesperson's argument is that prison is too comfortable, and that this is proven by the large numbers of prisoners reoffending in order to have access to the comforts of the prison. At no point has it been stated that the prisoners would not reoffend if prisons were less comfortable, and we can see that if this is not true the spokesperson's conclusion is no longer valid from their reasoning. Therefore A) is a valid conclusion.

D) is completely irrelevant to the spokesperson's argument, whilst C) does not affect his conclusion that the levels of reoffending prove that prison is too comfortable, so can be ignored. B), meanwhile, actually weakens his argument if true, and is therefore not an assumption. E) actually strengthens the prison officer's argument, if true, so therefore E) is not an assumption either.

Question 6: D
If 1974 and 1983 are both years in which Arthur's birthdays have been on dates when there were 8 different digits, and then there cannot be a 1 or a 3 in his date and month of birth.

For there not to have been a 1 in his month of birth, it must begin with 0. Additionally, if there is not a 0 (because it has already been used), 1 or 3 in his date and month of birth, the date of his birth must begin with 2. Hence we so far have 2?/0?/1974 and 2?/0?/1983.
Hence his date of birth is either 25/06 or 26/05 as 5 and 6 are the only two digits left. Hence in 1974, the two digits not in the 8 digit format of Arthur's birthday are 3 and 8, and in 1983, the two digits not in the 8 digit format were 4 and 7.
Given that the years are 9 years apart, Arthur must have been 38 in 1974 and 47 in 1983. Hence Arthur must have been born in 1936 (1974 – 38). Hence the answer is D.

Question 7: D
From the criteria given in the question we can see that in order to qualify for a bonus, a worker must have:
  - An attendance figure of higher than 90% (i.e. absences of less than 10%)
  - An Over Production figure that is not negative (thus either meeting or exceeding targets)
  - A Product accepted figure of greater than 92% (i.e. rejects less than 8% of total output)
We can quickly see now that Smith, Patel and Owololu meet all of these criteria, and that the other workers do not.

Question 8: B

We can follow the local's directions from Akeland. By doing this, we find that Ducton is **south** of Akeland, Cranton is **west** of Ducton and Eksburg is **north** of Cranton. Therefore, we know that Eksburg must be West of Akeland.

However, we do not know how far South of Akeland Ducton is, or how far North of Cranton Eksburg is. Without knowing these relative distances, we cannot know if we need to travel North or South. We only know we need to travel West. Therefore, B) is correct.

Benford is completely irrelevant, and serves to distract you from the real answer.

Question 9: D

The argument gives many reasons to support the conclusion that people in rural areas have to travel far to get to pubs and clubs, and have no choice but to drive home afterwards. It then claims that without more pubs/clubs being built in rural areas, the number of people drink-driving will increase. This is much more likely to be true if the population of rural areas will increase in the future, so D) is the correct answer. A) and B) are irrelevant to the argument's conclusion. E) does provide further reasons why people in rural areas may drink and drive, but does not do anything to support the idea that this will increase in the future. C), meanwhile actually weakens the argument, by suggesting that people in rural areas do not choose to drink close to their homes even if pubs/clubs are available.

Question 10: B

The passage describes how media personalities employ agents which generate large amounts of income for them, more so than their original activity. It then concludes that talent is no longer being rewarded. Answer B) correctly points out that the original talent may also be rewarded, which is a valid flaw in the passage's reasoning. C), D) and E) are irrelevant and do not affect the conclusion of the passage (that talent is no longer being rewarded). A), meanwhile, actually strengthens the argument by suggesting that personalities without talent can still generate significant income via agents, suggesting that talent is not the decisive factor in profit.

Question 11: A

Answer A) correctly identifies the main conclusion to the passage, namely that the government should invest in the film industry.

The other answers are a combination of reasons in the paragraph, and intermediate conclusions which can be drawn from the passage, all of which contribute towards supporting the notion that the Government should invest in the film industry. Therefore, A) is the main conclusion.

Question 12: B

The starting balance is £0, and each month £50 is paid into the account. Thus, at the end of the first year, the balance will be 12 X £50. Thus, the finishing balance at the end of the first year will be £600.

The average balance for this year is calculated from the average of the starting and finishing balance. Thus the average balance will be (0 + 600)/2 = £300. The interest will be 5% of this balance, thus the interest will be 300X0.05 = £15.

The starting balance for the second year will therefore be £600 + Interest (£15), giving £615. Each month another £50 will be paid in, giving a final balance at the end of the second year of £1215.

Thus the average balance for the second year will be the mean of £615 and £1215. This is £915. The interest paid on this amount will be £915 X 0.05 = 45.75.

Thus, the final balance, once interest for the second year has been paid, will be £1215 + £45.75, resulting in a final balance of £1260.75

To the nearest £10, this is £1260. Thus the answer is B)

Question 13: B

Marilyn spends 10 hours making 60 cakes, working out as 6 cakes for each hour. Since she charges £6 per hour of time spent, this results in a charge of £1 per cake for the time involved in making them.

Thus each cake costs £1.60 for ingredients, plus £1 for time, resulting in a total cost of £2.60 for each cake.

Thus, each cake would ordinarily be sold at a cost of £4.55 (175% of £2.60).

10% of £4.55 is 45.5p. Thus, friends receive a 45p discount, resulting in a cost of £4.10 per cake for friends.

Question 14: C

Let X be the % change in wages each time.

If the original change was a decrease, the wage would decrease by X% of the original wage. The next change would be an increase by X% of a smaller amount, thus it would not be as large as the original decrease, and would not raise the wage as high as the original wage.

If the original change was an increase, the wage would raise by X% of the original wage. However, the next change would then be a decrease of X% of a larger amount, thus being larger than the original increase, and bringing the wage *below* the level of the original wage.

Thus, the new wage *must* be smaller than the original wage.

Question 15: A

E) is irrelevant to the reasoning of the argument and can be safely ignored. D) and C) are incorrect because the argument does not say whether traditional examinations are fairer, or whether there are any entirely fair ways of assessing students.

B) is incorrect as the argument does not claim or imply that we should only assess A Levels via examinations. It casts doubt on the fairness of assessment by coursework, but this reasoning does **not** necessarily follow on to say that we should only assess A Levels via examinations.

A) correctly identifies a conclusion from this argument, that assessment by coursework is not necessarily fairer than assessment by examination.

Question 16: C

The passage argues that factory farming is cruel, and that if people are concerned about animal welfare they should therefore purchase game. At no point is it stated that game meat is not produced via factory farming methods, and if this is not true it weakens the conclusion that people concerned about animal welfare/factory farming should purchase game. Therefore, C) correctly identifies an assumption in the argument.

None of the other possible answers would directly affect the conclusion of the argument if true, and so they are not assumptions.

Question 17: C

A) is irrelevant as the argument is discussing waste, not energy consumption. D) is also irrelevant as the fact that councils already have programs to promote washable nappies does not affect the conclusion that the government must do more to promote this. E) is also completely irrelevant.

B), meanwhile, would actually weaken the argument if true, by suggesting that disposable nappies will not cause waste problems, as they are compostable. Only C) would strengthen the conclusion that disposable nappies cause significant issues of waste, and washable nappies must be promoted instead.

Question 18: C

The car travels 3 times as fast as Sven on his cycle. Therefore, without the breakdown Helga should take 10 minutes to arrive. She travelled two thirds of the way before the car broke down, so she would have been travelling for 6 minutes and 40 seconds before the breakdown.

Helga then had to travel the final third of the journey on foot, travelling at 1/3 of the speed of Sven's cycle. Therefore it would take Helga 90 minutes to walk the full journey, and would take her 30 minutes to walk the final third of the journey.

Therefore Helga would take 36 minutes 40 seconds to arrive. This is 6 minutes 40 seconds longer than Sven (who takes 30 minutes as stated in the question). To the nearest minute this is 7 minutes.

Question 19: E

The only way it is possible to make a hexagon from one straight cut across the cloth is by starting the incision in either the left-most side (labelled A below) or the right-most side (labelled B below), and cutting to the **nearest** of the 2 sides labelled X (i.e. along one of the two dotted lines).

As can be seen, these cuts will result in a triangle, and not a quadrilateral. We can therefore see that it is impossible to produce a hexagon and a quadrilateral from one straight cut in this cloth.

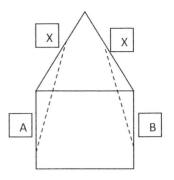

Question 20: E

The question states that Thomas is only free on mornings, so all afternoon sittings can be ignored. We are only considering morning tests.

He wishes to take the test in the main hall, so is looking for a test which has more than 30 candidates sitting it. The number of candidates currently booked onto a given test will be 100 minus the number of spaces currently available. Thus, if there are more than 70 spaces available, there are currently less than 30 people taking the test, and it may not take in the main hall. Therefore, Thomas will only book a test which currently has fewer than 70 spaces available. As we can see from the list, all tests except Monday currently have fewer than 70 spaces available, so we should consider all tests except Monday.

However, he also wants to be with the smallest number of other candidates possible. This will result from booking onto a test which currently has the largest number of spaces available (as long as it is less than 70). As we can see, from the tests we are considering, Friday has the largest number of spaces available.

Therefore, Thomas should book a test for Friday.

Question 21: E

A) and D) are completely irrelevant statements.

B) does not necessarily strengthen the argument as the fact that politicians have high-profile affairs does not necessarily support the notion that the personal aspects of politicians' lives should be reported.

C) actually weakens the argument, suggesting that there are negative consequences to reporting on politicians' private lives.

E) strengthens the argument, if true, in that it describes how politicians claim to be honest in aspects of their lives. Thus, by reporting on the private aspects of a politician's life, the media can provide the public with important insights into whether these claims of honesty are genuine, and thus provide important aspects into the politicians' values. This ties in with the argument's reasoning.

Question 22: B

The argument's reasoning can be summarised as "we can conclude that A is happening because B happened and we know C." In the passage, "A" is a person being a criminal, "B" is a person living a lifestyle that they cannot legally afford, and "C" is that people living a lifestyle they cannot legally afford are often criminals.

Answer B) follows the same pattern of reasoning. In this instance, "A" is someone spending more than half an hour on a piece of work, "B" is writing more than 4 pages, and "C" is the fact that it is impossible to write more than 4 pages in half an hour. Therefore, when "B" happens and someone produces more than 4 pages, we know "C", so we can conclude "A".

D) is the answer which most appears to follow this reasoning on first glance.

However, when we assess answer D), we find that the reasoning can be summarised as "A is often followed by B. A is happening, so we can expect B to happen soon". Here "A" is a person saving up, and "B" is that person going on holiday. This is not the same pattern of reasoning as in the question.

C)'s reasoning can be summarised as "For A to happen, B must have happened. A happens, so we know B must have happened". Here, "A" is the bank being robbed, and "B" is very careful planning, with attention to detail.

E) follows similar, but slightly different reasoning to C). E) can be summarised as "For A to happen, B must happen. We want A to happen, so we do B". Here, "A" is the police catching criminals, and "B" is watching how people spend their money.

Meanwhile, A) follows a completely irrelevant style of reasoning, simply concluding that one possible reason for an event has not occurred, and trying to find other possible explanations.

Question 23: C

The principle of the question is that those who are best at a given task should be rewarded for it. Therefore we look for an answer which follows this principle.

A) and D) are incorrect as these both refer to a situation where people are rewarded for *how much* work they do, rather than *how good* they are at a given task. E) is incorrect as it essentially reverses the principle by deciding who is best based on how much money they make, rather than basing how much money someone makes on how good they are. B) is incorrect as it refers to eliminating poorly performing people, rather than rewarding high-performers.

C) follows the principle. It identifies an important aspect of work, then says that someone was picked out for being best at this aspect, and rewarded for it. This follows the principle used in the passage.

Question 24: C

The showroom is 24m by 12 m, resulting in a total area of $288m^2$. The showroom thus has 2 edges 12m long and 2 edges 24m long, so there is 72m of tape required to cover the edges of the showroom.

Each rectangle of carpet is 8m by 4m, so has a total area of $32m^2$. Thus, we can see that there will be 9 rectangles of carpet required to be taped along all seams.

Each rectangle of carpet has 2 sides 8m long, and 2 sides 4m long. Thus, each rectangle will require 24m of tape to cover all the sides of a given rectangle of carpet.

Thus, 216m of tape (24 X 9) would be required to cover all the edges of each rectangle of carpet. However, less tape than this is required because:

- The points where the carpet joins the edges of the showroom have already been accounted for, and do not need to be covered again.
- Each seam will only need to be covered once.

Thus, to calculate the amount of tape required to cover the seams between carpets:

- First we subtract 72m from 216m, to give us the length of tape required just to cover the points when carpet meets carpet. This gives us 144m.
- Then we divide this number by 2, as each seam only needs to be covered once. We do not need to apply tape to both bits of carpet in a given seam. This leaves 72m of tape required.

Thus, we can see that 72m of tape is required to cover the seams between carpets, and then another 72m is required to cover the edges of the showroom. Thus, 144m of tape is required overall.

Question 25: B

The show runs for 3 full weeks, plus one additional Saturday. Each week has the following performances:
- 6 Nightly performances between Sunday and Friday
- 2 Nightly performances on Saturday
- 3 additional Matinee performances

Thus, there will be 11 performances each week, resulting in 33 performances overall, just considering the number of weeks. Then we need to factor in the additional Saturday, which will have 3 performances, giving 36 performances

Then we need to account for the closure of the theatre on 25th December. If the 28th December is a Saturday, the 25th will be a Wednesday. Thus it would have had 1 night performance and 1 matinee performance, so we need to subtract 2 from the total number of performances.

This gives a final total of 34 performances during the run.

Question 26: E

Answers A) through D) all follow the same pattern as the question. Each thing in question can be paired with each of the others, giving 30. This counts each combination twice, so we half this number to get 15 as the total number of combinations possible.

However this does not apply to 6 friends sending each other Christmas cards. This time, each friend sends 5 cards, so we still multiply 6 by 5 to get 30. However, this time we do not half the number, as each friend will both send a car to each other friend, and receive one in return. Thus, person 1 will send a card to person 2, but will also receive a card from person 2.

Therefore, we do not half the number, as we do wish to consider each pairing twice. Therefore the total number of cards sent will be 30, 5 per friend.

Question 27: D

The argument begins by describing how a belief that family planning services can solve the problem of overpopulation is Naïve, and then goes on to give reasons why it can in fact only be properly tackled by economic development. Thus, the main conclusion of the passage is that given in D).

E) is actually a reason in the passage, which helps support this main conclusion. B) and C) also both go on to support the conclusion given in D).

A) is an irrelevant point.

Question 28: E

The argument's structure can be summarised as "If A could happen/was happening, B would happen/would have happened by now. B has not happened, so A cannot be happening".

Answer E) follows this structure, claiming if intelligent life existed, we would have evidence for it. We do not have any evidence for it, so there is no intelligent life.

From the other possible answers, C) is the closest. C) argues as "If A happened B would not happen. A hasn't happened, so B is happening". This is not the same structure as discerning that A has/has not happened on the basis of B happening/not happening.

A) reasons as "We know that A cannot happen because it has not happened outside of fiction", which is not the same reasoning as in the passage.

B) argues as "If A happened, B would happen. B has happened, so A must have happened". Meanwhile D) argues as "For A to happen, B must happen. B happens, therefore A must have happened". Both these arguments are incorrect, and neither follow the same structure as the passage.

Question 29: A

C) and D) are irrelevant statements, whilst E) actually contradicts the argument's conclusion, which concludes that video is as much a medium for great art as any other form of expression.

B) is not an assumption because the question explicitly states "if they [the jury] are right". Thus, it has not assumed that the jury are right, and is simply talking about a case which would be true *if* they are.

However, the question does **not** state that work with emotional force and complexity is necessarily capable of being great art. The emotional force and complexity of the video medium described by the jury is the main reason given to support the conclusion that this medium is capable of being great art. Therefore, if the statement in A) is not true, the argument's reasons no longer necessarily lead on to its conclusion. Thus, A) is an assumption in the passage.

Question 30: B

Dividing 20,000 by 40 gives us the number of gallons of fuel mixture required to drive 20,000 miles. However, since the mixture is only 75% ethanol, we must then multiply this number by 0.75 (i.e. 75/100) to calculate the number of gallons of ethanol required for this distance.

We must then divide the number of gallons required by the number of gallons 1 field of sugar beet produces (550) in order to get the final answer.

B) correctly follows this working, producing the correct answer of 0.68

Question 31: B
We can work out the distance each car can travel on each tank of petrol and then select the furthest.
➤ Clipper: 12 miles per litre, 60 litres per tank, = 720 miles per tank
➤ Ghia: 11 miles per litre, 70 litres per tank, = 770 miles per tank
➤ Sedan: 10 miles per litre, 75 litres per tank, = 750 miles per tank
➤ Estate: 8 miles per litre, 80 litres per tank, = 640 miles per tank
➤ Saloon: 5 miles per litre, 82 litres per tank, = 410 miles per tank
The Ghia travels furthest on one tank at 770 miles, hence the answer is B.

Question 32: B
A) cannot be concluded because we do not know how much of the population comes from each category, so we cannot conclude whether the overall % of people under 55 with no natural teeth is >50. Similarly E) cannot be reliably concluded without this information.

C) and D) cannot be reliably concluded as we cannot make any conclusions about the causes of tooth loss, or the effects of tooth loss on employment prospects, from this data. Any such inferences would be a confusion of cause and correlation.
B) can be reliably concluded as the % of Professionals, Employers and Managers with no natural teeth is lower than the % of semi-skilled and unskilled manual workers in the same age group with no natural teeth.

Question 33: C
The argument concludes that organic sales will only continue to rise if there is a nutritional benefit from eating organic food. However, C) correctly points out that organic sales have risen for some time now, supposedly without there being any nutritional benefit from eating organic food. Thus, C) presents the strongest challenge to the article.

A) does not necessarily present a challenge to the argument. It implies that the article in the independent has not prevented people from buying organic food, but this does not necessarily mean that a lack of nutritional benefit will not stop organic sales rising. It could be that people who read the independent are inherently more likely to buy organic food even without a nutritional benefit.

D) and E) are irrelevant. B) is relevant to the argument but does not affect the conclusion as it suggests the nutritional benefit will not affect whether people choose to purchase organic good.

Question 34: B

The argument concludes that if a Swiss political system were adopted in Britain, the populace would be happier. B) correctly identifies that this assumes the only reason Swiss people are happier is due to their political system. If this is not true, then we cannot state that adopting a Swiss political system *would* make the British populace happier so the argument's conclusion is invalid.

A), C) and E) do not affect the conclusion so are not assumptions, and can be ignored. D) is not a valid assumption because the argument does not assume there is only one reason why people are disillusioned with politics. Even if there are many reasons, this does not mean that removing one of them will not make the populace happier. Thus D) is not *required* to be true in order for the conclusion to be valid.

Question 35: B

A) is an irrelevant statement, whilst C) and D) are reasons given in the passage to help support the main conclusion.

E) is an intermediate conclusion, which helps support the main conclusion, which is the statement given in B). The statement in E) supports the statement in B), but the statement in B) does not readily support the statement in E). Therefore we can see that E) is an intermediate conclusion and B) is the main conclusion of the argument.

Question 36: B

After 16 days, the average was just over 6 miles. 6 miles per day for 16 miles is 96 miles. For the 9 days after 16 days, 2 miles were run each day and so after 25 days, the total miles run is 96+18=114 in 25 days.

➢ If I run 8 miles the day after, this will be 122 miles in 26 days which is less than 5 miles per day.

➢ If I run 8 miles for 2 days after, this will be 130 miles in 27 days which is less than 5 miles per day.

➢ If I run 8 miles for 3 days after, this will be 138 miles in 28 days which is less than 5 miles per day.

➢ If I run 8 miles for 4 days after, this will be 146 miles in 29 days which is more than 5 miles per day.

➢ Hence it will take 4 days until the average can be brought back up to 5 miles on average per day.

Question 37: C

The maximum number of times it can be activated will assume it always plays the shortest tunes possible. If it plays 3 different tunes, the shortest 3 it can play will be 10+15+15 seconds long which is 40 seconds.

In an hour, there are 3600 seconds. 40 goes into 3600 90 times, hence the bird can play 3 different tunes 90 times in the space of an hour. Hence the answer is C.

Question 38: E

The question has stated that the number of visitors *per hour* is higher for Tuesday and Friday than for the other days, yet less customers were received on Tuesday than any other day except Sunday, and on Friday the number of customers was the same as Monday, Thursday and Saturday. Therefore, both Tuesday and Friday must have had shorter opening hours than these days, so A), C) and D) are incorrect.

We can also see that Tuesday had ¼ less visitors in the day than Monday, Thursday and Friday. Since it had more visitors per hour, we can conclude that the opening hours must have been more than ¼ less than for Monday, Thursday and Friday. These days had 10 hours open time in total. Therefore, on Tuesday the shop must have been open for less than 7.5 hours.
The only possible answer which fits in with all of these conclusions is E)

Question 39: D

The passage's main conclusion is that the USA's actions in the Haiti crisis proves it is the only genuine superpower. The statement in D), if true, would weaken the argument as it suggests that the EU has a much greater military force than was seen in the Haiti earthquake crisis, but they were not used because they are not an integrated force that is mobilised for humanitarian crises. This implies that they may possess a force comparable to the United States that could react if necessary, and thus class as a superpower.

A) is an irrelevant statement whilst E) does not affect the argument's conclusion. B) does not affect the argument's conclusion as simply having as many men in the military does not necessarily mean that the EU is a comparable superpower to the USA.
C), meanwhile, would actually strengthen the argument's conclusion by suggesting that the EU's ability to respond is limited, and thus it is not a comparable superpower to the USA.

Question 40: D

A) is contradictory to a statement in the passage because it is stated that no-go areas for trawlers would enable fish to reproduce safely, which carries an inherent implication that fish cannot currently reproduce safely. B) is irrelevant as the passage simply states it should be top priority, not that current coverage is lacking. C) is irrelevant to the conclusion, and also contradicts directly a statement in the passage.

E) is not an assumption as the passage refers to no-go areas for trawlers of *any nationality*. Thus the idea of "foreign trawlers" being responsible for dwindling fish stocks is not required to be true for the argument's conclusion to be valid.

Only D) is required for the conclusion to be valid, yet it is not stated at any point that Fish farming is impossible without wild fish as food. It is stated that fish farming is "futile" without the wild fish, but not that it is impossible.

Question 41: C

A) and E) are irrelevant to the argument's conclusion, as they say nothing about whether investing in irrigation schemes would help poor countries to feed their populations. D) is completely irrelevant to the notion of solving world hunger.

B) meanwhile actually weakens the argument's conclusion, suggesting that lack of mechanisation is not the main cause of malnutrition in poor countries and that wars/natural disasters are major causes, which would not be solved by mechanisation.

C) suggests that currently much of the excess food cannot be used to provide for poor countries, and in doing so it strengthens the argument that investing in mechanisation for poor countries would be a better solution.

Question 42: C

The graph shows us that each application adds value to the crop as follows:
-   The first application adds £500 value to the crop.
-   The second application adds a further £2000 of value to the crop (giving a total of £2500 extra value, once we add in the value for the first application).
-   The third application adds a further £1500 of value to the crop (giving a total of £4000 extra value, once we include the value added from the first two applications).

We can immediately see that each additional application after the third adds only £500 extra value, and will cost £1000 per application, so after the third application, adding another application will reduce profit. Hence, D) and E) can be ignored, as these numbers of applications would not maximise profit.

We can see that 2 applications will add £2500 extra value, and will cost £2000, resulting in £500 total profit from 2 applications.

We can see that 3 applications will add £4000 extra value, and will cost £3000, so will result in £1000 profit from 3 applications. Thus, 3 applications is the most profitable.

Question 43: C

The passage is asking about a train from Teovil to Erd, departing at 20 minutes past 10. All other trains mentioned in the question can be ignored.

➢ Ordinarily the train would arrive at Erd 51 minutes after departure, so the expected arrival time is 11:11am

➢ The quickest way to calculate how many minutes late the train would be is to calculate how much delay has been encountered.

➢ The train has arrived in Uble station on time, so any time taken to reach Uble is irrelevant to how late the train is.

First, calculate how long the train should take to then travel on to Erd:

➢ The train would ordinarily wait 3 minutes in Uble station.

➢ It would then travel to Erd, covering a total distance of 24 km, as seen from the distances chart in the question. If the train were on time, it would cover this distance at 60km/h, thus taking 24 minutes to travel this distance.

➢ The train also needs to make stops at Ergen, Lowley and Aregon stations. Ordinarily it would wait 3 minutes at each station, giving a total of 9 minutes spent waiting at stations.

Thus, ordinarily there would be (3+24+9) = 36 minutes between the train arriving at Uble, and the train arriving at Erd.

Now calculate how long the train actually takes to make this journey:

➢ The train sits in Uble station for 22 minutes.

➢ The train would then cover the 24km to Erd station. Since it is late, it would now travel at 80km/h, a third faster than the train would normally travel. Therefore, it would cover the distance in ¾ of the time it would normally take, and would cover 24km in 18 minutes.

➢ The train would also need to stop at Ergen, Lowley and Aregon stations as usual. However, since it is late, it would only stop for 2 minutes at each station, giving a total of 6 minutes spent waiting at stations.

Thus, thanks to the delay there will be (22+18+6) = 46 minutes between the train arriving at Uble and the train arriving at Erd. Thus the train will arrive at Erd 10 minutes late.

Question 44: E

Answer A), the view from the East, shows a door in an East-facing wall. We have been told that the only doors are in the westernmost wall (which will thus only be viewable from the East), and in a North-facing wall (which will thus only be viewable from the North). Thus, A) is incorrect.

B), the view from the West, is not a possible view because there are no doors in sight. We have been told there is a door in the westernmost wall, and as we can see from the top-down view, the westernmost wall will be viewable from the West. Thus, there must be a door viewable from the West, so B) is incorrect.

C), a view from the south, is incorrect as there are only 2 windows in the image. We have been told there are 3 south-facing windows, which must be viewable from the south. Therefore, C) is incorrect.

D) shows the correct number of South-facing windows, but it is not a possible view because the layout of the church is wrong. As we can see from the top down view, the longer section of the church extends to the west side of the church. Thus, when viewed from the south, the longer section of the church would be on the left hand side. In D), the longer section is on the right-hand side, so this is not a possible view of the church.

E), a view from the North, is a possible view. The longer section of the church we discussed in D) should proceed to the right-hand side of the church when viewed from the North, which is what is seen in view E). Also, we are told that there are 2 north-facing windows and a door in a North facing wall. Thus, we should be able to see 2 windows and a door when viewing the church from the North. We see these features in view E).

Thus, E) is a possible view.

Question 45: A

B) is a fact stated in the argument, and is not a conclusion, because it is not supported by any other reasons given in the argument.

C), E) and A) are all valid conclusions that can be drawn from the argument. When we examine them further, we see that C) and E), if true, would support the statement given in A). Therefore, C) and E) are intermediate conclusions, and A) is the main conclusion of this argument.

D) can be treated as a conclusion in the argument, which can be drawn from the argument's description of how communities can exert control over behaviour. However, it is not the main conclusion, because it is only supported by a small section of the argument, whereas the main conclusion should be supported by the argument as a whole.

Question 46: D

The reasoning in the passage can be described as follows: "A always happens if B happens. A doesn't happen, so B can't have happened." Only D) follows this reasoning (with "A" being John enjoying the movie, and "B" being there being a big star in the movie).

C) reasons as "A happens if B happens. B happens, therefore A will happen". A) reasons as "If A happens, B will happen. A happens, therefore B will happen" (although the second part is stated in an inverse way). B) reasons as "If A happens, B happens. B happens, so A must have happened". B) is incorrect reasoning, and none of these follow the same pattern as the passage.

E) meanwhile simply describes a situation and states it happens frequently.

Question 47: C

The passage describes a principle of rewarding people for good performance, rather than as a matter of course. Only C) follows this principle, describing Tim getting a bicycle as a reward for his high grade.

B) is a different situation describing punishment for those performing poorly. A) is a direct opposite, describing how all employees get money because the company is in profit, rather than as a reward for their own performance. D) also describes a situation where everybody gets a financial reward, regardless of personal performance. E) meanwhile does not describe a reward specifically being given, it simply describes a positive situation resulting from good performance.

Question 48: B

Let the value of a Red note be termed "R", a Green coin be "G" and a Blue coin be "B".

The question states that the smallest denomination is worth 1k, and that each higher denomination is a whole number multiple of a smaller denomination. Thus, we know that the value of each denomination is a positive integer of "k". Thus, in all equations with a certain number of "k", the "k" can safely be discarded.

Hence from the amount of change you get when paying for something worth 135K with a red note, we can write the equation R-3G-B=135. Rearranging this, we get R=135+3G+B

We also know that something worth 33K is paid for with 4 green and 1 blue coins. Hence 33=4G+B

The question states that one of the denominations is equivalent to 1k, and we know R is more than 135k, so we know that either a blue coin or a green coin must be equivalent to 1k.

➢ If B=1,we can see that 4G=32 and so G=8. Hence from the equation R=135+3G+B we see that R=160
➢ If G=1, we can see that B=33-4G=29. Hence from the equation R=135+3G+B we see that R=167

Each higher denomination is a whole number multiple of the lower denominations. 167 is not a multiple of 29, so the answer cannot be G=1, B=29, R=167. 160 is a multiple of both 1 and 8, so B=1, G=8, R=160 is the only possible answer.

Hence B=1, G=8, R=160 is the answer. G=8 and R=160 hence 20 green coins are worth 1 red coin. Therefore the answer is B.

Question 49: A

The total number of votes in favour of the motion is 5, whilst the total number of votes against the motion is 8. Thus, there are currently 3 more votes against the motion than for the motion.

If 2 committee members who previously voted no decide to vote yes, and the same committee members abstain, then the total number of votes in favour of the motion will be 7, and the total number of votes against the motion will be 6.
Therefore, the minimum number of committee members who need to change their vote for the motion to be passed is 2. Hence, the Answer is A)

Question 50: E

Andrew *may* be able to calculate the number of houses in the street by knowing Amy's house number and that opposite, but *only* if the houses in the street are numbered consecutively, starting at one end of the street, going up to the end and back down the other side. Then he will be able to work out how many houses are either side of Amy's house. However, if the houses in the street are numbered with the odd numbers on one side and the even numbers on the other side, he cannot work out how many houses have a larger house number than Amy's house. Therefore, A) and B) are incorrect.

C) is also incorrect because if the house opposite Amy's is 26, then the houses are numbers with even houses on one side and odd numbers on the other, so he cannot work out how many houses there are. In fact, he can work out how many houses there are only if the house opposite Amy's house **is not** number 26.

Similarly, D) is incorrect because if the houses are numbered with odd numbers on one side and even numbers the other, knowing the numbers either side of Amy's house will not allow him to work out the number of houses on the street.

However, Andrew can work out the numbers of the houses either side of Amy's, as follows:
➢ If the house opposite Amy's house is number 26, then we know the houses are numbered odd numbers one side, even numbers the other. Therefore, the houses either side of Amy's will be 23 and 27
➢ If the house opposite Amy's house is **not** number 26, then we know that the houses must be numbered consecutively, going up one side and back down the other. Therefore, we know that the houses either side of Amy are 24 and 26.

END OF SECTION

Section 2

Can you ever know whether anyone else has thoughts and feelings like yours?

Introduction

> This is a complex philosophical question based on an empirical issue. In order to answer this question, which I would not advise unless you have a solid and wide philosophical background, it is first necessary to explore what is meant by knowledge. Explore and define the term in as clear a manner as possible. One such definition could be: 'facts, information, and skills acquired through experience or education; the theoretical or practical understanding of a subject.'

> However, this is definition is largely scientific in nature. While there is a large scientific element as explained below, it is important not to ignore the mention of 'thoughts' and 'feelings', which it could be argued go beyond the scientific realm.

Philosophical theory

> It is a good idea to explore a number of different epistemological approaches, if possible backed up by various philosophers such as Plato, Descartes etc. However, if you do include such thinkers, make sure you keep their arguments simple enough to be referred to throughout the essay, but not so simple as to misunderstand their arguments.

> Ensure you are confident with a thinker if you want to include them in your essay – it is better not to ascribe an idea to a thinker than to ascribe a false or erroneous one.

> Another area to explore would be the difference between being able to know 'thoughts or feelings' as opposed to other forms of knowledge, such as basic predictable instincts.

> Feelings for example have a range of levels of complexity – for example I can say with quite a lot of certainty that if you put your hand in a bowl of boiling water you will feel pain, but determining other, more complex feelings such as love or jealous are much harder to see.

Biological arguments

➢ While that our biological apparatus for sensing the world is fairly similar from person to person, that sensing process cannot in practice be decoupled from the processes of attention filtering and emotional interpretation, which are likely to vary widely between people: an interesting facet of this question is the role that emotions play in our perception of the world. Scientific understanding of how this works is still at a basic level, but experiments are showing that a change in emotional state can often affect one's perception. And of course the sense data we receive from the world has to pass through the filter of our attention as well, and this filter is highly sensitive to emotional context. All of this explains why, if we have a strong emotional association with a particular colour, taste, smell, sound or texture, we start to observe it more often (and possibly differently) in the world.

Nature vs. nurture

➢ You could use the Nature vs. Nurture debate (whether a person's development is predisposed in his DNA, or a majority of it is influenced by this life experiences and his environment) - even though the general wiring of the human brain is specified by genetics, a great deal is influenced by nurture. For example, in the visual system, each cell differentiates so as to handle only signals coming from one eye, and this is unique to every individual.

Conclusion

➢ Summarize the main points made on each side of the argument in the essay.
➢ You may wish to come to a decision either way, or it is equally fine to sit somewhere in the middle, so long as this is fairly justified

Should the supply and use of all drugs be legalised?

Introduction

➢ This essay is relatively simple to answer if structured correctly due to the wide availability of arguments both for and against drugs. However, it is important that the arguments you use are measured and focused in approach – merely writing down every single argument you can think of connected to narcotics will not lead to a good essay as you will fail to achieve sufficient depth or clarity of thought.

➢ This essay requires a clean and clear definition of drugs. Drugs can be defined as 'a medicine or other substance which has a physiological effect when ingested or otherwise introduced into the body.'

➢ Note that this term has a very open ended definition, and can be seen include a number of substances which would not conventionally be considered as a drug – such as alcohol, or caffeine for example.

➢ An important issue to note that not all drugs are the same in terms of the detrimental effect they have on the body- for example, some drugs such as caffeine have a negligible effect on one's health.

Arguments against

➢ A key issue at the heart of this question is liberty. One argument could be – it's my body, so why should I let the laws of the government constrain what I do with it? I could just as easily damage my body by sticking a metal fork into a plug socket as I could by taking an illegal substance. Any law which limits what one can do to their own body can therefore be seen as an affront to their individual liberty.

➢ Another issue is that not all drugs are illegal – for example alcohol and tobacco are drugs which, despite having a large negative impact on one's health, remain legal (albeit not available to those under the age of 18)

Arguments for:

➢ However, the counter argument is that of paternalism – that the government prevents the supply of drugs because it is in the best interests of an individual's liberty and wellbeing to do so – if they were to allow unlimited access to very addictive substances such as heroin, individuals would quickly become addicted and would be unable to stop taking the drug – leading to their eventual death.

➢ Eliminate the criminal market place - The market for drugs is demand-led and millions of people demand illegal drugs. Making the production, supply and use of some drugs illegal creates a vacuum into which organised crime moves. The profits are worth billions of pounds. Legalisation forces organised crime from the drugs trade, starves them of income and enables us to regulate and control the market (i.e. prescription, licensing, laws on sales to minors, advertising regulations etc.)

➢ The price of illegal drugs is determined by a demand-led, unregulated market. Using illegal drugs is very expensive. This means that some dependent users resort to stealing to raise funds. Most of the violence associated with illegal drug dealing is caused by its illegality. Legalisation would enable us to regulate the market, determine a much lower price and remove users need to raise funds through crime. Our legal system would be freed up and our prison population dramatically reduced, saving billions. Because of the low price, cigarette smokers do not have to steal to support their habits. There is also no violence associated with the legal tobacco market.

➢ Safety - prohibition has led to the stigmatisation and marginalisation of drug users. Countries that operate ultra-prohibitionist policies have very high rates of HIV infection amongst injecting users. Hepatitis C rates amongst users in the UK are increasing substantially. In the UK in the '80's clean needles for injecting users and safer sex education for young people were made available in response to fears of HIV. Harm reduction policies are in direct opposition to prohibitionist laws.

Conclusion

➢ An important distinction in the question is that it refers only to the supply of drugs – what could you say about the illegality of the demand of drugs?

➢ If you have a more nuanced argument, like the example given in the introduction, this should be restated here with the arguments that justify it.

➢ Restate your position and summarise the arguments and counterarguments you've presented above.

Do countries benefit from immigration?

Introduction

➢ Like with the drugs question above, this question is easy to answer due to the abundance of arguments on both sides, however, again, it is vital that arguments are deployed carefully in a sophisticated manner in order to create a convincing case one way or the other. It is therefore very important with this question to have a clear and concise opening paragraph in which you introduce the reader to the arguments that you are about to make. As well as framing the essay well, this has the additional benefit of helping you keep the rest of the essay structured.

➢ To answer this question you must define two terms – immigration, which is simple (the action of coming to live permanently in a foreign country) and benefit – which is harder to define.

➢ There are a number of different potential areas which immigration could be seen to be beneficial – economically, socially, culturally, or politically, to name a few. Pick a couple of these and focus your argument on these areas, but make sure you make it clear this is what you are doing.

Argument

If for example you take economic, you would need to assess the costs and the benefits of immigration.

➢ For example: benefit – immigrants have skills, cost: immigrants might use up resources such as social security.

➢ Another example, culture: benefit – a large number of immigrants will help create a vibrant and multicultural society, cost: cultural integration might be hard to achieve and will lead to friction between different communities.

A good distinction to make is between the impacts on host countries, and of origin countries. There are numerous arguments which can be used for either side.

To give a brief description of the possible arguments available:

Host countries:

Positive
- Job vacancies and skills gaps can be filled by immigrants, which will improve the competitiveness of the host country economy. This, in turn can lead to sustained economic growth which is maintained through the increase in the supply of labour provided by the immigrants.
- Social security can be improved by the contributions of new workers and they also pay taxes.
- Immigrants bring energy and innovation to a country's economic sphere.
- Host countries are enriched by cultural diversity brought by immigrants.

Negative
- There may be a depression of wages and employment as immigrants replace natives in the workforce.
- Having workers willing to work for relatively low pay may allow employers to ignore productivity, training and innovation, and migrants may be exploited.
- Increases in population can put pressure on public services, such as the NHS for example.
- There may be cultural integration difficulties and friction with local people.

Origin countries:

Positive
- Developing countries benefit from remittances (payments sent home by migrants) that now often outstrip foreign aid.
- Unemployment is reduced and young migrants enhance their life prospects.
- Returning migrants bring savings, skills and international contacts.

Negative
- Economic disadvantage through the loss of young workers
- Loss of highly trained people, especially health workers
- Social problems for children left behind or growing up without a wider family circle

Conclusion
- Summarize the main points made on each side of the argument in the essay.
- This is a very open ended question – ensure your answer reflects this.
- Be sure to link your conclusion back to the question by referring to immigration through a cost/benefit analysis.

How should we evaluate advances in science?

This is a difficult question in that it requires an in depth knowledge of both philosophy and science, and the interaction between them. It can be made simpler by clarifying in your opening paragraph the manner in which you are going to make the argument – i.e. from the points of view of profit and of societal benefit. Never the less, it remains a challenging question.

Introduction
- There are two main ways to evaluate advances in science – either through the amount of people the scientific advance helps in regard to lives saved or some other metric, or through the amount of profit that it creates for the scientist/company who invented it.
- From a moral point of view, the importance of a scientific advance is clearly the former – how it helps improve people's lives.
- From an economic, and possibly a more realistic point of view however, the reality might be different. In our capitalist society, profit is a huge driver of scientific advances. Whether this is a good thing or not is a good way of addressing wider political issues while answering this question.
- A key issue at the heart of this question concerns what the purpose of science is – should it be to improve lives or simply to make profit?

Assessing profit in science
- Due to the involvement of private, profit making corporations in the scientific field, you could argue that this is no longer the most important. A firm which creates scientific advances which make no money will quickly go bust and stop producing advances. This is an issue that you could explore morally – should this be the case? What are the implications for society? What are the implications for the future of scientific research?
- You could also explore the implications for having research publicly funded versus research which is privately funded. You could argue that private research funding is more likely to flow to issues which generate the most money rather than what is best for the people, leading to advances in areas such as arms and weaponry which might be at the detriment to society as a whole.

Counter argument

The other side to this argument is that you could argue this is a false dichotomy, and that given the nature of scientific research industry, any invention that helps people sufficiently will make money anyway. Should this be the case? Try and assess the issue from a moral rather than a purely scientific/profit-based viewpoint.

Time lag

Another angle of assessing the profit-based view of science is through timeframe – an advance might not be immediately profitable or beneficial, and it might take many years before an advance is recognised as being useful. An argument therefore could be made that focuses more on an advancement's long term impact rather than immediate impact.

Conclusion

➢ Make sure that you include potential counter arguments for any of the above points that you make – it is vital that your essay comes across as balanced and not one-sided.

➢ In your conclusion you could argue that this distinction is not absolute – for example a scientific advance could both save lives and make profit for a company.

➢ Another distinction you could make in your conclusion is between how we ought to evaluate advances, and how they are actually evaluated. How could the current situation in regard to the profit motive be improved? Could, for example the government introduce legislation to prevent the negative effects described above? If so, what kind of laws would they be? Exploring these political implications is a good way to end the question.

END OF PAPER

2014

Section 1

Question 1: C

The passage discusses reasons why spending money on trying to increase adult participation in sport is futile, citing research showing that it is what people do in their childhood that influences their sporting habits later in life. It them claims that schools should be given money to increase sporting participation amongst children. If we accept the other reasons in the paragraph as true, we have good cause to believe this claim. Thus, answer C) is the main conclusion of this passage. Answers A), B) and E) are all reasons given in the passage, which contribute towards supporting C). Thus, they are not main conclusions.

Answer D) is irrelevant, the passage is not discussing the technicalities of how schools are able to implement sport, it is simply discussing whether they should be given money to do so.

Question 2: C

The longest calendar months have 31 days in total. This is 4 weeks (28 days = 4 weeks), with 3 days leftover. The maximum number of working days will occur if the month starts on a Monday. Counting from this day, the 4th week ends on a Sunday, and thus the 3 extra days would be Monday, Tuesday and Wednesday, which are all working days.

The total number of working days can thus be calculated:
- Monday to Friday for 4 weeks is a total of 20 days
- Alternate Saturdays are worked, so there would be 2 Saturdays
- Adding in the extra 3 days after the 4th week ends, this gives a total of 25

Thus, there are 25 working days. We are told the neighbours alternate driving, so in this example, one will drive 12 days and the other will drive 13 days.

Question 3: C

This passage discusses how traditional book sales are declining whilst e-book sales are soaring, and concludes by saying that this means that this means e-books have attracted readers away from paper books and towards digital copies. Answer C) correctly identifies that this conclusion is not valid – e-books could have attracted new readers who never read before, and printed book sales could be falling for an entirely different reason. Nothing in the passage's reasoning necessarily means that e-books have attracted people *away* from hard copies.

Answers B) and D) are irrelevant because the issue at hand is whether e-books have attracted readers away from hard copies, not whether this is good or its economic impact.

Answers A) and E) are not flaws because for a critical thinking assessment we accept the reasoning given in the passage as true – assessing the quality of evidence is not part of the task, we are simply looking to see whether the reasons, if true, cause us to accept the conclusion.

Question 4: B

The passage discusses how Governor Schwarzenegger is concerned with reducing expenditure, and how he proposes the use of the electronic devices as a means to cut the cost of school textbooks. The passage says that this is common sense, implying agreement with the governor. It is immediately apparent that this conclusion is *not* valid if the handheld devices do not save any money compared to textbooks, but nowhere in the passage is it stated that this is the case. Thus, B) is a valid assumption.

All the other answers are irrelevant because they do not directly affect whether the governor's suggestion to save money on textbooks is sensible. Thus, none of them are *required* to be correct for the conclusion to be valid, and thus they are not assumptions. In addition, answer D) is actually stated as a reason in the passage, and thus cannot be an assumption even if it was required for the conclusion to hold.

Question 5: E

The passage describes experiments which have implied animals (pigeons) are better at maths than humans. However, it criticises these implications as "mistaken" and says that instead, the animals are simply learning from experience, whilst the humans are not. However, if we treat learning from experience as a mathematical process, then this criticism is not valid, and the experimental conclusions seem to be correct. Nowhere in the passage is it stated that learning from experience is *not* a mathematical process, so E) is a valid assumption.

Answers A) and C) are both over-concluding. The passage simply says how in this instance, the pigeons were learning from experience, and that therefore the conclusions that they are better at maths does not follow from the evidence. It does not say anything about whether the people were better or worse at calculating probability, so C) is incorrect. Equally, it doesn't make any claims about the ability to learn from experience (the fact the pigeons were doing it in this instance *doesn't* necessarily mean they are better in general at it) so A) is incorrect.

Answers B) and D) are not assumptions because neither is *required* to be true for us to accept the passage's conclusion. The passage is simply claiming that the experiments' conclusions do not follow from their results, because the process observed was learning from experience not mathematics. This is still a valid point even if B) and D) are not true, so neither of these are conclusions.

Question 6: D

In order to calculate the *longest* possible journey time, we need to know is whether it is possible for the cyclist to have to wait at both sets of traffic lights:
- The question tells us that the cyclist cycles at 5 metres per second
- There are 900m between the 2 sets of traffic lights
- Thus, it will take the cyclist 180 seconds to move between the 2 traffic lights

We know that the two traffic lights are green for 120 seconds, both at the same time. Thus if the cyclist sets off from the first lights as they go green, they will arrive at the second set 60 seconds after they turned to red. Thus, they will have to wait 60 seconds at the second set until they turn green.

Thus, the longest possible journey is as follows:
- The cyclist takes 80 seconds to get from home to the first traffic lights, arriving exactly as they turn red.
- They then wait 2 minutes at the first traffic lights (120 seconds)
- The cyclist then takes 180 seconds to get to the second set of traffic lights
- The cyclist then waits 60 seconds at the second set of lights
- The cyclist then takes 100 seconds to get to the office.

Adding this up, we get a maximum journey time of 540 seconds, which is 9 minutes.

Question 7: C

The simplest way to find the answer to this question is simply to calculate the price for each item in turn and add them up:

➤ We can clearly see that the dimensions for the first item exceed the maximum dimensions for a letter, so it will have to be sent as a parcel
  - The first 30 grams costs $1.22
  - The total weight is 300 g, leaving 270 additional grams to be paid for after the first 30 grams
  - 270 is 9x30, so we will need to pay 9x$0.17 (the price for each additional 30g is $0.17)
  - Thus, the total price for this item is $1.53+$1.22, which is $2.75
➤ The second item fits within the dimensions for the letter, and also weighs less than the maximum weight, so the cheapest way to sent it will be as a letter.
  - The first 30g costs $0.44
  - The total weight is 110g, so there are 80 additional grams to be paid for after the first 30 g
  - Each additional 30g or part thereof costs an additional $0.17. 80 is 2.67x30, so we will need to pay for 3x$0.17, which is $0.51
  - Thus, the total cost for this item is $0.95

Adding these costs together, the total cost for sending both items is $3.70. Thus, the answer is C)

Note: We are not given any information on what constitutes a postcard, and neither of the items are stated to be a postcard, so we can safely ignore the postcard information given in the table.

Also, perhaps the easiest trap to fall into in this question is attempting to calculate the proportion of postage for sending 2/3 of 30g with the second item. Reading the question clearly, we see that the $0.17 charge applies for each 30g *or part thereof*, so we simply add a full $0.17 for the 20g leftover for this item of post.

Question 8: B

From the viewing angle given in the picture:
Options A) and E) are both the bottom side, in different directions.
Option C) is the top side.
Option D) is the right hand side, where left to right in C) corresponds with top to bottom from the viewing angle in the picture
Option B) does not correspond to any of the sides, so this is the answer.

Question 9: C

The passage argues that steps must be taken to prevent child labour, and that nothing short of a ban is acceptable. One of its reasons is that children are more productive than adults, making child labour attractive to employers, so B) would *strengthen* the argument, not weaken it. Option E) would also strengthen the argument, suggesting that international pressure has failed to bring an end to child labour, so a ban may be necessary. D) also somewhat strengthens the argument by indirectly suggesting that child labour reduces the price of products, which is cited as a reason why child labour is attractive to employers.

A) does not strengthen or weaken the argument, and is actually an assumption in the passage, being required to be true for the arguments conclusion to be logical.

C) does weaken the passage as the passage discusses how child labour reduces the potential for education. However, if we accept C) to be true, then these children would not accept education without the wages from their work. Thus, C) is the answer.

Question 10: E

The passage says that canal usage declined due to other, faster/cheaper forms of transport becoming available. It then says that the use of lorries is becoming less practical and more expensive, and that this means canals will soon be used again. However, if there are other forms of transport available as alternatives to lorries, then the decline of lorries will not necessarily lead to the resurgence of canals. Nowhere is it stated that there are no other alternatives, so E) is an assumption from this passage, and is the main flaw.

Answers A) through D) are discussing reasons why the road network may still be preferable to the canals. However, the passage is discussing why the decrease in road networks will result in a resurgence of the canals, so none of these answers affect the argument as strongly as E). Thus, E) is the answer.

Question 11: A

The passage discusses how mentioning right and wrong in a statement does not alter the factual content of that statement, so A) expresses the main conclusion of this passage. Answer B) is referring to an example discussed in the passage to help explain/illustrate this point, and is not a main conclusion. C) and D) both disagree with the passage, which says claims about things being right and wrong are evincing moral approval/disapproval. Thus, neither of these are conclusions from the passage. E) is an intermediate conclusion, which then goes on to support the main conclusion given in A). We can see that if we accept E) as true, it gives us good cause to believe A), but this does not apply the other way round.

Hence, A) is the main conclusion.

Question 12: B

None of the answers mention Barcelona as a possible destination, so we can instantly discount this row.

Answering this question is now simply a matter of proceeding through the other answers, calculating the price of each one, and subtracting this from £2000, to see how much is left over for spending money:

➢ Option A) would be £500 for the Ferry and train (£250 per person for 2 people), then £1200 for Hotel (£120 per night for 10 nights). This is a total of £1700, leaving £300.

➢ Option B) would cost £390 for flights, plus £1020 for hotel (£42.50 per person per night, which is £85 per night, for 12 nights). This totals £1410, leaving £590.

➢ Option C) would cost £480 for car hire and fuel (£40 per day for 12 days), plus £960 for hotel (£80 per night for 12 nights). This totals £1440, leaving £560.

➢ Option D) would cost £220 for flights, plus £1440 for hotel. This totals £1660, leaving £340.

➢ Option E) would cost £160 for flights, plus £1260 for the hotel. This totals £1420, leaving £580.

Of these options, B) leaves the closest to £600, so B) is the answer.

Question 13: A

The volunteer wants exactly 5000 calories in the mix. Thus, the first step is to calculate how many calories are already present, to know how many calories are required from the sunflower seeds:

➢ 150g of mealworms, which are 150 calories per 100g, will provide 225 calories

➢ 150g of apples, which are 350 calories per 100g, will provide 525 calories

➢ 250g of raisins, which are 300 calories per 100g, will provide 750 calories

➢ 125g of suet, which is 800 calories per 100g, will provide 1000 calories

➢ Thus, the total number of calories already present is 1000+525+750+225 = 2500 calories.

➢ 5000 calories are required, so the sunflower seeds must provide 2500 calories.

➢ Sunflower seeds are 500 calories per 100g. 2500 is 5 times 500, so we need 5x100g of sunflower seeds, which is 500g.

Question 14: B

As Freya runs to collect the stick, the distance between the 2 will increase. The distance will then decrease as Freya returns the stick to Sue. Thus, the graph showing the distance must go up then down to reflect this. Only the graphs in B) and D) show this, so the answer must be one of these 2.

To decide whether B) or D) is correct, we need to look at the rate at which the distances will change. During the collection of the stick, Freya is running away, whilst Sue is walking slowly towards Freya. Whilst the stick is being returned, Freya is running towards Sue, whilst Sue is still walking towards Freya.

Thus, we expect the distance to change faster whilst the stick is being returned than whilst Freya is collecting the stick, because during this stage the two are walking towards each other. Thus, we expect the gradient of the graph to be steeper whilst the distance is decreasing, during the returning of the stick. Graph B) correlates with this, whilst Graph D) shows the opposite. Thus, the answer must be B)

Question 15: C

The passage describes how many people find the BBC license fee unfair, and describes 3 possibilities for continued funding of the BBC (continuation of the license fee, commercial funding or general taxation). It then goes on to highlight a problem with two of those possibilities (general taxation and commercial funding). The passage does not discuss how efficient/good at producing revenue the 3 possibilities would be, so D) and E) are not valid conclusions from the passage.

B) is also incorrect. The passage says how the commercial funding and general taxation funding options would put the BBC's independence at risk, but does not mention that this is the case for continuation of the license fee.

Option A) is not correct because the passage does not say any other options can be used for funding the BBC, it simply mentions how they would put the BBC's independence at risk. Thus, A) is not a valid conclusion.

Option C) is a valid conclusion. The passage mentions how many people do not like the licence fee, then criticises the alternatives. If we accept all these reasons as true, we have good cause to believe Option C). Thus, C) is the answer.

Question 16: C
Option A) actually disagrees with the passage, which says that teeth left in bones *are* evidence for predation, so this is not an assumption. Option B) is also not an assumption because the passage states that the speed of a dinosaur is hard to assess, so we assume this to be true. Thus, B) is irrelevant. Option D) is a flaw in the passage, but it is not an assumption because the passage discusses several pieces of evidence why T-Rex may not be a predator. We do not need all of this evidence to be true for some of them to be valid, so D) is not *required* to be true for the passage's conclusion to hold. Thus, D) is not an *assumption*. E) is not relevant to the arguments reasoning, so is not an assumption.

The passage discusses evidence given by a palaeontologist that T-Rex was not a predator, and says that instead, T-Rex *must* have been a scavenger. However, nowhere is it stated that T-Rex could not have been both, and without this, the conclusion it must have been a scavenger is not valid from the reasons given. Thus, C) is an assumption from the passage.

Question 17: C
The passage says usage of libraries has declined, but argues this is due to the style of libraries rather than a lack of interest in reading books. It concludes by saying this means the future of the current library functions will be better protected by restyling libraries.

Answer B) actually weakens this argument, as people looking for reference books are unlikely to be concerned with the style of the library. Answers E) also weakens the argument by suggesting that the rebranded library encourage use of *other* library functions, rather than preserving the current function of borrowing books. Answer D) is not relevant, because it does nothing to help determine whether the decline in library use is due to lack of interested in books or due to the poor branding of libraries.

Answers A) and C) both offer support to the argument, but Answer C) *most strengthens* the argument because it is discussing book usage in Britain. Answer A) discusses library usage in other countries, which may have patterns of library and book usage that differ from the UK. Answer C) refers to how the purchase of books in Britain has increased during the period in which library use has declined, offering direct support to the notion that poor branding of libraries may be responsible, rather than lack of interest.

Question 18: D

The longest period of waiting for traffic on the side road will occur when they wait for the pedestrian crossing phase, then for the lengthened green period on the main road. During this period, the maximum length traffic on the side road can wait will be:

- A 2 second period after the side road lights going red, when all lights are red
- A 10 second period whilst the pedestrian lights are on green
- Another 2 second period after the pedestrian lights turn red. All lights are on red
- A 35 second period for the main road lights to be green
- A final 2 second period where all traffic lights are on red

This adds up to 51 seconds. Thus, D) is the answer.

Question 19: D

We can see from the question that Ryan's Birthday (the earliest in the year) is on the 50th day of the year, and that since it occurs before the 28th February, it is unaffected by leap years.

All the other grandchildren's birthdays are affected by leap years, as they happen after the 28th February. Thus, in a leap year the other birthdays will occur on the 124th, 151st, 251st, 322nd and 351st days of the year.

For another birthday to happen on the same day of the week as Ryan's, it must happen a number of days after Ryan's birthday that is a multiple of 7. Thus, we simply calculate how many days after Ryan's birthday each of the other birthdays occurs on, and see which one is a multiple of 7:

- 124-50 = 74. This is not a multiple of 7
- 151-50 = 101. This is not a multiple of 7
- 251-50 = 201. This is not a multiple of 7
- 322-50 = 272. This is not a multiple of 7
- 351-50 = 301. This is 43 times 7

Thus we can see that Robert's birthday happens 301 days after Ryan's, which is 43 times 7. Thus, Robert's birthday must happen on the same day. Hence D) is the answer.

Question 20: E

The key to answering this question lies in looking at *how many times* each symbol in the code appears in the word, and where. Although the code changes each time Alistair writes, we can presume that within each message a given symbol always represents the same letter of the alphabet.

Looking at the symbols representing "Alistair" confirm this is the case. The 1st and 6th symbols are the same, just as the 1st and 6th letters in "Alistair" are both "a". Equally, the 3rd and 7th symbols are the same, just as the 3rd and 7th letters are both "i".

Now, if we look at the code for when Alistair is coming, we see two useful clues:
- The 3rd and 7th symbols are the same.
- The 4th and 8th symbols are the same.

Thus, we know that in the word representing when Alistair is coming, the 3rd and 7th letter must be the same, and the 4th and 8th letter must also be the same. The only word which fulfils this criteria amongst the options is "SOMETIME".

Hence, E) is the answer.

Question 21: B

The passage argues that university fees of £27,000 for a 3 year degree are reasonable, using a comparison with a similarly-priced car as justification for this point of view. Answer A) actually reinforces this point, suggesting that the degree is worth more, and therefore the fees are better value. Answer C) is simply a personal opinion that disagrees with the passage, and does nothing to affect the validity of its argument.

Answer D) is not a flaw because the passage states that the fees *will* lead to an increase in choice for students, so for the purposes of a critical thinking assessment we must accept this point as true. Answer E) is not relevant because the passage is discussing whether the *current* fee increases are reasonable. Future fee increases are irrelevant.

In contrast, answer B) correctly identifies that a person's car and a person's education are not intrinsically linked in anyway. Thus, discussing car prices when talking about education is irrelevant, and this removes a significant amount of the justification given in the passage for saying the fees are reasonable. Hence, B) is a flaw in the passage.

Question 22: D

The passage reasons that cats are interesting to most people in short doses, even if you are not a particularly keen cat lover. However, over long periods, cats are of interest only to a few people.

Answer A) claims that many subjects are interesting in short doses, but not over long periods. This is incorrectly extrapolating from the passage, which makes no claims about how many subjects are only interesting in small doses.

Answer B) follows the opposite pattern of reasoning, in which the first few bits (equivalent to the short film) are boring, but the further detail (equivalent to the longer film) is more interesting.

Answer C) reasons that many people may *not* share an interest in cats and/or babies. This is not the same as the passage, which claims that most people *do* have a short-term interest in these things, just not a long-term one.

In Answer D), the person is interested in short doses of photographs, but not in a long session of watching photographs. This is the same reasoning as the passage, where people may be interested in the short film but not in the longer one.
Answer E) describes whether cats are interesting enough to make a long film. This is not the same as the passage, which refers to the interest being dependent on the person watching it.
Hence, the answer is D)

Question 23: C

The issue raised with the University minister's comments is that a more qualified student is being charged more than a less qualified student. Thus, the less qualified student, by virtue of being less qualified, is getting a better deal. This principle is related to whether the students are being treated in accordance with their ability. Answer C) illustrates this principle, so this is the answer.

Answers A) and B) both discuss issues of timing, with no reference made to whether the later buyer/applicant is more deserving of the job/holiday, so these answers do not illustrate the principle used in the passage.

Answer D) is incorrect as the passage is actually discussing selling of education at different prices, not saying that it should not be sold. Answer E) is completely irrelevant, discussing logistical problems, and whether they should compromise the law.

Question 24: D

The fastest way to calculate the answer for this question is simply to calculate the largest expenditure possible, and then see what we can take off to get the amount as close to £28.50 without going over it.

The largest expenditure possible is as follows:

➢ Duck confit Salad for £6.95
➢ Rainbow Trout for £16.10
➢ Profiteroles for £6.20

This gives a total expenditure of £29.25. This is 75p over the allowance of £28.50. Thus, we are looking for the smallest reduction in price that is larger than 75p.

The smallest reduction in price possible that is larger than 75p is found by substituting Duck confit salad for smoked salmon, a reduction in price of 85p. This gives us a new total price of £28.40. Hence, D) is the answer.

Question 25: C

The first requirement of this question is to calculate how many calories Chris must burn in order to lose 7.5lb. The note at the bottom of the table says each lb in fat = 3500 calories, so to lose 7.5lb of fat, Chris must lose 26250 calories.

Now we need to see how many miles Chris is walking. He aims to walk 26 miles each week, for 10 weeks, giving a total of 260 miles of walking.

Now we can see how many calories Chris needs to lose for each mile of walking. Here, we can save ourselves some difficult calculating by taking into account a few useful points:

➢ 26250/260 is a difficult calculation to work out without a calculator. However, we can see that 260 multiplied by 101 is 26260, which is very close to 26250.
➢ Additionally, we can see that all of the values given in the table for calories burned per mile are integers.
➢ The question asks how many calories Chris needs to burn per mile to lose *at least* 7.5lb, *not exactly* 7.5lb.

Taking these points into account, we can round up the number to the nearest whole number, and assume that Chris needs to lose 101 calories per mile to lose the weight.

Finally, we look at the table and see which walking speed is required to lose 101 calories per mile of walking. We are told that Chris' starting weight is 180lb, so we simply look at that column in the table to find the slowest walking speed which will lose over 101 calories per mile of walking for a starting weight of 180lb.

We can see from the table that this walking speed is 4.0 mph. Hence, C) is the answer.

Question 26: D

We can see from the first graph that Arthur has the most money at the start, and Carol has the least, and since they have all spent the same amount this order must also apply to the end of the year, so we can instantly discount Option C), which shows more money in Carol's account than Belinda's.

If we treat the amount originally in Belinda's as X, we can estimate the amount in Carol's account as somewhere between 0.5X and 0.75X. Equally, we can estimate the amount in Arthur's account to be somewhere between 1.5X and 2X. We cannot calculate precisely since no numbers are given.

We are told that half of Belinda's money has been spent, so we can treat the amount spent by each person as 0.5X. Thus, as the end of the year, the amounts in each account will be the following:
➢ Arthur's Account – Somewhere between X and 1.5X
➢ Belinda's account – 0.5X
➢ Carol's Account – somewhere between 0 and 0.25X

We can now see that the amount in Carol's account should be less than Half of the amount in Belinda's account, and the amount in Arthur's account should be between two and three times the amount in Belinda's account. The only option which fulfils this criteria is Option D), so this is the answer.

Question 27: B

The passage describes using willow trees as fuel as *one of the most promising* solutions for high carbon emissions, and goes on to describe several advantages of using willow trees for fuel. It also mentions that this is already used in other countries, to further reinforce this point. All the reasoning given ultimately supports the idea that we should use willow trees to produce fuel. Hence, B) is the main conclusion of this passage.

Answers A), C) and D) are all reasons in the passage which support this conclusion, and are not themselves conclusions. Answer E) could be described as a conclusion, which follows on from the reasons in A), C) and D), but Answer E) itself then supports the Main conclusion in B). Thus, Answer E) is an *intermediate conclusion*, not the main conclusion.

Question 28: B

Answer A) is not a valid conclusion. The fact that the police strike coincided with a doubling of the homicide rate *does not* mean that the end of the strike will cause the rate to halve.

Answer C) is not a valid conclusion because the passage provides two conflicting view points, neither of which are stated as fact by the other, and which explicitly disagree with each other. Thus, we cannot *reliably* conclude that C) is true,
Answer D) is not a valid conclusion because the passage makes no reference to the police officers' opinions on the pay rise, and neither the government nor the police officers have claimed that this was the reason for ending the strike.

Answer E) is not a valid conclusion because no reference is made in the passage to why the government decided to offer the striking officers an amnesty from punishment, or to the government's opinions on policy pay.

Answer B) can be reliably concluded. We are told that the police officers accepted a 6.5% pay rise, so we know they will be on improved pay. We also know that the strike has ended before the carnival, so the carnival will be staffed by a full-strength police force. Whether the strike ended *because* of the carnival is irrelevant to this, the important point is that it *did* end before the carnival.
Thus, B) is a valid conclusion from the passage.

Question 29: B

The passage discusses how discussion between students, parents and teachers contributes to students doing well in exams by revealing problems. It concludes from this that if a school provide opportunities for meetings between these 3, it will contribute to its students achievements. However, it is not necessarily the case that that providing opportunities for meetings will lead to discussion, and this is not necessarily the case, and nowhere does the passage state that this is the case. If this is not the case, the passage's conclusions do not necessarily follow from its reasons, so Answer B) correctly identifies an assumption in the passage.

Answers C) and E) both strengthen the passage's conclusion, if true. However, neither is required for the passages conclusion to be valid, so they are not assumptions. Neither C) or E) is an integral part of the argument.
Answer A) is not an assumption, because the presence of other factors does not mean that highlighting emotional problems is not important. Thus, the passage's conclusion is not *dependent* on A) being true. Thus, Answer A) is not an assumption.

Answer D) is not an assumption because the passage discusses how it is import for students *not to suppress* emotional problems, and how the discussion between parents, teachers and students simply brings them out into the open. Here, the student's academic performance does not rely upon the problems being *solved*, it simply relies on them being openly discussed.

Thus, Answer D) is not required for the passage's conclusion to be valid, so it is not an assumption.

Question 30: D
We are told the following key pieces of information:
- Average speed of first Journey = 30 km/h
- Total time of first journey = 30 minutes (or 0.5 hours)
- Total mileage after 2nd journey = 24 km
- Average speed after 2nd journey = 32 km/h

This question is solved by using these facts and the equation of speed=distance/time as follows:

$$Total\ Speed\ after\ 2\ journeys\ = \frac{Total\ distance\ after\ 2journeys}{Total\ time\ after\ 2\ journeys}$$

Let T = Total time after two journeys

We know the Total speed and the total distance after 2 journeys, so we can plug these into this equation to calculate total time as follows: $32\ = \frac{24}{T}$

This gives: $T\ =\ 0.75\ hours\ =\ 45\ minutes$
We know the first journey took 30 minutes exactly, so the 2nd journey must have taken 15 minutes.

Now we need to know the total *distance* of the 2nd journey. We know the total distance after both journeys was 24 km, and the first journey was 15 km, so the 2nd journey must have been 9 km.

Now we know that the 2nd journey was 9 km long and took 15 minutes (0.25 hours). Plugging these figures into the $Speed = \frac{Distance}{Time}$ equation, we get the following:

$Speed\ = \frac{9}{0.25} = 36\ km/h$
Thus, the answer is D)

Question 31: B
There are 10 possibilities for the first digit (0, 1, 2, 3, 4, 5, 6, 7, 8 & 9).
For each of these possibilities, there are 9 possibilities for the second digit which will not be the same as the first digit (e.g. for a first digit of 0, the 2nd digit can be anything except 0).

For each of *these* possibilities, there are 8 possibilities for the third digit which will not be the same as either of the first two digits (e.g. if the first two digits are 0 and 1, the third digit can be 2, 3, 4, 5, 6, 7, 8 or 9).

The answer can be found by multiplying these 3 numbers: $10x9x8 = 720$.
Hence, the answer is B)

Question 32: D
This question is difficult to describe on paper, as it requires visualisation of 3-D shapes. The best way to prepare for these questions is to practice visualising nets, and then use cut-out nets to verify your answers (remember that you can always take scissors into your exam!).

Question 33: A
The passage discusses how people enjoy watching fictional violence on TV and in novels, but the recent increase in violent crime shows that increasing numbers of people are not satisfied with watching violence and need to take part in violence to be satisfied. However, Answer A) counters this by saying that most murders are not random killing of strangers to satisfy an urge, but pre-meditated and targeted at close family members. Thus, A) does weaken the passage.

Answer B) does not weaken the passage because the passage simply claims that increasing numbers of people are not satisfied with watching/reading about violence. It does not claim that an increase in violent films has caused the increase in violent crime.

Answers C) and D) are not relevant because the passage does not make any reference to the age of those carrying out crime, or whether the film classification system would make any difference.

Answer E) could actually be seen to strengthen the argument, because the argument refers to people not being satisfied with watching violence. If they are seeking real-world violence to instead satisfy their urges, then they would need to be able to tell the difference between real-world and TV.

Question 34: C

The passage describes a small group of anarchists causing violence during a presentation, but then goes on to discuss and criticise the action of describing all violent protestors as "anarchists".

Answer A) does not identify a flaw in this passage, because the passage does not claim that violent protestors cannot be anarchists – in fact it agrees with this. It simply disagrees that *all* violent protestors are anarchists.

Answer B) does not directly relate to the discussion about whether all violent protestors are anarchists, so is not a flaw in the passage.

Answer D) somewhat reinforces the passage. By questioning how possible it is to call someone an anarchist, it casts further doubt upon whether it is sensible to label all violent protestors as anarchists.

Answer E) also somewhat strengthens the passage, which claims that anarchists generally want an abolition of the state. If this group of violent protestors want an *increase* in state funding, then this suggests that they may not be anarchists.

Answer C) does detract from the passage, because the passage uses the fact that the violence occurred at a protest *against* decreased government spending as evidence that the violent protestors may not be anarchists (who the passage claims generally want an abolition of the state). However, Answer C) correctly identifies that the violent protestors may not agree with the protest's official aims, removing one of the reasons given why they may not be anarchists.

Hence, C) is the answer.

Question 35: C

The passage criticises government advice on milk, saying it makes false assumptions and ignores health benefits of full-fat milk. It then describes the advice as an example of unhelpful government intervention. This last sentence clearly follows from the reasoning given in the passage, so this is the main conclusion, and thus C) is the correct answer.

Answers A) and B) identify reasons given in the passage, which go on to support the conclusion given in C).

Answers D) and E) could be seen as conclusions from the passage, but both would require leaps of logic not made in the passage in order to be conclusions, and thus are somewhat criticisable as conclusions.

Also, if we accept either of these answers as true, they both go on to support the conclusion given in C), making them *intermediate* conclusions, not the main conclusion.

Question 36: E

First we calculate when she arrived according to her watch:
- The train was 10 minutes late
- The taxi was delayed 15 minutes due to the traffic
- Walking to the room took 5 minutes longer than expected

Thus, there was a total of 30 minutes delay. We know she intended to arrive exactly on time, so by her watch she will have been 30 minutes late.

We are told that the clock in the interview room was running 30 minutes slower than her watch, so according to this clock, she will have been exactly on time. Hence, the answer is E)

Question 37: C

First, we need to calculate what the cheapest option for membership will be under the conditions given in the price:
- Paying the discounted renewal price, because a change in membership counts as a renewal
- 12 visits during the year (Once a month for the full year)
- Locker hire (£2 a visit unless included in membership cost)
- Not entering any competitions

With 12 visits, the cost of a locker will be £24 throughout the year if not included in the membership price. Thus, the total cost of Bronze membership will be £32 (£8 for yearly membership plus £24 for locker hire through the year). The total cost of silver membership will be just the £28 renewal price, since a free locker is already included.

Thus, the cheapest option is a 1 year silver membership, costing £28.
We are told the person is currently a Gold member, that she made the payment 6 months ago, that she joined as a new member, and that the membership is about to expire. Thus, she must have paid the new member price for a 6 month Gold membership, which is £40.

Hence, the new payment will be £12 less than the payment 6 months ago, so the answer is C).

Question 38: A

104 x 11-year-olds participated in swimming, compared to 150 16-year olds. This is roughly a 2:3 ratio of 11-year olds:16-year olds. Thus we are looking for another sport with a roughly 2:3 ratio of 11-year olds to 16-year olds. Starting from the top of the column, we see that the first sport mentioned, football, had a 120:181 ratio, which is also very close to a 2:3 ratio.

We can verify this by checking the rest of the ratios in the other sports:
- Cricket is 120:133, which is closer to 1:1 than 2:3
- Hockey is 55:66, which is a 5:6 ratio, also not close to 2:3
- Tennis is 123:149, which is roughly 5:6, and not close to 2:3
- Squash is 51:97, which is closer to 1:2 than 2:3

Question 39: A

The passage discusses how some commentators have cast doubt on the idea that government campaigns have led to a decrease in car accidents, claiming that instead many may simply not be reported. It uses the increase in hospital admissions as evidence to back up this claim.

If we accept all these reasons as true, we have good cause to believe that those thinking road safety is increasing continually may be incorrect, and thus A) is a valid conclusion from the passage. However, all the points refer to how it *may* be the case that road accidents have increased. Nothing is stated for certain, so we cannot conclude that the government initiatives *have* been unsuccessful. Thus, B) isn't a valid conclusion.

Answer C) could be described as an assumption in the passage. The main supporting evidence in the passage is that hospital admissions have increased, and if this is true the argument's conclusion no longer securely follows from its reasoning. Thus, C) is an assumption, and not a conclusion. Answers D) and E) both *counter* the passage's argument, and are thus not conclusions.

Question 40: C

The passage argues that the UK government's policy of increasing university places is appropriate, arguing that graduate unemployment has decreased and the UK is wisely responding to the demands of a modern "High-Tech" economy.

Looking at the reasoning used, we can see that just because the graduates are getting jobs does **not** mean they are getting jobs *requiring degrees*. If this is the case, then the passage's reasoning no longer supports the conclusion that the extra university places are required for the economy's demands. Thus, C) is a valid assumption of the passage.

Answers A) and E) both refer to whether increasing university places is always a requirement or a response to economic growth. This does not directly affect the conclusion regarding whether the UK's increase is required to be a high-tech economy. Thus, neither of these are assumptions of the passage.

Answer B), if true, would reinforce the conclusion, providing additional strength to its reasoning. However, it is not *required* to be true for the conclusion to be valid, so this is not an *assumption* of the passage.

Answer D) would actually *weaken* the passage if it is true. Thus, it is not an assumption of the passage.

Hence, the answer is C)

Question 41: B

The passage discusses how more and more crimes are being committed by girls and how for several crimes, the increase is seen as linked with an increase in alcohol consumption, concluding that this means greater alcohol is responsible for the increase.

Answers D) and E) would both *strengthen* the passage. D) reinforces the point that girls are committing crimes not traditionally associated with them, whilst E) describes an increase in alcohol consumption. If these are both true, the passage's conclusion is reinforced.

Answers A) and C) are irrelevant. The passage does not refer to whether girls are committing more and more crime relative to other age/gender groups, it simply states that they are committing more crimes. Thus, the effects of alcohol on other groups are irrelevant to the passage's conclusion.

Answer B) does weaken the passage, as it suggests that the chances of prosecution have increased for girls. This provides another reason why the number of recorded crimes committed by girls may be rising, weakening the passage's conclusion that alcohol is responsible.

Hence, the answer is B)

Question 42: C

This question asks us to find the value for y, the 5-year moving average for the year of 1909.

We do not know the average maximum day temp for 2009 itself (value x), or next year's 5-year moving average (value z)

However, we *can* calculate the value of x, using the 5-year moving average for 1913. This average will be composed of the average of the mean max temps for the Years 1909,1910,1911,1912 and 1913. Since the table provides the information for the mean max temp for 4 of these years, we can use this information to calculate x as follows:

➢   5 year moving average for 1913 $= \frac{x + 13.3 + 14.9 + 13.7 + 14.2}{5}$

➢ $13.82 = \frac{x + 13.3 + 14.9 + 13.7 + 14.2}{5}$

➢ $69.1 = x + 13.3 + 14.9 + 13.7 + 14.2$

➢ $69.1 = x + 56.1$

➢ $69.1 - 56.1 = x$

➢ $13.0 = x$

Now, we can use this value, along with the values of the years 1905-1908, to calculate the value of y, following a similar procedure to before:

➢ $y = \frac{13.4 + 14.4 + 13.4 + 13.7 + 13.0}{5}$

➢ $y = \frac{67.9}{5}$

➢ $y = 13.58$

Hence, the answer is C)

Question 43: C

To answer this question, we must calculate the average number of fish per angler from each river *during each year* – since the question asks what the highest figure is *in any one year*, we cannot average these figures out over both years.

River Dark:
- Year 1 = 77 scale sets from 5 anglers = 15.4 per angler
- Year 2 = 125 scale sets from 30 anglers = ~4 per angler

River Fare:
- Year 1 = 85 from 20 anglers = 4.25 per angler
- Year 2 = 35 from 8 anglers = ~4 per angler

River Gwynt:
- Year 1 = 71 from 19 anglers = >4 per angler
- Year 2 = 132 from 2anglers = 66.5 per angler

River Tine:
- Year 1 = 105 from 43 = ~2.5 per angler
- Year 2 = 66 from 19 = ~3.33 per angler

River Yarrow:
- Year 1 = 80 from 18 = >4 per angler
- Year 2 = 150 from 25 = 7 per angler

*Notice that these calculations have frequently made use of estimation for tricky calculations here, which could be time consuming to work out exactly. We do not need to work them out exactly as the question only asks which individual figure is highest.

For example, once we have seen that in Year 1 River Dark returned 15.4 scale sets per angler, we can clearly see that the figure for the 2nd year was lower (~4). We do not need to work out the exact answer (4.1666) to see that 125/30 is less than 15.4, so we can save time by simply estimating approximate answers.

We can clearly see that the highest individual figure is year 2 for River Gwynt. Hence, C) is the answer.

Question 44: A

We are told that **two** of the lights in the display are not working, so we are looking for a number which, in this matrix, could be turned into an "8" by the addition of **one or two** extra lights being illuminated. We are told that the lift has **left** the ground floor, so he **cannot** be on the ground floor.

We can see that in the matrix show, figures 2, 3, 5, 6 and 9 could be turned into a figure 8 with 2 more lights being illuminated. Thus, there are 5 floors he could have got out on by mistake.

Figure 1 would require 5 extra lights, Figure 7 would require 4 extra lights and Figure 4 would require 3 extra lights to be turned into Figure 8, so none of these are possible. Hence, there are 5 possible floors and the answer is A)

Question 45: C

The passage argues against the claim that cooked food is less healthy due to loss of vitamins, claiming we should be "thankful" our ancestors developed cooking. If we accept all the reasons given in the passage to support this claim, we have good cause to believe this claim. Thus, C) expresses the main conclusion of the passage. E) is also a valid conclusion from the passage, but it goes on to support the statement in C). Thus, E) is an intermediate conclusion in this passage, *not* the main conclusion. A) could also be seen as an intermediate conclusion, supporting the main conclusion given in C).

Answers B) and D) are reasons given in the passage to support its conclusion.

Question 46: B

The reasoning in this passage can be described as "A is required for B. A is happening, therefore B will be possible". Here, "A" is the light level being low, and "B" is stargazing being possible.

➤ A) could be described as "A must happen for B to happen. A isn't happening, so B won't happen", with A being the train being on time and B making the flight. This is not the same as in the passage.

➤ B) reasons as "A must happen for B to happen. A is happening, so B will happen". This is the same as in the passage, so B) is the answer.

➤ C) reasons as "A is required for B to happen. A has not happened, so B must not have happened either", where "A" is the exceptionally high tide, and "B" is a flood happening. This is not the same as in the passage.

➤ D)reasons as "A must happen for B to happen. A didn't happen, so C couldn't happen", where "A" is the water being boiling, "B" is making an excellent cup of tea, and "C" is the aunt enjoying the cup of tea.

➤ E)reasons as "the best produce comes from France, therefore produce from France must be the best". This is not the same as in the passage.

Question 47: D
The passage discusses how in boxing, the negative events (i.e. damage to the players) are the object of the sport, rather than an unfortunate effect of something going wrong. It claims that because of this, boxing is unacceptable whilst other sports are not. Thus, the principle underlying the passage is that 2 things are not the same if one is designed to cause negative events, and one has risks of negative consequences if something goes wrong.

Answer D) follows a similar principle, in which negative things only occur from bonfires when something goes wrong. Thus, it should not be banned in the same was as arson, where negative things are the objective.

None of the other answers refer to differences between intentional negative consequences and problems resulting in unintended negative consequences, so these are not the principle in the passage.

Question 48: C
The average number of great-great-grandparents would be 16 (2 for each great-grandparent).

However, we are told that 2 sisters from one family married 2 brothers from another among her great-grandparents.

The two sisters would have had the same 2 parents. We would normally expect the 2 great-grandparents to account for 4 great-great-grandparents, so we subtract 2 from the average total. The same applies for the 2 brothers, with another 2 subtracted from the average total here.

Thus, we subtract 4 from 16, leaving us with a total of 12 great-great-grandparents. Hence, the answer is C)

Question 49: B
The maximum income from students will come when all canoes are being used by students. We are told that the school has 18 canoes, with the instructors expected to use their own. Thus, the maximum income will be from a group of 18 students.
For a two hour session, each student will pay £12 (£7 for the first hour and £5 for the second hour). For 18 students this will be a total of £216 of income from the students.

The minimum instructor : student ratio is 1:6, so a group of 18 students will need 3 instructors. The instructors are being paid £6 an hour, so this will be a total of £36 paid to the instructors. £216 - £36 = £180 of profit for the school for this session.

Question 50: B
We can see from the bar chart that the three groups accounted for approximately the following amounts of revenue:
  ➢ Adults = Just under £400
  ➢ Children = Just under 150
  ➢ Senior Citizens = Just under £150

Thus, we expect that the following numbers visited the Museum:
  ➢ Adults = ~400/7 = ~60
  ➢ Children = ~150/4 = ~40
  ➢ Senior Citizens = ~150/5 = ~30

Thus, we are looking for a graph which shows the number of adults, children and senior citizens visiting as a roughly 6:4:3 ratio.

Thus, it should clearly show the following things:
  ➢ Adults should account for < 50% of visitors (so A, D & E are incorrect)
  ➢ The number of senior citizens should be smaller than the number of children (so Graph C) is incorrect

The only graph left which fulfils these criteria is B). Hence B) is the answer.

END OF SECTION

Section 2

How should we evaluate advances in science?

This is a difficult question in that it requires an in depth knowledge of both philosophy and science, and the interaction between them. It can be made simpler by clarifying in your opening paragraph the manner in which you are going to make the argument – i.e. from the points of view of profit and of societal benefit. Never the less, it remains a challenging question.

Introduction
- There are two main ways to evaluate advances in science – either through the amount of people the scientific advance helps in regard to lives saved or some other metric, or through the amount of profit that it creates for the scientist/company who invented it.
- From a moral point of view, the importance of a scientific advance is clearly the former – how it helps improve people's lives.
- From an economic, and possibly a more realistic point of view however, the reality might be different. In our capitalist society, profit is a huge driver of scientific advances. Whether this is a good thing or not is a good way of addressing wider political issues while answering this question.
- A key issue at the heart of this question concerns what the purpose of science is – should it be to improve lives or simply to make profit?

Assessing profit in science
- Due to the involvement of private, profit making corporations in the scientific field, you could argue that this is no longer the most important. A firm which creates scientific advances which make no money will quickly go bust and stop producing advances. This is an issue that you could explore morally – should this be the case? What are the implications for society? What are the implications for the future of scientific research?
- You could also explore the implications for having research publicly funded versus research which is privately funded. You could argue that private research funding is more likely to flow to issues which generate the most money rather than what is best for the people, leading to advances in areas such as arms and weaponry which might be at the detriment to society as a whole.

Counter argument

The other side to this argument is that you could argue this is a false dichotomy, and that given the nature of scientific research industry, any invention that helps people sufficiently will make money anyway. Should this be the case? Try and assess the issue from a moral rather than a purely scientific/profit-based viewpoint.

Time lag

Another angle of assessing the profit-based view of science is through timeframe – an advance might not be immediately profitable or beneficial, and it might take many years before an advance is recognised as being useful. An argument therefore could be made that focuses more on an advancement's long term impact rather than immediate impact.

Conclusion

➤ Make sure that you include potential counter arguments for any of the above points that you make – it is vital that your essay comes across as balanced and not one-sided.

➤ In your conclusion you could argue that this distinction is not absolute – for example a scientific advance could both save lives and make profit for a company.

➤ Another distinction you could make in your conclusion is between how we ought to evaluate advances, and how they are actually evaluated. How could the current situation in regard to the profit motive be improved? Could, for example the government introduce legislation to prevent the negative effects described above? If so, what kind of laws would they be? Exploring these political implications is a good way to end the question.

How much should we test a medicine before making it widely available?

When answering this question, you should keep in mind the ambiguity of the question. Is 'we' whoever is producing the medicine, the government, or an independent medical authority of some kind? This will affect what kind of tests are had in mind. If it's not widely available before extensive testing, does this mean it is limited to certain people before this point, and they are the test? In this case, the access to the medicine is limited because those who take it will require very close monitoring. Is it unfair to limit access to a potentially life-saving medicine in this way?

Before beginning to answer, consider these questions; because of the time limit, you will most likely have to choose one or two such scenarios to discuss. You should choose the ones that you think are most ethically interesting – perhaps the borderline cases. For example, you might argue that we should test a medicine as much as possible to ensure that it is safe before making is available to anyone, but untested medicine should be available to people who are dying, as a last shot chance at life, as there are no risks involved for them, but it has the potential to help them live and to further medical science.

Introduction:

➤ Begin by defining your terms, as above. Indicate what you consider to be 'widely' available, and whether tests in this instance would include human tests (i.e.: are you imagining untested medicines to be available to a limited number of people?)

➤ Clearly state your opinion within these defined parameters, and outline the main arguments you'll be discussing.

➤ Though it may seem obvious, it is worth briefly discussing *why* we test medicine before making it available to the public, and why your opinion either finds the balance between flooding the market with untested drugs and over-cautious withholding, or why the extremes of a complete lack of testing, or extremely rigorous testing, are in fact desirable.

Potential arguments in favour of less testing:

➢ You could make an argument for bodily autonomy and informed consent; so long as a patient know that a medicine is untested, and knows the risks of taking a medicine about which we know very little, they should be able to make the informed decision to try it.

➢ Many medicines treat fatal conditions; if a patient is terminal anyway, they ought to be given the opportunity to take a potentially life-saving drug.

➢ The only testing that really holds weight is human testing – testing on animals is flawed as their biology is so different to ours. As above, when a drug is deemed safe enough to test on humans, participation in these tests ought to be *widely* available, as limiting a potentially life-saving treatment to only a few people for doctors to experiment on is unfair.

    o **Counter-argument**: because of the arguments below (patient safety, doctors need to monitor patients on new drugs), it ought to be limited. However, as soon as human trials are successful, it ought to be widely available.

➢ Conversely, you could argue that human testing isn't nearly as important as people make it out to be. We can test on animals to measure the safety of a drug with great success, and we can now also test on artificially grown human organs, the results of which are strongly indicative of how a medicine will actually react in a human body. When these tests are successful, we ought to treat a medicine as being as thoroughly tested as if it had actually been in a human body, and make it widely available.

Potential arguments in favour of more testing:

➢ Patient safety ought to be a priority. While a new drug that is entering the human testing stage might be an amazing treatment in a few years, it's unlikely to be a ready, finished product during the initial testing stages. Limiting availability to a few test subjects also limits the damage that a new drug can do before it is refined after the results of human trials.

➢ On this note – patients subject to relatively untested drugs need to be closely monitored, precisely because the medicine is new and untested. It is simply not feasible for doctors to give that kind of attention to the huge number of patients that might request access to a new medicine for a common condition.

    o Counter-argument: isn't this an argument in favour of more funding for health services and training medical professionals so that more monitoring of patients that need it can be provided, rather than an argument against providing necessary medicine?

➤ Patients might think they're making an informed decision about their body when they choose to try a new medicine, but they're simply not as educated on medical matters as their doctors and the medicine's developers. The decision to let humans take a medicine ought to be up medical professionals.

  ○ **Counter-argument**: this is paternalistic. While doctors might understand the risks involved, they are able to convey these to a patient, and only the patient can decide whether these risks are worth it for them.

  ○ **Counter-counter argument**: the patient is naturally more emotionally invested in this, and might not be able to make a clear-headed decision, especially if it's a potentially life-threatening illness, and could grasp at straws.

➤ Further, many of the arguments in favour of less testing make it out to be a life or death situation every time, but this is melodramatic. Most medicines treat conditions that aren't fatal, and many new medicines treat conditions that are already treated in other ways. It would be fool-hardy to risk serious side-effects trying out a new drug on otherwise fairly well cared for patients before it's tested enough to be declared sufficiently safe. (You might here give your argument some depth by saying that terminal patients are an exceptional circumstance, in which you might favour the use of untested drugs).

Conclusion:

➤ Restate your opinion, and summarise your arguments.

➤ Be sure to link your conclusion back to the question by referencing the purpose of testing before making medicine available, and why you feel the arguments you've favoured outweigh the arguments in favour of more/less testing.

➤ Given that you will most likely have had to restrict what you are saying to a few specific situations, it might be nice to make reference to other scenarios in which your opinion would be different. For example, if you've argued that making relatively untested medicine widely available is necessary as only human subjects can provide accurate information on the medicine's usefulness, you might add that, of course, if some other method were developed to test new medicines – computer simulations of chemicals affecting human bodies, for instance – then you would revise your position. This indicates that you've thought about scenarios you haven't been able to discuss in detail in this essay.

Should statistics be a compulsory subject of study at school? Why, or why not?

In this sort of question, 'statistics' is, in part, a stand in for any subject – much of your essay should be spent arguing for a set of criteria for a compulsory subject of study, focusing on the criteria that statistics fits if you are arguing in favour of it being compulsory. Alternately, you could argue that no subject of study should be compulsory – in this case, you should make it clear why you believe this is the case and reject counterarguments, and use statistics to demonstrate your case (e.g.: you might argue that no subject is necessary for every day functioning, and then explain why statistics specifically isn't necessary). It is probably worth restricting your answer to secondary education, or even just the second half of secondary education.

Not only is statistics completely irrelevant to primary education (one is unlikely to prescribe making it compulsory for under 10s), but it is often also not engaged with in any depth until the later secondary years. You can mention, when answering the question more broadly, why a subject ought to be compulsory at any level (because it's necessary in later life, but also appropriate for that age group, etc.), but your answer ought to be focused on the areas to which the question directly applies – in this case, from the age when statistics generally becomes appropriate to study in depth and older.

Introduction:
➢ Link your answer into a broader understanding of the concepts mentioned in the question by stating why a subject (if any) ought to be a compulsory subject of study at school, and thus whether statistics does not does not fit this criteria.

Potential arguments for:
➢ Statistics arise in day to day life more often than we realise: it's used to back up scientific data that we read about and believe in the newspapers; it's used to predict the results certain actions will have; it's used to manipulate data so that people believe what the manipulator wants them to believe. A more complex understanding of statistics would help us make more informed choices in these circumstances.
  o **Counterargument**: art and music also arise in day to day life, and we could equally make the argument that a more complex understanding of these means of expression would help us understand each other better and lead us to have more fulfilled lives – as social and expressive animals, these are both hugely important – but one is far less likely to prescribe art as a compulsory subject of study.

- o **Counter-counterargument**: if art is truly as essential as statistics then the answer is to make the study of both compulsory, not neither.
- ➢ Studying statistics doesn't only benefit us where statistics can be directly applied. It involves logical thinking which helps develop our reasoning powers, which can be applied to any number of areas of study as well as day to day life.

- ➢ The kind of abstract logical thinking that it's involved in statistics isn't found in other areas of study in school. Geography, history, philosophy, politics, economics, etc. all involve the same sort of reasoning applied to different sets of knowledge, and the applied sciences (physics, chemistry, biology) involve very similar reasoning abilities. Statistics involves using very precise, unbiased logical reasoning to reach necessary conclusions – an education in this way of thinking is found by studying any other subject.

Potential arguments against:

- ➢ No subject of study should be compulsory past primary education. While it is true that basic reading, writing, and arithmetic are extremely helpful, if not necessary, for functioning in the world, these skills should be acquired by the time someone starts secondary school, or at the very least before they begin studying advanced enough maths that statistics is a subject of its own.

- ➢ The reason we generally don't prescribe art as a compulsory subject (see counterargument to the first argument in favour) is that we recognise people's differing abilities in varying fields. If we can see that some people have less interest in and predisposition towards artistic study, and so should not be forced to fruitlessly spend time on it, we ought to see that the same is true of statistics.

- ➢ Forcing people to study statistics because we feel it's in their best interests for the reasons described in the arguments in favour section is not only paternalistic, it also cuts into the time they have to study subjects that actually interest them, and that will benefit them specifically (i.e.: we can recognise that statistics is broadly a good thing to be studied, without forcing every person who wants to, say, be a historian, to study it, while taking time away from their study of history).

Conclusion:
Once again, engage with the question on a wider level by restating why any subject should or shouldn't be a compulsory subject of study, and describe how statistics fits into this.

Should Western nations refuse to trade with countries in which child labour is used?

There is some ambiguity in this question, regarding what constitutes a 'Western' nation. Most likely, they mean rich economies – also known as the developed world, the first world, and MEDCs. It is worth noting briefly in the introduction exactly how you interpret 'Western world' to avoid confusion, and to show you have thought about it. It is also worth briefly defining 'child labour', since this probably doesn't mean any work by children under 18. A definition such as "legal full time work engaged in for the sake of sustenance by people under the age of 16" would suffice. Before answering, consider carefully the economic, social, and symbolic impact of such a refusal to trade, and your priorities regarding economic flourishing, human well-being, and international cooperation.

Introduction:
➢ Clearly state your opinion and outline your arguments for it, as well as your reasons for dismissing counterarguments.
➢ Although not addressed in the question directly, you ought also to state whether you think child labour is a good, bad, or neutral thing. This will obviously affect whether you think we ought to refuse trade with countries in which child labour is used; it might be that you think we shouldn't because child labour is acceptable, or it might be that you think we shouldn't because, although child labour is unacceptable, a refusal to trade won't help. Addressing this issue will help give your argument more nuance if you're arguing for trade, or a more substantial moral backing if you're arguing against it.

Potential arguments for:
➢ By participating in trade with nations in which child labour is legal, they not only implicitly endorse these practices, they also directly fund them.
➢ By refusing trade, they put pressure on Governments, who rely on healthy economic activity, to change their laws and end child labour.
➢ Refusing trade with nations in which child labour is legal won't only stop the funding of child labour, it will increase funding to more morally acceptable industries (since people won't stop demanding these goods, they will simply acquire them elsewhere), which will increase employment among adults.
➢ Western nations have higher standards of living and better working conditions; they ought to set an example for other nations. These nations realise that child labour is wrong, and have made it illegal for their own children to work; trading with nations in which child labour is legal is hypocritical, and shows a xenophobic prioritising of their own children above children in other countries.

> Western nations are among the strongest world economies; they have an unmatched ability to use this economic influence to make a real difference to economic activity in other countries.

Potential arguments against:
> Why do 'Western' nations have moral superiority regarding how our goods are produced? Though child labour is widely outlawed, workers often face dangerous conditions, long hours, earn lower than living wages, and aren't guaranteed sick leave.

> Refusing to trade with countries that use child labour won't actually raise the living standard for these children – it will put them out of work, and they will be left with even less.
>   o **Counterargument**: without child labour to rely on, supply of labour in these countries will fall, and the price of labour (wages) will subsequently rise, as labour will be in higher demand relative to supply. Wages for adults will therefore be higher, which will benefit the working class of the country, and adults are more likely to be able to support their children.

> Punishing whole countries, often very poor countries, for industries that use child labour isn't fair; we ought to simply not fund goods that were produced by child labour.
>   o **Counterargument**: the Governments that run these nations get tax money from every industry. By supporting any of them, we support the Government and its laws. By refusing trade, we threaten the Government's tax revenues and put pressure on them to change their laws.

> Child labour occurs in the majority of nations, and in particular in nations where manufacturing industry dominated the economy. Refusing to trade with all these nations simply isn't sustainable; we don't produce enough ourselves to fulfil demand.

> While children shouldn't be working, refusing to trade with nations where this happens will simply damage our relationship with them. The children will continue to work, and we will have no influence over it. We ought instead to negotiate with these countries to change their laws and use our economic pull to pressure them into doing so.

Conclusion:
Link your conclusion back to the question by referencing your definition of child labour, and discuss why children should or should not be working in such conditions, and why a refusal to trade with nations in which this happens would or would not prevent it, or whether other factors outweigh this.

In our country, every citizen has one vote. A scheme is proposed which allows anybody to buy additional votes if they want to, with the proceeds being used to pay for good causes. Would this be a good scheme?

The sort of question that asks you to discuss a hypothetical such as this is asking you discuss the issues surrounding the concepts it makes reference to. Here, those are the concepts of democracy and a good cause. Before answering, consider your feelings about both, the reasons they are widely considered beneficial (and whether you agree), and which, if either, you prioritise. Try to consider the full social, economic, and political impact such a scheme would, or could, have.

Introduction:

> Clearly state your opinion and outline your arguments for it.
> Link your argument to the concepts of democracy and good causes as discussed above – what are the underlying principles and values that have lead you to hold the opinion that you do? Simply arguing that, for example, the scheme will corrupt democracy, is not enough; you must defend the implicit position that democracy is something that ought not to be corrupted.

Potential arguments for:

> Many things that are widely considered 'good causes' – free health and education, food banks, care for those unable to care for themselves, etc. – are currently hugely underfunded.
> > o **Counterargument:** the solution is not to sell off democracy but, rather, to acknowledge the wealth gap between those who rely on free services and those who have enough money to hypothetically pay for votes, and forcibly correct it.

> This scheme would motivate people to put their money towards these causes in exchange for something they really care about; political pull. Importantly, political pull doesn't cost money to make. Unlike, to use a simplistic example, a bake sale, where what is sold has a cost in materials and labour power, political power has no production cost. In the case of the bake sale, we are essentially relying on people to give more money than must be spent on the material costs of making the goods, which they do because they understand the money is going towards a good cause. This relies on altruism. The proposed scheme does not rely on altruism; in exchange for money, people acquire something they really want, and do not pay more than what is considered its worth. Since people are fundamentally selfish, this will be far more effective than other means of raising money.

- o **Counterargument:** but currently people DO put their money towards good causes without selfish motive, and without any personal acquisition as desirable as political power.

➤ People with money have the right to use it how they wish. They can buy power in other ways – hiring staff, donating to political causes, setting up activist groups – why do we baulk at the idea of selling votes?

➤ People with a lot of money deserve to buy votes; they're rich for a reason, because they worked hard and were clever enough to get rich. Since political activity affects economic activity, they have a right to use their well-earned wealth to affect how the economy will be run.

Potential arguments against:

➤ This scheme clearly undermines democracy by allowing the rich to buy more votes than the poor can afford, so they can influence Government unfairly.

➤ Since they influence Government, who are presumably who decides what constitutes a 'good' cause, they also influence where the money they use to pay for votes goes – it could easily be back into funds that benefit them. They would get richer, and subsequently be able to buy more political power, which in turn would make them richer.

➤ There is already a power imbalance between the rich and the poor, this scheme would only exacerbate it and make it worse for the reasons stated above.

➤ Currently, poorer people are still able to exert political pressure by pooling resources and taking collective action. Richer people can act independently, due to their individual affluence, but, despite being able to donate to campaigns and organise political action groups, etc., they don't hold the pull that large groups of people have; they can exert influence precisely because they are many in number, and their cause is widely supported. This scheme would undermine this dynamic.
  - o **Counterargument:** couldn't poorer people pool their affluence to buy more votes together?
  - o **Counter-counterargument**: even if they did, they wouldn't hold the pull that one rich individual did. This is partly because of the huge wealth disparity in our country, and party because the votes per person would still be much smaller than the votes assigned to one richer person. Each poor person would therefore still have far less political power than each rich person.

> This is key to political health – that a decision is made because it benefits the majority. Voting is the way in which we measure public preference. This scheme would defeat the entire object of voting at all.

Conclusion:
> Restate your opinion and summarise your arguments for it.

> Link your conclusion back to the question by making reference to democracy, and the concept of a 'good cause'.

> It's nice to conclude this sort of question, as discussed in the opening paragraph, with a sentiment regarding the concepts discussed as a whole, and the conclusions you had to reach to make the arguments that you did. For example, you might conclude that democracy is a universal good which is necessary to protect against corruption by the powerful. Or, you might conclude that charity and redistribution of wealth are far greater virtues, for the sake of which we can have some humility and sacrifice some political power.

END OF PAPER

2015

Section 1

Question 1: E

The passage discusses reason why it is important to realise that drug crime is not solely related to illegal drugs such as heroin and cocaine, but also includes counterfeit and homeopathic medicines, citing examples of how each can also be harmful. It then suggests that previous efforts to tackle drug crime have not included counterfeit medicines, and this approach should be changed. If we accept the other reasons in the paragraph as true, we have good cause to believe this claim and so and E) must be the main conclusion of this passage.

Answer A) specifically focuses on the first line of the passage, and so does not encompass the real argument of the passage, which is to tackle counterfeit drugs.
Answers B) and D) are both reasons given in the passage, which contribute towards supporting E). Thus, they cannot be main conclusions.
Answer C) is irrelevant because homeopathic remedies are not the central issue of the text. Although the passage says that they do not work as advertised, there is nowhere in the passage which states that they are not effective, and so C) is false.

Question 2: D

The simplest way to do this question is by using algebra.
  ➤   Let x = number of 50p coins and Let y = number of 10p coins
The information provided allows us to construct two separate equations which we can us together to find x and y.
We know that the total value of the coins added must be £8.50 and so:
  $50x + 10y = 850$. This can be simplified to $5x + y = 85$
Secondly we know that the total number of coins added is 25 and so: $x + y = 25$
We can then solve these simultaneous equations by elimination:
  $4x = 60$ Therefore x = 15 and y = 10
This tells us that the woman inserted 15 (50p) coins and 10 (10p) coins into the machine. However the question asks us what combination is **retained** by the machine. As 5 (10p) coins are returned, the machine must retain all 15 (50p) coins and 5 (10p) coins.
Therefore the correct answer must be D, the machine retains three times as many 50s and 10s. Note that if you ignored the fact that the question is specifically asking for the combination retained by the machine, you would have instead gone for answer B, thus highlighting the importance of reading the question very carefully.

Question 3: B

This passage discusses how in recent years voting has declined to such an extent that less than half of the population actually voted for the party currently in office, and so argues that the governing party does not have the support of the majority of people. B) correctly identifies this conclusion as not valid – it suggests that the party may still have the support of those who did not vote, and so would have an overall majority. Therefore B) represents the greatest flaw in the argument.

Answers C) and D) are irrelevant because the issue at hand is whether the current government has the support of the majority of the people, not why the voting has declined or who is responsible for the lack of legitimacy.

Answers A) and E) are not flaws because for a critical thinking assessment we accept the reasoning given in the passage as true – assessing the quality of evidence is not part of the task, we are simply looking to see whether the reasons, if true, cause us to accept the conclusion.

Question 4: E

The passage discusses how there appears to be double standards in the advertising industry which has allowed certain retail groups to utilise sentimental marketing techniques to outperform all of their rivals. The passage explains how John Lewis' advertisement has been extremely popular online, despite using themes that people may describe as sexist or out-of-touch, as it displays a more stereotypical view of a woman. Although there is evidence that A) might be true, this statement is far too bold to be supported and does not encompass the whole argument, which is about the use of sentimental marketing techniques.

There is no evidence to support B) and D) in the passage even though these might be underlying assumptions of the argument. In addition, C) cannot be right as it represents the stereotypical, politically incorrect view that women are trying to escape from. Hence E) in the main conclusion of the passage.

Question 5: C

This passage discusses how the rise of extremist parties across Europe in the 1920s and 1930s was a major factor in starting the Second World War. Furthermore, it warns that as extremist parties have recently gained more popularity, it is possible that history may repeat itself and lead to new conflicts in the near future. The passage then suggests that the only way to reduce the likelihood of future conflicts is to educate children about the dangers associated with extremist parties.

It is immediately apparent that the conclusion of the passage is not valid if educating children about the dangers of extremist politics does not cause fewer people to vote for them, but nowhere is it stated in the passage that this is the case. Thus C) must be the underlying assumption of the argument.

Answers A) and D) are both over-concluding and are too strong to be underlying assumptions. For example in the case of answer A), although the passage suggests that it is possible the dangerous situation will get worse, there is no concrete evidence which proves that history will definitely repeat itself. Furthermore, although extremist parties were directly involved in starting the Second World War, there is no evidence that the main reason for starting all wars is extremism (this might be the case in reality but there is no evidence in the passage to suggest this).

Answers B) and E) are not assumptions because neither is required to accept the passage's conclusion. The passage simply states that schools should educate children about the dangers of extremist politics to reduce the chances of future wars. Thus, none of them are *required* to be correct for the conclusion to be valid, and thus they are not assumptions. In addition, E) is a very bold statement, and there is nothing to suggest that the success of extremist parties will definitely continue to grow.

Question 6: D
In order to calculate when he should put in the potatoes, the first thing we need to know is how long the beef will take to cook.
- The question tells us that William is cooking for himself and 4 friends. Therefore this is a total of five people.
- He needs to allow 300g per person.
- He is cooking the meat medium rare in a **Hot** oven

Therefore, total weight of beef = 5 x 300 = 1500g

We know that in a hot oven, cooking time = 15 minutes per 500g plus 15 minutes and then an additional 10 minutes standing time.

Cooking time = (15 x 3) + 15 + 10 = 70 minutes

As we are cooking the potatoes in a hot oven, the table shows that they will be ready in 30 minutes. Hence, to ensure that both will be ready at the same, the potatoes should be put in 30 minutes before the beef is ready.

Therefore, we should put in the potatoes 40 minutes after putting the beef in, as they will both be ready after 70 minutes.

Hence, the answer is D).

Question 7: E

The simplest way to find the answer to this question is by the process of elimination.

➢   If we look at the first condition it says the prize cannot be given to anyone who has been late more than twice. We can use this to eliminate the Grace first.

➢   The second condition is that the prize cannot be given to anyone who has failed to complete more than two pieces of homework by the set deadline.
   -   Andrew had been set 60 pieces of homework and completed 56. Therefore he had missed 4.
   -   Edward had been set 59 pieces and only completed 56, and so had missed 3, thus ruling him out of the prize.

➢   After the first two conditions have been satisfied, this leaves Carole and Ian left. Out of them, the one to receive the prize is the one with fewest non-A-grade pieces of work.
   -   For Carole, 53/56 pieces of homework were awarded grade A, meaning only 3 were non-A-grade.
   -   For Ian, 52/53 homeworks were awarded grade A, meaning only 1 was less than a grade A.

Therefore by following through the conditions, we can see that the prize will be awarded to Ian.

Question 8: D

This question requires us to read the information very carefully. It specifically asks us for a representation of plankton production in southern Polar Regions.

Firstly, the fact that we are in a polar region suggests that the variations throughout the year will be quite pronounced and easily distinguishable on the graph. Secondly, the fact that it is in a southern region suggests that there will be a surge in numbers of plant plankton in the months of December, January and February, as it would be summer during these months in the southern hemisphere. Using this information we can then see that the only graph to satisfy both criteria is D), hence it is the right answer.

Option A) this is the same graph for plankton production in northern tropical region so it cannot be correct.

Options B, C and E) The surge in plant plankton occurs during the months of July and August. In the southern hemisphere this would be during winter and so all 3 options must be incorrect.

Question 9: C

The passage concludes that armed people are more likely to be shot than unarmed people. it cites the study conducted at the University of Pennsylvania as a main reason, which pretty conclusively showed that those who were armed had a greater chance of being shot.

Option A) is fairly irrelevant – whether the weapon is visible or concealed does not detract from the overall conclusion of the passage. Furthermore, option D) actually *strengthens* the argument if we accept this to be true, it gives a possible reason as to why those who are armed are more likely to be shot, because they are more likely to be involved in violent situations.

Options B) and E) neither strengthen nor weaken the argument, as they provide simple facts which provide additional information, yet do not counter the overall conclusion.

If we imagine that being armed is variable A and being shot is variable B, the principle of the argument states that A causes B. Hence C) does weaken the passage as it suggests that in fact, B causes A which reverses the whole argument. Thus, C) is the answer.

Question 10: B

The passage says that recurring dreams contain messages that could potentially be very important; hence these dreams are repeated to ensure that you retain the information. However, there is no evidence to suggest that the explanations or information you receive in the dreams are true or beneficial. In fact, recurring dreams could simply contain useless information that is being repeated for an unknown reason. Therefore B) undermines the reasoning which supports the main conclusion of this passage, and so is the main flaw in the argument.

Answer A) is incorrect as we cannot completely discount supernatural explanations as having no value – the fact is that we do not know. Hence A) is not the main flaw. Answers C), D) and E) are irrelevant as they do not undermine the main conclusion of the passage – although they suggest that not all dreams are useful or that people can forget dreams, they do not discuss anything regarding recurring dreams (which is the main topic of the passage). Hence these are not flaws in the argument.

Question 11: D

The passage discusses that buying expensive items and being materialistic do not necessarily make us happy; merely these actions are used as signal to show others certain qualities. The main argument of the passage states that in order to achieve true happiness, we should try to emulate our ancestors and devote more time to simple, traditional activities, so D) expresses the main conclusion of the passage.

Answer A) is a bold statement, which can only be, inferred from the first half of the passage, and so does not encompass a view of the overall argument. Answers B) and C) are not really supported by any evidence from the passage, whilst E) seems to be an intermediate conclusion, which then goes on to support the main conclusion given in D).

Hence, D) is the main conclusion.

Question 12: B

When looking at the table, it is important to note that the same numbers of people were surveyed in each age group. Therefore this makes comparing between the different age groups much easier as we can say that that there were 100 people in each group. We can then solve the problem by considering each option in turn.

- Option A) we can see that Drink A is more popular than Drink B for all age groups except age 25-35. Therefore A) must be incorrect.
- Option B) the total number of people with a preference for Drink B = 20 + 31 + 33 + 19 = 103.
- Total number with no preference = 33 + 12 + 22 + 34 = 101. Therefore B) is the correct answer.
- Option C) we can see that 48% of people expressed a preference. Therefore 52% either expressed no preference or don't know and so C) must be incorrect.
- Option D) we can work out that the total number of people who expressed a preference was 103 (total for B) + 122 (total for A) = 225. As this is greater than 50% of the total number D) must be incorrect.
- Option E) we can prove this is incorrect by estimating an average of the percentage of people who did not know what they preferred. The Average = (19 + 19 +12 +23) / 4 = 18.25%, hence E) is wrong.

Therefore the only correct option is B).

Question 13: D

This question seems quite difficult as we have two unknown variables to deal with, the standing charge and the amount per unit used. The best way to tackle this problem is to therefore solve it using algebra.

Let x = standing charge value and Let y = amount charged per unit

To work out x and y, we need to construct two equations and then solve them simultaneously. As the tariff could have been changed in any of the given months, we can only use May, June or July in our equations as the tariff must have been constant during these months. Using May and June as an example:

$39.50 = x + 95y$ and $37.50 = x + 75y$

Solving these equations by elimination, $20y = 2$

Therefore $y = £0.10$ and $x = £30.00$

Therefore we know that the standing charge is £30 pounds and the amount per unit used is 10p.

We can then check the remaining months to see when the tariff must have changed.

We can see that the tariff is consistent for all months including August.

E.g. $£70 = £30.00 + 70 \times 0.1$ Therefore August is in the same tariff.

If we then check September we can see that it is the first month, which does not obey the same tariff. Under the old tariff, the monthly charge would be $£30.00 + 80 \times 0.1 = £38.00$.

Therefore the tariff was changed in September and so D) is the correct answer.

Question 14: E

When tackling this question, it is necessary to understand what both tables show. The first table suggests that children of parents working in professional or managerial roles tend to do better at GCSEs than those of manual labourers. The second table shows a different link between GCSE performance and type of school attended, with those in independent schools doing better than local authority schools. However it is important to note that although parental occupation and type of school affect success at GCSE level, there is no evidence that they are linked and so any connection between the two variable cannot be inferred from the tables, hence A) and B) are incorrect.

There is no evidence stated that one variable is more important than the other and so C) cannot be correct. Finally, although D) might seem plausible, it is not supported by any information provided and so must be incorrect.

Hence the only option which can be inferred is E) as both type of school and parental occupation clearly affect educational success in their own way.

Question 15: A

This passage discusses the importance of learning at foreign language at school, as it increases one's confidence in communication and travelling. However the majority of British children do not study a foreign language, which could potentially limit their opportunities later on in life.

Option A) is a valid conclusion. There is a great emphasis on how British school children are not being taught a foreign language, and so the lack of education is holding them back in the business world. If we accept all the reason to be true, A) represent the correct conclusion of the passage..

C) is not a valid conclusion as the passage does not imply that the closing down of university language department has put teachers out of work, and therefore we cannot jump to this conclusion. D) Directly contradicts the passage – if we accept the reasoning in the passage to be true, we can see that there is a great need for Britons to learn a foreign language to succeed in the international business world.

B), and E) are both over concluding. The passage says that knowing a foreign language makes us more comfortable in interacting with foreigners. It makes no explicit claim about enjoying your holidays or losing out on business deals. Neither of these focus on the main point of the argument and instead make an indirect conclusion, hence they are incorrect.

Question 16: B

The passage discusses how banning fun science activities have apparently led to a decreasing percentage of students enrolling on science courses at universities. The passage stresses that in order to increase the popularity of university courses; the regulations must be relaxed to allow exciting activities, as they rarely caused harm. This is directly based on the assumption that the 'exciting practicals' have a profound role in encouraging students to take up science. Thus, B) is an assumption from the passage.

Option C) actually disagrees with the passage, which states that some science practicals, even those that are minimally dangerous should be banned on health and safety grounds, so this is not an assumption. Option A) is also not an assumption of the argument, because the passage does not imply that the death of a few does not matter at all, rather than in the context of other factors such as the decreasing number of students taking science at university, this bears less significance. Hence A) is not the correct assumption as the main conclusion is not dependent on this being true.

Option D) is not an *assumption* because it actually strengthens the passage, as it provides further reasoning to relax health and safety regulations. Finally the passage does not necessarily imply that science can only be fun when dangerous and in fact many of the activities suggested are not dangerous at all, rather just more creative or interesting. Hence E) is not an assumption.

Question 17: A

The passage emphasises how owning a home today is unaffordable for many people, as house prices have continued to rise due to increased levels of borrowing. This housing bubble created was a major factor, which contributed to the financial crisis, as it explained how homeowners were unable to repay their debt to pay back their loans. Thus, the main conclusion is that the government should prevent house prices from rising more to avoid a similar crisis in the future.

Answer B) actually weakens the argument, as it suggests that the passage is no longer relevant as house prices are no longer increasing, and so is incorrect. Answer E) also weakens this argument, as it suggests that house prices rising more than inflation rates is good for homeowners as it aides in paying back their mortgage, therefore undermining much of the reasoning in the passage. Finally D) also counters the argument, as it suggests that there is little that the government can actually do to lower house prices, therefore rendering the argument invalid.

Answer C) is fairly irrelevant, because it does nothing to help determine whether the government can do anything to prevent a continued rise in house prices, and so is incorrect. Therefore the correct answer is A) as it provides further reasoning why the government must act to reduce house prices – as the gap between prices and salaries has continued to widen, which suggests that home ownership is becoming even more unaffordable. Hence A) is the correct answer.

Question 18: C

The best way to do this question is to work out the method yourself and then try and match it to one of the given answers. We know that out of 420 candidates, 210 will be sitting in the sports hall.

- Therefore we must share the remaining 210 students between the rest of the rooms.
- There are a total of 11 rooms.

The wording of the question here is very important: instead of asking for the same number of candidates in each room (which would be a far simpler calculation) we want to leave the same number of empty desks in each room.

- Hence, we must determine the total number of empty desks that will be left after all students have been accommodated for.
- Therefore, we need to work out the total capacity of the rooms
  Capacity = 26+20+24+28+24+20+24+16+20+18+26 = 246
- The total number of empty desks = 246 – 210 = 36
- Therefore, number of empty desks per room = 36/11 = 3.2727...

We can see that this method most closely agreed with C) and so this is the correct answer.

Question 19: D

We can see from the question, there is a lot of key information that we need to take careful note of.

- There are a total of 80 people at the wedding reception.
- The marquee must allow a minimum of 3 metres squared per person.
- The couple want the most expensive chairs, and so they will be buying the gilt chairs.
- The couple want eight people per table, and so will be buying the round tables.
- The couple will purchase the complete package, and so the individual costs are irrelevant.

Firstly, we need to calculate the minimum area covered by the marquee.

Minimum area = 80 x 3 = 240 metres squared

Therefore, the smallest size marquee that the couple can order is the 9 x 27, as this will give an area of 243 metres squared. Hence, the price of the complete package is £1,385.

Next we must work out the price of the tables. As the couple need 10 round tables, cost = 10 x 6 = £60

Finally, the couple also requires 80 gilt chairs (as these are the most expensive). Cost = 80 x 2.40 = £192

Total cost = 1385 + 60 + 192 = £1,637. Therefore the correct answer is D).

Question 20: E

The key to answering this question lies in looking at the results table and the graphs provided, and using the table to generate a scale for the x-axis of the graphs. After that it is possible to match each score to the correct bar of the bar chart.

The easiest way to start this question is to use the highest and lowest average marks on the test. The Lowest score was 20 by set 7MO and the highest score was 82 by set 7EV.

Looking at graph A, we know that the top bar must equal 20 marks. Therefore, this tells us that the x-axis is scaled in units of 20 marks each (each line goes up in 20 marks).

Therefore B) and C) must be incorrect as the top bar is greater than 20 marks. We can then use the highest mark achieved to discount graph A) as the bottom bar shows only 80 marks, whereas the highest average mark achieved was 82.

We then must compare graphs D) and E). The only clear visible difference between them is the fourth bar from the top, which should correspond to the mark 57. As in graph D) the bar for this mark is greater than 60, D) must also be incorrect. Hence E) is the correct answer.

Question 21: C

The passage states that certain illegal drugs interfere with a person's driving ability. The reasoning in the argument leads the author to suggest that driving with any level of any illegal drug should be a criminal offence, as this should ensure that driving ability is not impaired due to drugs. However, C) states that some legal drugs can also impair driving ability, and so as there is nothing in the passage to counteract this fact, this significantly weakens the argument. Thus, C) is the correct answer.

Answer A) is irrelevant to the main conclusion of the argument. Although some countries have legalised the drugs that impair driving ability, the problem still exists in this country. Answer B) is also not significant as the drugs referred to in the passage are illegal drugs – hence the possession or consumption of these drugs even if they do not impair driving ability is still a criminal offense.

Answer D) actually strengthens the passage as it emphasises how many drivers are unaware about the dangers of taking drugs and driving. Therefore, new laws to ban drug-driving as suggested in the passage should help eradicate driving under the influence of drugs. Finally E) does not represent the main flaw in this argument – yes, although some illegal drugs may improve driving ability, most others drugs (indeed the most common ones such as cannabis) have been proven to impair driving ability as is mentioned in the passage, and so E) is incorrect.

Hence C) is the answer.

Question 22: A

The passage reasons adding fluorine to water does not improve dental health, drawing upon the example that people who drink fluorinated water regularly do not have healthier teeth than those who do not. Therefore the reasoning in the argument is along the lines of: "Let us assume that A causes B. If you have A, then B will happen". A is drinking fluorinated water and B is having healthier teeth. However since this is not the case A cannot cause B.

Answer A) uses a similar reasoning to the one in the argument. Let us imagine that badgers living there is variable X and the presence of badger droppings is variable Y. It uses the assumption that X causes Y. Therefore if X happened, Y would happen. But since Y has not happened, X cannot be true. This most closely follows the reasoning in the argument and so is correct.

Answer B) follows the opposite pattern of reasoning. It claims that the presence of little piles of soil indicate that moles are present – the reasoning in the passage instead uses the lack of a particular feature to prove that something is not present. Hence this does not parallel the argument's reasoning.

C) warns that since foxes may kill chickens and are present in the area, the chicken house should be guarded against them. Therefore this introduces the idea of actually doing something, which is not mentioned in the argument.

Answer D) introduces the notion of ambiguity and doubt into the argument. Whereas the original argument uses the reasons to come to a definitive statement based on a logical fact. Answer D) suggests that the animal is probably a hedgehog simply as the person cannot think of anything else.

E) uses a slightly different reasoning to the argument, as it is along the lines of, "If A happened, B might happen. As A has happened, B probably has happened" where A is the presence of grey squirrels and B the absence of red squirrels.

Hence, the answer is A)

Question 23: A

The issue raised in the passage is that people who live in towns with peculiar names find that their property values are lower. Therefore, they should feel able to rename their towns if it is in their best interests. This principle is related to whether the people of a community/town are being given the right to exercise their own will regarding their own towns. Answer A) illustrates this principle, so this is the answer.

Answers B) and E) both give the decision making ability to an external source (outside agencies and school staff) which is in contradiction to the principle of the passage.

Answer C) is completely irrelevant, discussing on what basis officials should be elected, but not by whom. Answer D) disagrees with the passage, as nowhere in the passage does it state that new residents cannot expect to be part of the local community. Therefore, D) is also incorrect.

Question 24: B

The fastest way to calculate the answer for this question is to see how much personal allowance and married couple's allowance Mary is eligible for and then calculate what her taxable income is.

- Looking at the column 2000-01, as Mary is aged under 65, her personal allowance is £4385.
- The table shows that the elder spouse (Mary' husband) is aged Under 65 too, she is not eligible for any married Couple's allowance.
- Her total income is £5,585

Therefore taxable income = 5585 – 4385 = £1200

As this amount is within the 10% tax band, she must pay 10% of £1200. Hence the total tax paid = 120/10 = £120

Hence, B) is the correct answer.

Question 25: D

The fastest way to answer this question is to work out the total rainfall between the beginning of June to the end of September and then divide by the number of months (which in this case is 4).

We can see from the graph that at the end of September the cumulative rainfall was 400mm. At the beginning of June, cumulative rainfall was approximately 180mm.

Therefore total rainfall in these months = 400 – 180 = 220mm

Average monthly rainfall = $\frac{220}{4}$ = 55 mm. The closest answer is 57mm/month and so D) must be the correct answer.

Note, we know that although C) is quite close to our answer, it cannot be correct as we can see the total rainfall in these months it clearly over 200mm and so our average must be greater than 50mm/month.

Question 26: B

We are told that the bath has a capacity of 360 litres.
The hot tap can fill it in 15 minutes.
Therefore, the rate of filling for the hot tap = 360/15 = 24 litres/min
The cold tap can fill it in 10 minutes.
Hence the rate of filling for the cold tap = 360/10 = 36 litres/min

In the first 1.5 minutes, both taps are running. Therefore the amount of water in the bath = $(1.5 \times 36) + (1.5 \times 24) = 54 + 36 = 90\ litres$
We can use this information to work out the scales of the axes on the graphs. The x-axis must go up in units of 1.5 minutes each and the y-axis must go up in units of 90 litres each.

As we are told that the bath is left ¾ full, this would mean that the final volume is 270 litres. Hence, C) and E) must be incorrect as the total volume of water in these graphs is 360 litres.
After 1.5 minutes, we are told that the cold tap is switched off leaving only the hot tap still on. The amount of water left to fill up = 270 – 90 = 180 litres.
Time taken to fill remainder = 180 / 24 = 7.5 minutes.

Therefore, the bath would be at the correct level of 270 litres after a total of 9 minutes. As we know the scale of the graphs, this would correspond to the 6th line along the x-axis. Hence B) is the correct graph.

Question 27: B

The passage describes the potential dangers of storing personal data on computers on our privacy, and explains how the Data Protection Act ensures that this information is kept confidential except in extenuating circumstances. It also mentions that, as there is a possibility of this information being misused in the future, we *must not allow the principle to be abandoned* (referring to the Data Protect Act). All the reasoning given ultimately supports the idea that the Data Protection Act should not be abandoned for our own safety. Hence B) is the main conclusion of the passage.

Answers A), C) and E) are all reasons in the passage which support this conclusion, and are not themselves conclusions. Answer D) is irrelevant to the overall conclusion and we cannot be sure to what extent the Data Protection Act might potentially interfere with crime detection, hence D) is also incorrect.

Question 28: C

The passage describes how politicians use sound bites to justify their proposed actions as it allows them to take advantage of the sentiment of the public and so get away with their decisions.

Answer A) is not a valid conclusion. The second line clearly states that sound bites are used to justify a politician's action, rather than use a sound bite to avoid a proper explanation.

Answer B) is not a valid conclusion because the passage does not state that politicians always believe that their actions are right, rather than the sound bite is a tool to justify their actions, even if they are unsure whether it is right or wrong. Thus, we cannot *reliably* conclude that B) is true.

Answer D) is not a valid conclusion because the passage directly contradicts this statement. The passage suggests that sound bites are used to appease the public or quieten public discontent; rather it is only the author of the passage that seems alienated. Hence D) is incorrect.

Answer E) is not a valid conclusion because no reference is made in the passage to whether politicians actually prefer to use sound bites rather than provide a proper rationale. Instead the sound bite could be a last resort that politicians use if they cannot properly justify their actions. Notice how A) is extremely similar to E), and so in this case is seems likely that both answers are wrong.

Answer C) can be reliably concluded. We are told that the use of sound bites in many ways is immoral and is effectively a way of manipulating the public. We also know that instead of sound bites, the moral thing to do for politicians would be to accurately explain the reasoning behind their actions. Hence C) encompasses the whole argument and so is the main conclusion.

Question 29: D

The passage discusses how the British Constitution has greatly benefited over the years by not being too rigid and following logic, but instead being guided by following common sense. It concludes that the reason we have avoided several problems in the past is because we have always followed common sense and never been guided by logic. However, it is not necessarily the case that using logic in the past would not have avoided problems wither, as we have never tired using it and so do not know what would have been the consequences. If this is not the case, the passage's conclusion that ignoring logic and following common sense is far better do not necessarily follow from its reasons, so Answer D) correctly identifies an assumption in the passage.

Answer C) strengthens the passage's conclusion, if true. However, it is required for the passages' conclusion to be valid, so it is not an assumption, as it is not an integral part of the argument.

Answer A) is not an assumption, because it directly contradicts the passage. The opening line states how logicians did not devise the British Constitution, and so A) is incorrect. Furthermore B) is also not an assumption, as there is nowhere in the passage which implies that the British Constitution even today is written down, and so it would be wrong to assume this in the argument. Hence B) is not correct.
Answer E) is not an assumption because although the passage discusses the benefits of ignoring logic and following common sense, this is a great over conclusion of the argument. There are several advantages of using common sense, but we cannot assume that it must always be right to ignore logic to produce the best result. Hence answer E) cannot be an assumption of the passage.

Question 30: D

The best way to do this question is to work out which teams cannot mathematically win the league.
Firstly we need to calculate the total number of games played by each team. There are 6 teams in the league and we are told that all teams played each other 4 times. Therefore total games played = (6-1) x 4 = 20 games. We can then start from the bottom of the table to work out which teams cannot win.

Starting with Bottom Albion. We know that they only have 5 games remaining. Therefore, the maximum number of points that they can win with 5 wins = 5 x 3= 15 points. This would give them a total of 30 points, meaning that they would still be below East Rovers, and so they cannot win the league.

Although Top Town, are second from bottom, they have 7 games remaining. Therefore, the maximum number of points they can achieve is 17 +21 = 38 points. Provided East Rovers lose or draw the rest of their games, Top Town could mathematically still win the league.

South United have 3 games remaining and so could only score a maximum of 31 points which would make them level with East Rovers. We are told that in this case, the team with the most wins will win the league. Even if South United win all of their games, they would only have a total of 7 wins, which is less that East Rovers, and so they cannot win the league.

Although North Rangers also have 22 points, with 3 wins out of 3, they could score 31 points in total with 9 games won (more than East Rovers if they lose all their remaining games). Hence North Rangers can win the league.
It is clear that West Athletic and East Rovers can win the league, which means that only Bottom Albion and South United cannot win. Hence only 4 teams can win the league and so D) is the correct answer.

Question 31: C
This seems like quite a long question as there are 9 different classes to choose from, and so to calculate the price per hour for each class would be quite time consuming. Therefore, the quickest way to do this question is to eliminate answers by working out which do not satisfy the conditions stated before working out the price per hour.

The first condition states that she does not want to leave home before 09:15 and return by 16:15.
-    We can therefore eliminate Painting Class 3
-    We can eliminate Dancing Class1 and Class 2
-    We can eliminate Pottery Class 1
We must then work out the price per hour of the remaining classes
➢   Painting Class 1 = 30/2 = $15 per hour
➢   Painting Class 2 = 40/1/5 = $26.66 per hour
➢   Pottery Class 2 = 40/2 = $20 per hour
➢   Writing Class 1 = 35/2.5 = $14 per hour
➢   Writing class 2 = 24/1.5 = $16 per hour

Therefore she will choose writing Class 1. The price of this class is $35 and so C) is the correct answer.

Question 32: D
This question is difficult to describe on paper, as it requires visualisation of 3-D shapes. When looking at the remote from the direction of the arrow, you would see a row of five small buttons, regardless of any of the larger buttons.
Therefore the answer is D as the small button in the first column is missing and so cannot be a possible view.

Question 33: C
The passage discusses how the apparent fall in crime rate in many towns and cities such as Kings Lynn is thought to be due to the implementation of CCTV cameras, and so they have been a great success in controlling "opportunistic" crime. However C) greatly weakens the association between CCTV implementation and reduced crime as it introduces a confounding variable: extra police presence, which may have caused the fall in crime rather than the CCTV cameras. Thus C) is the correct answer.

Answers A) and E) are not relevant as the passage simply states that CCTV reduces crime rates. Whether they are recording or not, or can be used in court convictions is not important to the overall conclusion.

Answer D) seems irrelevant as it does not counter or weaken the effectiveness of the CCTV cameras. Even if they are an overreaction, they have produced great results and so this does not oppose the main conclusion. Finally B) could actually be seen to strengthen the argument – as even though the cameras are situated in the centres of towns and cities, they still great reduce crime rates (probably because so called "opportunistic" crime is greatest in the busy city centre).
Hence C) must be the correct answer.

Question 34: A
The passage describes how learning a foreign language at school is essential if people want to work at the highest level. The argument stated here is along the lines of, for X to happen, Y is required – where X is working at the top level and Y is learning a foreign language. The argument then suggests that is people have Y, then X will happen. Therefore by replacing the variables with X and Y, we can see how the argument has treated a necessary condition for success as a sufficient condition. Just because A is necessary does not mean that if you have A, B will definitely happen. Hence A) is the correct flaw in the argument.

Answer B) does not identify a flaw in this passage, because it is the opposite argument to what the passage is actually suggesting. For business success, learning a foreign language is necessary, not sufficient – therefore it disagrees with the passage.

Answer C) does not directly relate to the discussion as the passage does not in fact include any main examples, and rather just states assertions that we should accept to be true. Therefore it is not the main flaw in the argument.

Answer D) can be seen as a flaw in the passage as the author assumes that learning a foreign language will directly help students succeed in the business world. However due to the reasoning given in the passage, which we assume to be true, there is no evidence to suggest that this relationship is not causal. Furthermore, this small flaw is outweighed by the much larger flaw in A) and so in not the *main* flaw of the argument.

Answer E) also somewhat is irrelevant. Nowhere in the passage does it mention the past; rather the passage suggests that this is a current problem which should be dealt with now to prepare for the future.
Hence the answer is A).

Question 35: B
The passage criticises banks, which pay large bonuses to their employees, saying that it cannot be justified. This statement at the beginning of the passage is then supported by several reasons, which argue that it discourages young people from taking jobs in the industrial sector and also promotes adverse risk taking with shareholder's assets. The remainder of the passage explains why firms pay large bonuses, but then again highlights how the cost for these can fall on to the consumer. Therefore, the main conclusion of the passage must be B).

Answers A) and C) identify reasons given in the passage, which go on to support the conclusion given in B).

Answers D) and E) could be seen as conclusions from the passage, but both would require leaps of logic not made in the passage in order to be conclusions, and thus are somewhat criticisable as conclusions.

Also, if we accept either of these answers as true, they both go on to support the conclusion given in B), making them *intermediate* conclusions, not the main conclusion.

Question 36: C
First we calculate the total time available to sign autographs in minutes:
-    There are 9 hours available between 9am and 6pm.
-    This means that there are 9 x 60 = 540 minutes to sign autographs.
Next we are told that he can sign ten times per minute and has to have a ten-minute break after each hour. Therefore the easiest way to do this is to find out how much the organisers can earn each round of 70 minutes.
-    Amount earned per minute = £10
-    Amount earned per hour + 10 minute break = 10 x 60 = £600
Therefore we can split the 540 minutes available into 7 rounds of 70 minutes and a remainder of 50 minutes.
Therefore total amount raised = (7 x 600) + (50 x 10) = 4200 + 500 = £4700
Therefore the answer is C).

Question 37: D
First we need to calculate how many cubic metres of mulch are required for each plot of land.

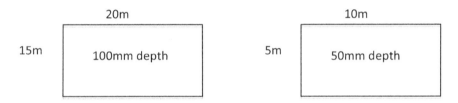

Area of Plot 1 = 10 x 5 = 50 metres squared
If we then look at the table, underneath the 50mm depth column, we can see that we would require 2.5 cubic metres of mulch.
Area of Plot 2 = 20 x 15 = 300 metres squared
If we then look at the table underneath the 100mm column, we can see that 100 metres squared requires 10 cubic metres of mulch.

We can then extrapolate this, so that 300 metres squared requires 30 cubic metres of mulch.
Total mulch required = 2.5 + 30 = 32.5 cubic metres
Total weight of mulch = 32.5 x 0.65 = 21.125 tonnes
(NB: This is a hard sum to calculate without a calculator. A simpler way to do this is to work out 50% of 32.5 = 16.25. You can then increase this by 10% and then 5% to work out 65%)
Therefore, we would require 22 one-tonne bags to ensure we have enough to complete the mulching of the two plots. Hence D) is the correct answer.

Question 38: E

This is a question that involves many steps to find the correct answer. Firstly, we are told that the time is supposedly nine minutes past ten.

➤ Therefore, the first thing we must do is work out how much time has passed since he reset his watch and looked out again across the road this morning.

➤ He reset his watch at 22:05 and again looked out at 10:09. Therefore, we can see that the time passed was 12 hours and 4 minutes.

➤ Next we can work out the actual time when he reset his watch last night. As the reflection showed a time of 22:05, this means the actual time was 20:55.

➤ Therefore, the actual time this morning must be 12 hours and 4 minutes after 20:55. Therefore the actual time is 08:59.

➤ Hence, when he looked across the road, he would see a reflection of the time 08:59.

Therefore, E) is the correct answer, as it is the correct reflection of the time 08:59.

Question 39: C

This passage highlights how many consider that homeopathic medicines work solely due to the placebo effect, and so are only effective as patients believe they are useful. This stance is countered by a particular study in cows which tested the effects of homeopathic medicines compared to a placebo, and found that there was a difference in beneficial effects between the two. Therefore, if we accept the study to be fairly conducted and the result true, the most logical conclusion from this is that the beneficial effects of homeopathy in cows cannot be due to the placebo effect, so C) is the right answer.

Answer A) contradicts the findings of the experiment as the study showed more cows developed mastitis with a placebo than the homeopathic remedy, and so the effects of homeopathy cannot be solely due to the placebo effect, hence A) is incorrect. B) Criticises the validity of the experiment conducted, however there is no evidence to suggest that we should discount the findings of the study with the cows, and so we cannot conclude B).

Although in this case, the experiment was carried out on cows, D) seems to be an over conclusion as we cannot be sure that homeopathy is only beneficial to animals. If humans or other species were tested, they may see the benefits of homeopathy. Finally E) could be described as an intermediate conclusion, as it goes on to support the notion in C). Although the study does suggest that there are several beneficial effects of homeopathy, there is no further evidence we can use to extrapolate these results to humans and other species. Furthermore, the sample size maybe too small and so these results maybe unreliable. Therefore much of the criticism maybe justified and so we cannot conclude E).

Hence C) is the correct answer.

Question 40: C

This passage emphasises that insurance must be compulsory for dog owners, arguing that it is unfair that victims must take the owner to court to receive compensation, which can be an arduous and expensive process. This would mean insurance companies pay for injuries caused as they do for damage to cars and homes.

Looking at the reasoning used, we can see that the argument stresses that just because a law being passed would make dog owners have to take out insurance for their dogs, it does **not** mean that they would do it. If this is the case, then the passage's reasoning no longer supports the conclusion that all injuries would be paid for by the insurance companies. Thus C) is a valid assumption of the passage. Answers A) and E) both weaken the argument. A) Suggests that if the law was passed, dog owners may not be able to afford the insurance and so may not opt to buy it and their dogs would not be covered by insurance. Similarly E) weakens the reasoning to make dog insurance compulsory as it suggests that injured victims can easily take owners to court and receive compensation. Therefore both of these are not assumptions.

Answer B), if true, would reinforce the conclusion, providing additional strength to its reasoning. However, it is not *required* to be true for the conclusion to be valid, so this is not an *assumption* of the passage.

Answer D) is irrelevant to the overall conclusion of the passage. The fact that dogs are illegal or legal makes no difference to whether passing a law to make insurance compulsory would ensue that injuries are funded by the insurance company, rather than the taxpayer.

Hence, the answer is C).

Question 41: D

The passage discusses how there is a disproportionate number of students who study at elite universities to those who attend private schools. This increased proportion is seen as linked with better teaching in private schools, which allow students to achieve better examination results and therefore gain admission into better universities. Thus, it concludes that the teaching in private schools must be better than state schools. Note that we are asked for the answer that would **most weaken** the argument – so we may see multiple answers which would weaken the argument and must choose the one with the most direct link as the strongest.

Answer E) would *strengthen* the passage. It suggests that as private schools accept students from poorer backgrounds and still are better at getting their students into better universities, family background does not really determine or affect the grades students achieve, rather the better performance of those in private schools must be down to the better education they receive.

Answers A) and C) are irrelevant. The passage does not refer to whether students in private schools do better in just A-levels, but that they achieve higher grades overall. Answer C) also suggests that a majority of those in Oxbridge are from state schools. However this number of students in private schools (7%) is still disproportionately small to those in Oxbridge (40%), so this in fact strengthens the argument. It is adding no new information that cannot be deduced from the question.

Answer B) does weaken the passage, as it suggests that family background and wealth might be the reason more private school students go to elite universities, rather than better education. The implication is that factors other than the school's performance may influence attainment. However there are a few missing steps between this background and A-level results, so it is not a very strong argument.

Answer D) is the strongest and therefore the correct answer, as if fewer state school students sit A-levels, this could be the reason why fewer get the opportunity to go to Oxford and Cambridge. In other words state school exam results might not be worse, but the good results might be enjoyed by fewer pupils. Now this is not a wholly satisfactory answer as the underlying reason behind fewer people sitting A-levels could be a lower standard of teaching and attainment in previous years – but as it is a solid and direct reason why despite comparable teaching fewer state school pupils might make Oxbridge selection it is the strongest answer to the question.

Question 42: C

We know that the examination contains five questions:

| 1 | 2 | 3 | 4 | 5 |

To make the question simpler, we can split the 5 questions into two groups, which allow us to test each condition individually.

Group 1:   1   2   3

For this group, we must choose at least one of the first two questions. Therefore the combinations allowed are:

1	2	3
1	2
1	3
2	3

Group 2:   4   5

For this group, we must choose not more than one. Therefore, we can either choose question 4, 5 or indeed none of them.

Now that we have established which questions we can pick from each group, and knowing that we must pick choose 3 questions in total, the possible combinations to choose are:

1	2	3
1	2	4
1	2	5
1	3	4
1	3	5
2	3	4
2	3	5

Therefore the total number of combinations possible is 7 and so C) is the correct answer. If we had not split the initial five questions into 2 groups, then it is more likely that we would have missed the combination of questions 1,2,3 and so would have incorrectly chosen answer B).

Question 43: E

To answer this question, we must calculate the total time taken for each of the possible journeys – although some options may take less time, it is important to check that they satisfy Hester's conditions and she has enough time to spend in each town before the next train.

Option A:
- Leave Birmingham at 09:00 → Arrive at Tamworth at 09:30
- Spend 1 hour in Tamworth until 10:30
- Catch 11:30 train → Arrive at Derby at 11:50
- As she must spend 1.5 hours here she cannot catch 12:15 train

Option B:
- Leave Birmingham at 10:00 → Arrive at Tamworth at 10:28
- Spend 1 hour in Tamworth until 11:28
- Catch 11:30 train → Arrive at Derby at 11:50
- Spend 1.5 hours until 13:20
- Leave Derby at 14:00 → Arrive back at 15:00
- Total time is 5 hours

Option C:
- Leave Birmingham at 11:00 → Arrive at Tamworth at 11:30
- Spend 1 hour in Tamworth until 12:30
- Catch 12:45 train → Arrive at Derby at 13:05
- Spend 1.5 hours until 14:35
- Leave Derby at 15:20 → Arrive back at 16:12
- Total time is 5 hours and 12 minutes

Option D:
- Leave Birmingham at 12:00 → Arrive at Tamworth at 12:45
- Spend 1 hour in Tamworth until 13:48
- Catch 13:45 train → Arrive at Derby at 14:00
- Spend 1.5 hours until 15:30
- Leave Derby at 16:10 → Arrive back at 16:55
- Total time is 4 hours and 55 minutes

Option E:
- Leave Birmingham at 13:30 → Arrive at Tamworth at 13:45
- Spend 1 hour in Tamworth until 14:45
- Catch 14:45 train → Arrive at Derby at 15:05
- Spend 1.5 hours until 16:35
- Leave Derby at 17:00 → Arrive back at 18:15
- Total time is 4 hours and 45 minutes (shortest time taken)

Question 44: D

Again this question is difficult to describe on paper, as it requires visualisation of 3-D shapes. The best way to prepare for this question is to practice with dies, as these types of questions are common in this exam. Alternatively, you can use cut-out nets in the exam to make the die if you have enough time (remember you can always take scissors into your exam!).

Without a cut out net, this question is very difficult. The best way to tackle it is to first be sure of exactly which numbers are on the sides you cannot initially see.

➢ Opposite the 5 is a 2
➢ Opposite the 3 is a 4
➢ Opposite the 1 is a 6

Using this information, you must look at each of the options and attempt to do this question by elimination. But if you do have time, try to make a cut out net, as it will make the question much easier.

Question 45: C

The passage argues against the claim that you can work out what a particular sentence in a book means by simply asking author or guessing what he intended to mean, as the true meaning of a sentence will inevitably depend on your own interpretation of it. If we accept all the reasons given in the passage to support this claim, we therefore find that C) expresses the main conclusion in this passage as it encompasses the whole argument.

E) is also a valid conclusion from the passage, but it goes on to support the statement in C). Thus, E) is an intermediate conclusion in this passage, *not* the main conclusion. A) Could also be seen as an over conclusion, but it seems too far stretched that no one can determine what the sentence means, as one can work out what the sentence means to them. Answers B) and D) are reasons given in the passage to support its conclusion.

Question 46: C

The reasoning in this passage can be described, as "For A to happen, B is required. Since A did not happen, you did not have B." Here, "A" is getting a job, and "B" is writing a **good** application letter.

Answer A) could be described as "If you have B, then A will definitely happen. Since A did not happen, you did not have B", with A being having a place in the final and B recording the best time in the heat. This is not the same as in the passage as you did not need to write the best application letter to get the job - the use of the superlative means A) must be incorrect.

Answer B) reasons as "For A to happen, B is required. You don't have B, so A will not happen". This is not the same as in the passage, so B) is incorrect.

Answer C) reasons as "A cannot happen, with B. Since A did not happen, you did not have B". This most closely parallels the reasoning in the argument; hence C) is correct.

Answer D) reasons as "A will only happen if B has happened. As B has happened, A will happen", where "A" being promoted and "B" is working hard. This is not the same as the passage so D) is incorrect.

Answer E) reasons as "For A to happen, B is required." However it then says that as B has nearly happened, A should happen. This is not the same as in the passage.

Question 47: A
The passage discusses how the credit crisis as well as previous government policy decisions has caused many pensioners to be at risk of poverty. It claims that, as we have had a pension crisis looming for years, which the government is partly responsible for, it should be willing to face the consequences of its actions and act to restore them. Thus the principle underlying the passage is that since it was one's fault that an error occurred, they should be the ones to try and correct their mistakes.

Answer A) follows a similar principle, in which the person could have avoided dropping plates had he not carried so many (similar to the pension crisis which could have been avoided by the government taking better decisions). Furthermore, as he dropped the plates and is responsible, he feels compelled to replace the broken ones, thus making up for his actions.

None of the other answers refer to both notions that if better decisions were taken beforehand, the mishap could have been avoided **and** the fact that it is the responsibility of the one who is culpable to redeem their actions, and so these are not the principles in the passage.

Question 48: A

To solve this problem, we must first calculate the how many containers are used each quarter (from Jan-March, Apr – Jun etc.)

➢   Quarter 1 = 2000 + 3000 + 1000 = 6000
➢   Quarter 2 = 3000 + 2000 + 2000 = 7000
➢   Quarter 3 = 1000 + 1000 + 3000 = 5000
➢   Quarter 4 = 1000 + 2000 + 3000 = 6000
➢   Therefore the total usage in the year = 24000 containers

We are told that the takeaway currently has 2,000 containers left. Therefore the total amount that needs to be delivered is 22,000. We can use this information to then eliminate any of the answers, which do not deliver 22,000 containers.

D) is incorrect as the total number of containers delivered is 24,000 which would leave a remainder of 2000

B) And C) must both be incorrect as we are told that the maximum number that can be delivered at one time is 6,000 and for both, it says 7,000 will be delivered in quarter 2. Therefore these two options are wrong.

We can then compare answer A) and E). Although both have a total of 22,000 containers delivered, we must consider each quarter individually.

For E) 6,000 containers need to be used in Quarter 1. Therefore, the takeaway would have to use all 4,000 delivered and the 2,000 remaining. However, this means that they would not have enough containers to meet the usage for quarter 2 (only 6,000 containers are delivered and the usage is 7,000). Hence E) must also be incorrect. Hence A) is the correct answer.

Question 49: C

The quickest way to do this question is by the process of elimination, starting with the lowest amount provided in the question, A) 58p and then working upwards. For each amount provided, it is necessary to see whether it is possible to make up the amount with less than 3 stamps, and so, if we find an amount for which it is not possible to do so, that will be the correct answer.

For A) we can make up 58p = 56p stamp + 2p stamp. Therefore A) is incorrect.
For B) 65p = 56p + 9p. Therefore B) is also incorrect.

For C) we cannot use only two stamps to make up 68p. A possible combination could be 62p + 5p + 1p although there are several others available. Thus C) is the correct answer.

It is important to note that it is not possible to make D) 75p with two stamps either, and so if you miss C) then the only other possible answer would be D). This highlights how starting from the lowest amount first and then working upwards could avoid choosing this answer.

For E) 79p = 62p + 17p. Therefore E) is incorrect.

Question 50: E

The best way to tackle this question is to imagine taking photographs from different points on field and then writing down the order or trees you would see from left to right.

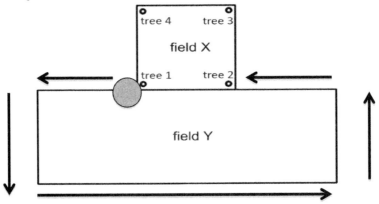

To ensure that you find all the possible combinations, you should start on the edge of Field Y at the marked point and then work around the perimeter of field Y noting every time you find a different combination. Therefore if we start at that point and work round in the direction stated the orders seen are:

> 4 – 3 – 1 – 2   > 1 – 4 – 2 – 3
> 4 – 1 – 3 – 2   > 1 – 2 – 4 – 3
> 1 – 4 – 3 – 2

Therefore as there are 5 different orders from left to right, the correct answer is E).

END OF SECTION

Section 2

Would society be better if there were more scientists in positions of political power?

This is a difficult question in that it requires knowledge of both politics and science, and the interaction between them. It can be made simpler by clarifying in the opening paragraph the manner in which you are going to make the argument – i.e. from the points of view science can benefit society. Nevertheless, it remains a challenging question.

Introduction

➢ Begin by defining your terms, as above. Indicate what you consider to be 'political power', and whether in this context it refers to positions in government. It is important to have an opinion regarding the question from the beginning – it is advisable to argue one side and acknowledge the other side of the argument later in the essay.

➢ Clearly state your opinion within these defined parameters, and outline the main arguments you'll be discussing.

➢ There are many ways in which society can be improved, which could be categorised into economically, socially, culturally etc. Therefore when addressing the question it is important to acknowledge how diverse society is and therefore state which aspects of society you will be focussing on.

➢ From an economic point of view, society might benefit, as scientists may potentially be able to allocate resources more efficiently, whilst also devising an efficient economic plan to aid the country. In contrast, from a social, and possibly a more realistic point of view however, the reality might be different.

➢ A key issue at the heart of this question's concerns is to evaluate the main qualities of a scientist – and then use this to either suggest why/why not they would be used to benefit society.

Potential arguments why society would be better:

➢ You could make an argument that a major aspect of science is using research and empirical evidence to make informed decisions. This would be of great benefit to society, for example in allocating resources to particular sectors or making decisions, as one could argue that a scientist would consider all the possible variables to arrive at the most logical conclusion. For reasons like this, it is often beneficial to give an example, e.g. how much money to allocate to the NHS.

  o **Counter-argument**: It is worth noting that not all arguments can simply be made on factual evidence. Furthermore, when confronted with a new problem, the time needed to research the problem may not be available. Hence a scientific approach may not always be the most practical approach. Give an example of a situation where this may be the case.

➢ Having more scientists in political power may lead to a more balanced government. Currently, the majority of politicians are from a political, economic (humanity based subject) background. If there were more scientists, this may help to even out the demographics of parliament so that it more closely represents the demographics of the country, rather than simply being composed of political graduates.

➢ If more scientists are in political positions, this may help to increase the popularity of scientific subjects at school and the numbers of those who choose to study science at university. It is worth mentioning here what science has achieved in the past: greater healthcare, discovery of antibiotics, extensive space exploration to name a few. Increased scientific interest in society therefore will inevitably lead to greater discoveries in the future.

➢ Finally, with certain aspect of society such as health, energy and the environment, a scientist is more likely to understand the consequences of new policy better than a non-scientist as it relates to a subject that the scientist has expertise in. Therefore they would be better placed to decide issues in government.

Potential arguments why society would be worse:

This is arguably the easier side to argue for this particular question. When stating why society would be made worse, there are several opportunities for counter-arguments which themselves can be further challenged (something that will make the essay much better).

➢ Although scientists may excel in their particular field, it needs to be mentioned that many will have had no experience governing or leading a country before. To be in a position of political power, we need to consider all the other qualities that are required: being a good listener, communicator, leader etc.

➢ One of the biggest dangers of promoting more scientists to political power is the fact that several atrocities in the past have been allowed under the banner of science. This provides an excellent opportunity to cite meaningful examples. For example, the rise of science in society might lead to eugenics – the selective breeding of people for the so-called benefit of society, or even the rise of Nazism and the pursuit of the pure Aryan race. Therefore it is necessary to consider the possible social implications of promoting more scientists to political power.
   o Counter-argument: there is always an argument to be made that no one is perfect and that arguably scientists have done more good than bad. The great number of scientific discoveries have saved more lives than were taken due to absurd scientific theories.
   o Counter-counter argument: we can mention how several scientific discoveries have the capacity now to completely ruin the society in which we live. An example of this is the discovery of nuclear fission and the atomic bomb, which could potentially destroy modern society.

➢ Another point to mention is that increasing the number of scientists to political power, especially in other more religious countries, might increase tensions between religious and secular communities in society. It is worth noting that several societies disagree with the theory of evolution and see science as a means of destroying their beliefs. This is a controversial topic and so should be discussed with caution, but is worth mentioning.

Time lag

Another angle of assessing the potential benefit to society is through timeframe – and evaluating what would be the short and longer-term consequences of having more scientists in political power. An argument therefore could be made that focuses more on advancement's long term impact rather than immediate impact.

Conclusion

➢ Make sure that you include potential counter arguments for any of the above points that you make – it is vital that your essay comes across as balanced and not one-sided.

➢ In your conclusion you could argue that there would be certain benefits to society, but at the same time other ways in which society might suffer.

➢ Another distinction you could make in your conclusion is between how we ought to evaluate the overall benefit to society and whether the economic or social argument is more important. Would it be right to allow great scientific advancement whilst at the same time allowing for the deterioration of the arts sector in society? Exploring these political implications is a good way to end the question.

Is it possible to justify abortion without justifying infanticide of recently born babies?

Before answering the question, it is important to fully understand what the question is actually asking. This is not a debate for /against abortion – instead whether abortion and infanticide are equally justifiable or fundamentally different. In what ways are they similar? How are they different? What are the moral and ethical objections of each? Before beginning to answer, consider these questions, as they will form the basis of your answer. For example, you might argue that infanticide cannot be justified despite allowing abortion due to the fact that a living baby is tangible being, but a foetus (or embryo) is still an intangible object.

Introduction:

➤ Begin by defining your terms, as above. Indicate what you consider to be 'abortion' and "infanticide" – it does not matter that you know the actual medical definitions, rather a sensible understanding of the topics at hand.

➤ Though it may seem obvious, it is worth briefly discussing *why* abortion and infanticide occur.

➤ Clearly state your opinion within these defined parameters, and outline the main arguments you'll be discussing.

Potential arguments to justify abortion without justifying infanticide:

➤ You could make an argument abortion and infanticide are fundamentally different. In the case of abortion, since the foetus has not been born it is not considered to be a person and therefore should have no rights. Hence the decision whether to keep or terminate the fetus' life should lie with its mother. In contrast, once the baby is born, infanticide could be deemed as murder as the baby is legally a person and so has fundamental human rights.

○ **Counter-argument**: it is possible to argue that all forms of life, whether born or still in the womb is sacred, and so both abortion and infanticide are morally wrong.

➤ Abortion could be justified under the grounds that an embryo is not a developed enough being to feel pain as its nervous systems or organs may not have formed yet. Therefore terminating the embryo's life at this stage would not cause any hurt to the baby. In contrast, once a baby has been born, its senses have developed to feel pressure, and pain and therefore infanticide would cause hurt to the baby.

> The risk to women during childbirth is substantial especially in less well-developed countries, and therefore abortion (particularly in the earlier stages) can be seen as a safer method of terminating the pregnancy if the child is unwanted – rather than waiting till after the child is born giving risk of birth complications. This would provide an argument to justify abortion without necessarily allowing infanticide.

> There is a strong argument to be made that abortion in this country at least, is justifiable as it is only allowed if the pregnancy was unwanted or if the baby has a genetic defect (rather than terminating after finding out the baby's sex). However, in other countries, the practice of female infanticide is common, as boys are preferred in these male-dominated societies. Hence, since the reasons for abortion are more justified than for infanticide, abortion can be allowed.

Arguments why abortion cannot be justified without justifying infanticide:

> All forms of life, whether born or still in the womb is sacred. This can be supported by considering duty-based ethics, and suggesting that we all have a moral obligation to preserve life in all forms. Hence there is no ethical difference between abortion and infanticide, and both cannot be justified.

> In both cases, it is possible to argue that it is not the child's own decision as in neither case, the child is competent enough or able to state whether he wants to live. On this note, we can argue that abortion and infanticide are both not acting in the best interests of the child and so both should not be justified.
>   o **Counter-argument**: we can argue that since a foetus isn't a person, it should not have the same rights or deemed to have any interest of its own. Therefore it should be legally and ethically moral that this decision can be taken by the mother.

> There is a strong argument that infanticide and abortion are effectively the same phenomenon, as they both represent ways of ending a baby's life – abortion can be thought of as the modern solution to terminating pregnancy through the use of technology which is often not accessible or unaffordable for many in poorer countries. In contrast, infanticide provides a more practical, accessible option to end a baby's life. If we assume that there are no moral objections to ending a baby's life, then it can be argued that there are no significant differences between abortion and infanticide – hence one cannot be justified without the other.

Conclusion:

> Be sure to link your conclusion back to the question by referencing the fundamental difference or similarities in ethical issues regarding abortion and infanticide, and why you feel the arguments you've favoured outweigh the arguments in favour of more/less testing.

Should 'whistleblowers' be encouraged or discouraged?

In this sort of question, 'whistleblowers' is, in part, a stand in for any subject – much of your essay should be spent arguing for whistleblowers to be encouraged, focusing on the benefits that whistle blowing allows. Alternately, you could argue that whistleblowers should be discouraged – in this case, you should make it clear why you believe this is the case and reject counterarguments, and cite examples to demonstrate your case (e.g.: you might argue whistleblowers can potentially expose severe problems and that despite the initial loss of confidence in the institution, the long term benefits are far greater). It is worth including several examples of where whistleblowers have helped or not, and therefore using these to support our argument.

You should aim to highlight the industries or areas of society where whistle blowing has been used in the past e.g. the NHS, athletics. You can mention how many people who notice wrongdoing often choose not to expose the truth, due to pressures from their peers and their seniors. Therefore, this question asks you to draw both on the ethical as well as the practical arguments for/against whistle blowing.

Introduction:

➢ Define what a "whistleblower" is and provide an example demonstrating your knowledge of whistle blowing.
➢ Clearly state your opinion and outline your main arguments.
➢ Link your answer into a broader understanding of the concepts mentioned in the question by stating why "whistleblowers" ought to be encouraged or discouraged, and the implications that might have on certain aspects of society.

Why they should be encouraged:

➢ The main reason whistleblowers should be encouraged is because the truth that they expose can be extremely important. For example, it could unveil a crisis with a particular industry or highlight an impending disaster. This reason is best supported with an example. An example which can be used is whistle blowing in NHS trusts such as the Mid-Staffordshire Trust scandal which exposed how several patients were treated with extreme negligence, and often left for hours unattended unable to go to the toilet. Whistle blowing allowed an investigation to take place so that patient care could be improved to adequate levels, thereby helping to improve patient care and survival rate in the future.

➢ Another example that could be used (especially in the recent climate) is that whistleblowers exposed cheats in sport. For example, due to whistle blowing there has been an investigation into state sponsored drug cheating in Russia which has caused Russian athletes to be banned from the Olympics, thereby hoping to help eradicate doping in sport.

➢ The next argument to be made in support of whistleblowers focuses on a more ethical aspect, and that is the freedom of speech. If people are aware of a problem, they should be allowed to highlight this problem to the general public so that it may be treated. As humans, we all have a right to say and do what we want as long as it is in accordance with the law – hence whistleblowers should be encouraged.

    ○ **Counterargument**: Although whistleblowers have a right to freedom of speech; we can look at the ethical debate from a different angle, which focuses more on the consequences of one's action. This theory of consequentialism states that an action should be deemed right or wrong by the effects it has. Hence, as whistle blowing can lead to a loss of confidence in the profession, which would be a disaster for some industries like the NHS, it should be avoided.

    ○ **Counter-counterargument**: On the other hand, we may counter this argument by considering duty based ethics. It is possible to argue that we all have a duty to do the right thing and expose the truth, and therefore morally, whistle blowing should be encouraged.

➢ It is possible to argue that whistle blowing is essential to help create a fully functioning democracy. In a democracy, all members have the right to know all the information so that they can come to an informed decision as to how they want to vote in the future. Withholding information form the public therefore undermines the current democratic system.

Why they should be discouraged:

➤ One of the main reasons why whistleblowers should be discouraged is because they can cause a loss of trust in the profession. For example, the vast number of scandals concerning cheating and blood doping in sport has led to a vast decrease in the confidence of certain sports such as athletics. This problem has become so great that many athletes now live under the continuous suspicion of cheating even though they have been meticulously tested and are clean. This problem is especially serious in the healthcare profession, where the confidence is critical to establishing a trusting doctor-patient relationship. Anything, which weakens this relationship, such as whistleblowers, should be avoided.

  ○ **Counterargument**: One may consider the timeframe when assessing whether whistleblowers should be encouraged. Although in the short term it might lead to loss of confidence, over time the confidence in the profession may increase and patient safety standards increase.

➤ When employees join an organisation, they are required to sign a confidentiality agreement. This is important as it states that they cannot divulge sensitive information about the company or its employees to others, and so "whistleblowers" are effectively breaking the law.

➤ Whistleblowers often are sacked by their employers and may even face death threats from those whose information they leak. An example of this is Edward Snowden, who founded the website WikiLeaks – an online platform where it is possible for whistleblowers to share sensitive information. Wanted by the USA, he currently seeks political asylum in Russia. Hence, whistle-blowing can have a great negative effect on one's life and so should be discouraged.

Conclusion:

Once again, engage with the question on a wider level by restating the ethical and practical reasons whistleblowers should be encouraged/discouraged and the implications this may have for certain sectors, such as the NHS.

If inward migration is bad for a country, does it follow that outward migration would be good for that country?

There is some ambiguity in this question, regarding what their terms "bad" and "good" mean. Most likely, they refer to the effect of society, which can further be categorised into economic and social factors. It is worth noting briefly in the introduction exactly how you interpret "migration" to avoid confusion, and to show you have thought that it represents both short and long term migration. With this type of question, we must accept that inward migration is bad for a country, rather than dispute the claim made in the question. Therefore it is worth noting the disadvantages of inward migration, and using these to either support or counter your proposal of why outward migration might be good/bad for that country.

One of the most important things to consider when answering this question is the exact wording of the question. It is not asking for the advantages and disadvantages of outward migration. Instead, the question asks you to consider the problems associated with inward migration, such as pressure on service, and then evaluate whether or not outward migration would help remediate this issue at all.

Introduction:
➢ Define your terms as discussed above.
➢ Accept that inward migration is bad for a country, and highlight some of the reasons why this may be the case, e.g. social, economic reasons.
➢ Clearly state your opinion and outline your arguments for it, as well as your reasons for dismissing counterarguments.

Potential arguments why outward migration would be good:

➢ One of the main problems with high levels of inward migration is potential overcrowding, which puts pressure on public services such as the NHS. Therefore, outward migration might help to reduce this strain on public services, thereby helping to improve patient care for example, but overall contributing to a better quality of life for the remaining citizens.
➢ Since inward migration can lead to depression of wages due to increased supply for limited demand, it is possible than outward migration may help to increase wages.
➢ There is an argument to be made that outward migration can be beneficial to a country in the long term. Although there is a loss of a working population, outward migration provides an opportunity for those emigrants to go to other countries, learn their trade and gain skills, which they can bring back to their original country.

Potential arguments why outward migration would not necessarily be good:

➤ One of the major disadvantages of inward migration is the larger influx of unskilled workers, which reduce wages for lower paid jobs. However, this does not necessarily mean that outward migration would be better, since it can result in highly skilled workers leaving the country in search of better prospects economically. This "brain drain" is prevalent in third world and developing countries, where talented individuals leave their country of origin to move to developed nations like the USA and so provides a great example of where outward migration is bad for that country.

➤ Outward migration can be bad for that country due to the fact that most emigrants are usually young, working class individuals. Therefore emigration often reduces the size of the workforce in the country of origin, thus causing the economy to shrink and with less tax collected by the government to spend on public services.

➤ Inward migration can often lead to overpopulation within a country. However, although outward migration may counteract this, the outward migration of young individuals can lead to an age imbalance in the country of origin, as the demographic is often skewed to a much older population. This has a great effect socially as it can lead to several towns losing their character and atmosphere whilst even leaving other areas completely deserted.

➤ Inward migration is often deemed "bad" socially as it can lead to increased tensions and even conflict between the native and arriving populations, eventually leading to segregation in society and local communities. There is nothing to suggest that outward migration does anything to resolve this problem, as regardless of who emigrates, the segregation between different communities still exists.

Conclusion:

Link your conclusion back to the question by stating to what extent outward migration may benefit a country, and discussing whether this outweighs the negatives of inward migration.

END OF PAPER

2016

Section 1

Question 1: D

This passage starts off discussing the increase in rainfall over the past 50 years. It then moves on to suggest that India and China are prepared for heavy rainfall but this is not the case in the UK. It finally gives another reason for the increased rainfall. Therefore, the main argument of the passage is that the UK should do more to prepare for flooding and hence the answer is D.

Let us look at why the other options are wrong:

➢ A- This at first sight seems like a plausible answer but it is not the main argument. We can infer that the UK has been underprepared for flooding in the past but the main issue in the passage that the UK needs to be more prepared now because of the increased risk of flooding
➢ B-This is not the main *conclusion* of the passage. The conclusion is that the UK could learn from India by planning its infrastructure to deal with flooding
➢ C-There is no mention of political will in this passage
➢ E-There is no indication of this in the passage

Question 2: C

The quickest way to do this is to find some solutions and look for a common number. Working modulo 2, it is obvious that we need to select either 2 odd numbers and 1 even number or all 3 even numbers. This gives us the following valid combination (8,18,24) and (18,11,21). The answer is therefore **C**.

Question 3: C

Reading the passage, the sudden conclusion does not seem like a legitimate argument and we are asked to find the main flaw. With this question, it is sometimes worth spending 10 seconds trying to find the flaw without looking at the answer choices. If you can find a flaw without any hints, you are most likely to be right. We are told in the passage that there is a correlation between brain structure and sleeping and there is a link between brain structure and mental health. There is nothing in this passage that suggests changing one of these things will lead to a change in another and therefore the answer is **C**.

Let us look at why the other options are wrong:

➢ A- While this group is neglected, this group of people are not central to the argument so this cannot be the main flaw
➢ B- Completely unrelated to the argument
➢ D- The argument states that night owl should try this change 'if they wish' so there is no reliance on the night owls wanting to change their sleeping patterns
➢ E- This is actually a flaw of the argument but it is not the main flaw. If C is false, then the whole argument is false. If E is not true, then the argument is only partially flawed.

Question 4: E
The "conclusion" style questions are very common in the TSA and you should practise these until you are confident in them. A popular method is to attach each option to the end of the paragraph and see if it makes sense. With this paragraph, the start is about the method of phasing out small denominations and it then goes on to say how such a move would hurt charities and consumers. The conclusion of this article is therefore **E**.

Let us look at why the other options are wrong:

➢ A-The paragraph suggests that charities benefit from small coin donations but nothing about whether people should donate to charities
➢ B-The paragraph only discusses small denomination coins so such a general conclusion cannot be true
➢ C-There is no suggestion of this in the paragraph
➢ D-Although the paragraph does suggest that those who save small coins would eventually benefit, it does not say that this course of action should be followed

Question 5 :B
These questions are usually more subtle than other reading questions on the TSA and as such can be harder. It is often helpful to think of the underlying assumption when reading through the passage. The main argument of this passage is that when people lie, they have small micro-expressions which other people recognize and realize that the first person is lying. An assumption of this argument is that we are able to recognize micro-expressions so the answer is **B**.

In this case, it is also useful to arrive at the answer by eliminating the other answers:

➤ A- while the statement might be true, it is not an assumption of the main argument but a side case that should be considered

➤ C- this is an unusual one because it is an assumption of the text. However, the main argument of the text is that one shouldn't lie because people will recognise the micro-expressions. One of the examples of this is pretending to recognise someone so it is just an example of the argument and not an assumption of the core argument

➤ D- Just as the answer to C, the example of meeting someone in a supermarket is an example and assumptions do not lie in examples

➤ E- This assumption does not really make sense as the advice "do not lie" does not apply to someone who never lies. If an answer choice is confusing you, remember that this could be its purpose.

Question 6: B
This is a wordy question that aims to confuse the reader so we must read the question carefully before attempting to answer. The first thing to do with time zone questions is to convert to one standard time zone; let this be GMT. Converting 06:15 local Auckland time to GMT give 18:15 GMT on 20 August, exactly 24 hours and 45 minutes after takeoff. Two and a half hours were spent on stops so total time flying was: 24.75-2.5=22.25 hours

Question 7: C
This a reading comprehension question that is easy once all of the question is understood. We are simply required to find the row of the table that satisfies all of the requirements in the question. The maximum limit of $400 leaves Intimidator, Top Thrill Dragster, Voyage and Kingda Ka as the only possible options. The min height requirement of Intimidator and Top Thrill Dragster eliminate these two as Anton's height is only 143cm. This leaves Voyage and Kingda Ka as possible options. Of these, only Kingda Ka had a speed of greater than 90mph.

Question 8: D
These 3D non-verbal reasoning questions are often the hardest of TSA section 1. To solve this question, we will look for certain conditions imposed by the two views and rule out certain nets based on these conditions. Looking at the first view, we can see that the top of the letter A is adjacent to the bottom of letter B. In cases C and E, the bottom of letter A lines up with the top of letter B so these two answers are wrong. Looking at the second view, it is clear that reading from letter E to the right gives letter A. In answer choice A, B is to the right of E and in answer choice B, an upside down A is to the right of E. The only correct answer is therefore D.

Question 9: A

The main argument of the passage is that to increase blood donors, only those willing to give blood or those who have given blood should be eligible to receive blood. They argue that this is a fairer system of blood donations. This system is clearly not fair if there exist individuals unable to give blood so the answer is A.

Let us look at why the other answer choices are wrong:

B. The greater demand for certain blood types suggest that we should place more emphasis on getting blood donors from these types but does not weaken the fairness of the system in question

C. This suggests many blood donors have had transfusions but does not say anything about the number of blood transfusion patients who are donors

D. This statement fully supports the passage so cannot be the answer

E. This fact is irrelevant because the passage is about blood donations

Question 10: C

When dealing with this kind of question, first try to summarise the steps of the argument. Then look at how each step leads on to the next and try to identify the flaw. The argument in question is that social media increases revenue. Since social media will become big in the future, it must be utilised to maximise profits. The key flaw in this question is that revenue is used interchangeably with profits. While social media use seems to increase revenue, it is wrong to assume that it increases profits. The answer is therefore C.

Let us look at why the other answer choices are wrong:

♦ A- the argument states that if a business uses social media, its profits increase. The argument is conditional on a business using social media so A cannot be right

♦ B- there is simply no such assumption made

♦ D- once again, the argument is conditional on a business using social media and does not say anything about a business using other forms of communication

♦ E- it assumes that social media use maximises profits but does not say anything about getting the maximal 18% growth rate

Question 11: B

One of the best way to deal with conclusion questions is to see which answer choice would most naturally append to the paragraph in the question. The passage states that the apostrophe is of limited use because we can speak without indicating its presence. The passage also states that is decreasing in use in business and there is frequent misuse. All of this suggest that there will be no loss if the apostrophe is lost from the English language leading to answer choice B.

Let us look at why the other answer choices are wrong:

- A- Although the passage accepts that misuse of the apostrophe is rampant, it does not condone this behaviour
- C- The passage states that the apostrophe is becoming less frequent in business correspondence but does not say anything about its necessity in business correspondence
- D- This is definitely true and can be inferred from the passage. This is however not the main conclusion, it is only an example of the main conclusion
- E- The passage does not suggest that we should or should not use apostrophes- it only suggests that apostrophes have very little use

Question 12: C

This is another "riddle-style" problem that we must approach with a logical mind. If Tom works four nights without a consecutive period of more than 2 nights, he must be on shift for: Monday, Tuesday, Thursday and Friday. This means that Tom and Robert are on duty Friday night; Sheila therefore cannot be on duty on Friday. If Tom is off duty on Wednesday, bother Robert and Sheila must be on duty on Wednesday. The only possible answer choice satisfying these two criteria is C.

Question 13: C

This question clearly has a straightforward approach: calculate the cost for all possible combinations and choose the cheapest. This is going to be time intensive and we must find a quick way of doing it for the TSA. The younger sister will only be three years old and so gets free entry. This means that they can be completely ignored for the purposes of calculating the minimal cost. This leaves: one employed adult, one unemployed adult, one senior citizen, one senior citizen spectator and two children. The party is happening on a Saturday afternoon so this is clearly going to be during peak hours. With only two children, we can get one spectator ticket so we need to figure out how to get this ticket to minimize cost.

Spectators have the lowest ticket cost so it makes sense to pay 70p for a spectator ticket. We can then either get the mum an adult ticket (£3.80) and a concession family ticket (£4.80) or we can get the grandpa a senior citizen ticket (£1.90) and a family ticket (£9.50). These give a total cost of £9.30 and £12.10 respectively. The previous is therefore the minimal cost. This was quite arduous and not fully rigorous but a rigor is not needed for the TSA.

Question 14: B

There is nothing challenging about this question; we must simply look at the five answer choices in the question and identify if they are present in the pattern. Answer choices A and E are both present at the bottom of 'W'. Rotating answer choice C by 90 degrees gives the central tile of the letter 'S'. Rotating choice D by 90 degrees counter-clockwise is also a tile in the letter 'S' so the answer to the question must be B.

Question 15: B

This is a classic logic question where we must use only the information given in the passage. The main idea of the passage is that children with less regular sleeping schedules performed worse on a series of tests. It is therefore clear that having bedtimes at different hours would decrease cognitive development in children giving answer choice B.

Let us look at why the other answer choices are wrong:

- ♦ A- This statement suggests the opposite effect which has no grounds in formal logic and therefore this answer choice is wrong
- ♦ C- There is no mention of parents so this answer choice must be wrong
- ♦ D- There is no indication that the damage occurs throughout life so this answer choice is not correct
- ♦ E- There is no mention of cognitive disorders so this answer choice must be wrong

Question 16: B

The paragraph suggests that spending priorities in prisons are wrong as more money is spent on the internet and TV compared to the money spent on books. It then suggests to reduce reoffending rates, literacy rates must be improved. The assumptions of this passage are: increases in literacy rate correspond to decreases in reoffending and internet/TV have no literacy benefit. The latter corresponds to answer choice B so this is the answer.

Let us look at why the other answer choices are wrong:
♦ A- There is no indication that prison is easy for the inmates
♦ C- There is no mention in this passage of prisoners rights
♦ D- The passage makes no assumptions about intelligence of the prison population; it just suggests that no matter how clever prisoners are, increasing their literacy prevents reoffending
♦ E- The only wish of the author is to reduce reoffending rates- they do not express an opinion on the purpose of prisons

Question 17: C
The passage can be summarised as follows: religion does not provide a basis for moral framework. The Greeks considered how to live life and invented the word "ethics". However, Greek gods often misbehaved with some in ancient Greece being atheists. Therefore lack of religion does not imply lack of morality. Clearly, if the ancient Greeks had doubts in the purpose of morality, then this argument would be significantly weakened so the answer choice is C.

Let us look at why the other choices are wrong:
♦ A- This statement does not change the fact that some Greek gods were adulterous
♦ B- We do not have any information on Greek poetry or drama so the answer cannot be B
♦ D- This does not suggest anything to do with morality
♦ E- While this may be true, it does not indicate anything about the link between morality and religion

Question 18: C
This is a hard question to do in a rigorous manner but we must be careful to check all cases before coming to a conclusion. The easiest way to approach this is to start with answer A, see if it is possible and if not, move down the list. Note that the this network is configured such that waking two paths always has a greater distance than one path. Our path must therefore consist of four edges with each town being visited only once. The first answer is 78km and this can be achieved if the four minimal paths are taken (17,18,20 and 23). This cannot form a full path so we move onto 83km. This path is achieved by the following edges: 17,18,23,25. This is also not a full path so we move onto 86km. This can be formed by: 18,20,23,25. This is a full cycle and is therefore the answer.

Question 19: A

This is a very wordy comprehension question with a paragraph whose only purpose is to confuse the reader. If we keep the final goal in mind, the question becomes trivial. We are asked for the number of non-fatal serious injuries on non-built-up roads. We are given the number of serious/fatal injuries on non-built-up roads (1724) and the number of fatal injuries on non-built-up roads (187). The difference between these two numbers gives the required answer: 1724-187=1537

Question 20: E

This is another 3D non-verbal question that is hard to verbally explain. To do this question, we must view the structure from the direction indicated by the arrow and visualise the image. In this case, we would see 1 cube on the top row, 3 on the middle row and 4 on the bottom row. This leaves answer choices B or E. It is clear that the row of four extends the row of three to the left giving answer choice E.

Question 21: A

The argument of the passage is that farmers in Africa should be allowed to poach lions as Europeans killed bears. When stated in such simple terms, the flaw in this passage becomes clear: Europeans failing to protect their wildlife does not justify Africans failing to protect their wildlife. This is an example of a *Tu quoque* error- the argument that something is right is based on the fact that someone else does it.

Let us look at why the other choices are wrong:
B. This statement provides evidence for the example given in the argument so it strengthens the argument, not weakens it
C. This again strengthens the argument that African farmers should be allowed to kill lions
D. This is a valid reason for lion conservation but does not address the argument in any way
E. This is once again another valid reason for lion conservation but it fails to address the crux of the argument

Question 22: B

To see why the answer is B, we will show the equivalent statements from the question and answer:

1. The essay is of a far higher standard= My partner has given me flowers
2. The student is clever or the student copied= He must be feeling guilty or this must be a special occasion
3. The student is of average intellect= This is not a special occasion
4. The student copied= My partner is feeling guilty

Essentially, an occurrence implies two possible options. One of these options is wrong so it must be the other.

Let us look at why the other options are wrong:
- A- There is no statement detailing the two possible options
- C- There is no statement detailing the two possible options
- D- There is no conclusion after ruling out one of the two options
- E- Again, there is no conclusion mentioned after the two options are detailed

Question 23: E
The argument in the paragraph is that it is wrong for the companies to be paying their workers below a living wage and expecting the government to subsidise the difference. The principle behind this statement is that companies should be paying their employees enough to live on and the government should not be paying the difference. The main principle however relates to the living wage so the answer is therefore E.

Let us look at why the other answers are wrong:
- A- This statement is false and not supported by the text- it is the companies that are leaving holes in millions of paycheques
- B- The argument is about how the government has to assist people on low incomes because of companies
- C- This is true but simply restates part of the paragraph- it is not the underlying principle
- D- While this is true and in some sense relates to the underlying principle, it makes no mention of the companies which should be paying the living wage

Question 24: B
Let x be the number of incorrect answers in Round 1, y be the number of incorrect answers in Round 2 and z be the number of incorrect answers in Round 3. We can form the two following equations: $x + y + z = 9$ and $x + 2y + 5z = 22$

We also have that x is the largest of the three variables implying that x >3. Note that if z=2, there is no way to satisfy the second equation and the incorrect answers in round 1 or 2 cannot make the 22 points lost. Therefore z=3 and the equations simplify to: $x + y = 6$ and $x + 2y = 7$

This can be solved to give x=5 and y=1. The question asks for the value of x which is 5.

Question 25: D
The condition that the roll must have a width of 210mm rules out the first paper roll. The diameter must be less than 25.4mm ruling out the fourth paper roll. Buying in bulk is going to be more economical than buying a single roll but we cannot afford to buy the third roll in bulk. This means that the only remaining options are:

1. Buying the second roll in bulk- price/m= 13.14/125=10.5p/m
2. Buying the third roll as a single roll- price/m= 7.49/100= 7.49p/m
3. Buying the fifth roll in bulk= price/m=20.94/300= 6.98 p/m

The last option is therefore the most economical so we choose answer choice D

Question 26: A
The sizes of the patches are: 2,3,4,5 and 7. These patches are stitched together to form a rectangle whose height is twice its width. This means that the area of the patch will be a number of the form $2x^2$ where x is an integer. Note that removing an even number from the above set would produce four number with odd sum so cannot form the correct answer. This eliminates two answer choices. Now consider the sum when each odd number is removed:
♦ If 3 is removed, the sum is 18
♦ If 5 is removed, the sum is 16
♦ If 7 is removed the sum is 14

Only the first of these is a number of the form $2x^2$ and we therefore get the answer if ignore the piece with 3 squares (shape V). This short method without actually looking at any of the shapes will likely save time during the TSA.

Question 27: C
A lot of conclusion questions reveal the answer within the very first sentence. In this paragraph, we are told that there is no point to historical re-enactments before we are given more reasons for this to be the case. It is clear that the main conclusion from this passage is the pointlessness of historical battle giving answer choice C.

Let us look at why the other answer choices are wrong:

♦ A- While this statement is true, it is not the main conclusion; it is evidence that lends itself to the main conclusion

♦ B- This is not true as the passage states that there is a meticulous attention to detail

♦ D- This is true but there is no mention of this in the passage so it cannot be correct

♦ E- This is another point that leads on from some of the evidence in the passage

Question 28: A
The passage states that there is a correlation between levels of leads in the body and the violent crime even though the former precedes the latter by 20 years. It also states that lead has been banned in certain products in Europe for about 20 years so it is possible that there will be a fall in violent crime just about now (20 years after the 1990s). This leads to answer choice A.

Let us look at why the other answer choices are wrong:

♦ B- the passage only explain that lead is a cause of violent crime- it does not state that lead is the only cause

♦ C- once again, the passage does not say anything about lead being the only reason for violent crime so this answer cannot be the case

♦ D- while this may be true, there is no indication of this in the passage so cannot be true

♦ E- the passage states that the group in question are *more* likely to go on to commit violent crimes not that they are *highly* likely

Question 29: C
This passage is about the reasons for employees leaving a company. It cites discontent with superiors as the main reason. It then argues that people leave companies because they do not have conversations with their superiors about their expectation. It is suggested that staff turnover could be reduced if these honest conversations were had. The assumption in this statement is that people do not have these honest conversations so they are not honest when they are leaving their companies.

Let us look at why the other answer choices are wrong:

♦ A- It assumes that some expectations are realistic, not all of them
♦ B- The supervisors being difficult does not preclude workers from having honest conversations
♦ D- The argument states that if staff turnover is to be reduced, then honest conversations must be had- it does not assume that staff turnover should be reduced
♦ E- It actually assumes the opposite

Question 30: A

Let the length of the margin be X. Then we can form a quadratic equation and solve for X:

$$(24 - 2X)(18 - 2X) = \frac{18 \, x \, 24}{2}$$

$$432 - 84X + 4X^2 = 216$$

$$X^2 - 21X + 54 = 0$$

$$(X - 18)(X - 3) = 0$$

Since X=18cm is not a valid solution, we have that the margin is 3cm.

Question 31: A

This question is a lot of text for a very simple answer. We are given a set of prices and are asked to find the cheapest option. The weekend prices are clearly more expensive so these options can be ignored. The box tickets come to £80 per person so are more expensive than the Balcony tickets. The box tickets can therefore be ignored. Finally, 85% of £95.50 is greater than £78.20 so these balcony seats are indeed the cheapest option.

Question 32: D

I will refer to the graphs as 1-4 with graph 1 being on the left and graph 4 being on the right. It is clear that the regular structure of graph 1 lends itself to container C. Similarly, the two part linear structure of graph 3 lends itself to container E. Graph 2 has a linear portion followed by a portion with decreasing gradient. This suggests that there is a regular section followed by a section with increasing width giving answer A. Graph 4 suggests an initially widening portion followed by a narrowing portion and then a portion of uniform width. This suggests that glass vial in B leaving D as the answer.

Question 33: A
The paragraph suggests that the independence of constitutional courts and central banks is only in name as they are appointed by politicians. Furthermore, giving too much power to these unelected institutions would be undemocratic. The argument in the passage is that if a politician chooses the independent members, then these members are likely to be partisan going against the independence of these institutions. This argument would therefore be weakened if these appointees go against their nominators politically.

Let us look at why the other options are wrong:
B. While this may be true, the passage is about the principle of independent officials and not the logistics
C. A politician vouching for an independent candidate does not make the candidate seem any less partisan
D. This supports the argument that independent candidates are likely to be involved in the political process
E. This supports the argument that political appointees are likely to have vested interests

Question 34: C
The argument goes as follows: genius is either due to genes or environment. There are cases of 'genius' in very early life when environment can have little effect therefore genius is wholly due to genes. The flaw in this argument is that although environment seems to have little effect in one example, it is not possible to say that it has no effect.

Let us look at why the other options are wrong:
♦ A- Although there is an example with genius at an early age, this is not an assumption of the argument
♦ B- This might be true but it is not assumed by the passage
♦ D- This is a weakness of the argument style but not a flaw in the argument itself
♦ E- This is also a flaw of the argument but it is not a main flaw

Question 35: D
The article explains that George Osborne's policy to remove housing benefit from council homes with spare rooms (bedroom tax) did not bring in sufficient savings. It then postulates that providing universal childcare would increase employment leading to more tax revenue. Therefore, the conclusion of this passage is that the government should implement a policy of universal healthcare. This question can be tricky as some of the other options look quite enticing.

Let us look at why the other answers are wrong:
- A- This statement is completely true but it is only a reason given in the passage and not the main conclusion
- B- The passage does not mention that the bedroom tax only affects a small number of people
- C- Similar reason as above
- E- This is a tricky choice and it is very tempting to choose this as the main conclusion. However, the passage talk about both hardship and government income. The conclusion must therefore relate to both of these results.

Question 36: D
Let the price of a coffee be C, the price of tea be T and the price of the service charge be S. We have the following equations: $5C + S = 121$ and $4T + S = 82$.

There may be clever ways to solve these equations but we will start will the smallest option and work our way up.
- S=1 implies 4T=81 and this has no integer solutions
- S=2 implies 5C=119 and this has no integer solutions
- S=4 implies 5C=117 and this has no integer solutions
- S=6 implies 5C=115 and 4C=76. There are integer solutions to both of these equations so the answer is D

Question 37: A
This question looks like a complicated mathematical exercise but the solution is mushrooms are growing at a certain rate. Let us try to identify the pattern:
- On day 1, the mushrooms form a 2x2 square
- On day 2, the mushrooms form a 4x4 square
- On day 3, the mushrooms form a 6x6 square

We see that on day n, the mushrooms form a 2nx2n square. We need to know when the mushrooms will take over a 100x100 square. This clearly occurs when n=50 which is 48 days from Wednesday (today is day 3).

Question 38: E

This question has a straightforward method: calculate the scores of each participant and identify the odd one out. The scores can be calculated as follows:

- Pip=28*54
- Eve=27*56
- Bob=24*63
- Viv=22*68
- Nan=21*72

Before you start trying to remember the day of year 4 when you were taught how to do long multiplication by hand, stare at those products for a bit. It should become clear that four of these are a multiple of 3 (found by summing the digits) while one is not. Viv's answer is equivalent to 1*2 modulo 3 while the other answers are 0 modulo 3. This must therefore be the odd one out.

This is an important takeaway for the TSA, you will very rarely need to engage in tedious computation; there is often a much simpler shortcut.

Question 39: D

To summarise the paragraph: patients are not eating too well because the quality of hospital food is very low. This is leading to patients 'fading' away and their health suffering. The conclusion of the article is that hospital food should be made more appealing in order to increase patient's willingness to eat it.

With a conclusion question, the best strategy is often to see which answer choice can be most appropriately appended to the passage.

Let us look at why the other answers are wrong:

- A- This is a general point that is implied by the article but the conclusion is that these better systems involve better food
- B- There is no mention of nurses in the passage
- C- There is no mention that the food currently provided does not satisfy the dietary requirements of the patients
- E- This could be inferred from the passage but it is not a conclusion of the main argument

Question 40: B

This paragraph is about democracy as a whole and can be summarised as follows. Political legitimacy is given to the government by the people of a country voting in elections. Therefore, a higher electoral will correspond to a more legitimate political system. The idea behind this argument is that people give a political system legitimacy by voting but there is an implied assumption that people consent to the political system as a whole by voting. The answer is therefore B.

Let us look at why the other answers are wrong:

♦ A- The argument is that democratic political systems have a higher turnout so this cannot be an assumption

♦ C- This is just a very general point that is not actually addressed in the paragraph

♦ D- Political legitimacy and common interests are different topics and should not be confused

♦ E- Non-democratic systems are not mentioned in the paragraph

Question 41: A

This paragraph argues that high-street banks should not be able to sell financial products because their staff are not trained to explain them. We are therefore looking for evidence that banks are mis-selling financial products. This evidence comes in the form of answer choice A so this is the answer.

Let us look at why the other answer choices are wrong:

♦ B- This could be seen to support the argument that many customers are tricked into buying financial products. However, the argument clearly states the issues is with bank workers not understanding financial derivatives so this cannot be used as evidence.

♦ C- This actually weakens the arguments as it suggests that customers will have all of the necessary information when they make a decision

♦ D- This again weakens the argument as it suggests that customers can benefit without understanding the actual financial product

♦ E- This does not strictly relate to the point about workers not understanding financial products so cannot be used

Question 42: C
This question almost gives us too much information and we can solve two different equations to arrive at the same answer. Firstly, let X be the weekday price of potatoes in pence. Using the first statement that £3 would buy 3 kilos less potatoes on a Saturday morning, we can get the following equation:

$$\frac{300}{X} = \frac{300}{(X+5)} + 3$$

This is a simple quadratic equation that can be solved to give X=20 or –25. Since the price must be positive, we have X=20p/kg. Note the same answer can also be solved by forming an equation based on the second statement:

$$\frac{300}{X} = \frac{300}{(X-5)} - 5$$

This shows that solving quadratic equations quickly is a key life skill. In this case, both equations could be solved to confirm that you have arrived at the correct answer

Question 43: A
We have seen numerous examples of similar questions on the TSA and the first step is to rule out options that are not possible given the set of conditions. This leaves the following cars:

- Rover 820
- Renault Laguna
- Rover 825
- Ford Sierra

We then have to calculate the depreciation per mile for each of these. This is done by subtracting the mileage from 100000 to get the miles driven. The price loss is calculated by subtracting £1000 from the cost price and this is divided by the miles driven to arrive at the answer:

- Rover 820: (7000-1000)/(100000-30000)=6/70
- Renault Laguna: (7000-1000)/(10000-20000)=6/80
- Rover 825: (1500-1000)/(100000-90000)=1/20
- Ford Sierra: (2000-1000)/(100000-70000)=1/30

The lowest of these is the Ford so this is the answer.

Question 44: D

With this kind of question, a systematic approach is needed to arrive at the correct answer. We will go through each statement and see if it is true:

A. The female numbers are higher than the male numbers above the ages of 34 so this is true
B. This is also true and can be seen by comparing the numbers in each age group
C. There are 417k men aged 85+ and 856k women aged 85+. This statement is therefore true
D. There are about 1.32 million in the 80-84 category while only 1.26 million in the 85+ age category. This statement is **not true**
E. This is true as it is the largest age group for both men and women

Question 45: C

The main argument of this paragraph is that with the advent of technology, only young people are fully equipped to understand the challenges of the day. They are therefore uniquely poised to set the moral standard that we should live by and this is the conclusion of the passage. The answer is therefore C.

Let us look at why the other answer choices are wrong:

♦   A- Although this can be inferred by the passage, it is not the conclusion. This is the reason why only young people should set standards
♦   B- This is true and again is the reason that young people should set moral standards
♦   D- This is an example of how the older generation's standards are no longer valid
♦   E- This again is a reason for them to set the moral standards and not a conclusion of the passage

Question 46: B

This is another logic question and we must clearly identify the formal logic that is being used in this statement. In this case, the "contrapositive" is used to arrive at a conclusion I.e. event A is predicated on event B, event B is not happening therefore event A is also not happening. We will show how this framework is shown by statement B:

♦   Rain only when clouds are present= solar eclipse when new moon is present
♦   No clouds therefore no rain= no new moon therefore no eclipse

Let us look at why the other options are wrong:

♦ A- this argument is as follows: A depends on B. A is happening therefore B is happening (notice the difference)

♦ C- blood clotting is not used in the second statement

♦ D- this argument is as follows: A is a result of B. Therefore when B occurs, so will A

♦ E- this argument is as follows: A depends on B. B will happen at a certain time so A will also happen at this time

Question 47: B

This question illustrates that we must only use the question paragraph to answer the question no matter how ludicrous the actual answer sounds. To summarise the paragraph: prostitution should be legalised because it will always happen and the money spent on prosecution could be spent elsewhere. If prosecution is replaced with murder we get answer choice B so this is the answer, no matter how silly it sounds.

Let us look at why the other answer choices are wrong:

♦ A- This is contradictory to what is mentioned in the text so must be wrong

♦ C- The passage does not justify prostitution based on the personal circumstances of those involved

♦ D- The focus of police is not mentioned- we are only told that prostitution should not be the focus

♦ E- The passage makes no mention of rehabilitation

Question 48: B

The easiest way to do this is to find out the location of each moon at each of the 5 options:

	Othello	Hamley	Romeo
After 36 Days	$16/20^{th}$ of 2nd orbit	$36/45^{th}$ of 1st orbit	$36/120^{th}$ of 1st orbit
After 72 Days	$12/20^{th}$ of 4th orbit	$27/45^{th}$ of 2nd orbit	$72/120^{th}$ of 1st orbit
After 132 Days	$12/20^{th}$ of 7th orbit	$42/45^{th}$ of 3rd orbit	$12/120^{th}$ of 2nd orbit
After 180 Days	$0/20^{th}$ of 10th orbit	$0/45^{th}$ of 5th orbit	$60/120^{th}$ of 2nd orbit
After 216 Days	$16/20^{th}$ of 11th orbit	$36/45^{th}$ of 5th orbit	$96/120^{th}$ of 2nd orbit

Note that for every 72 days, the ratios all equal 0.6. Therefore, this is the only answer where all three moons are at the same phase and hence will appear collinear.

Question 49: E

We look at 12m van column and extract the following information:

♦ 4 hour van hire, 40 miles included, initial cost £47 and cost per mile extra is 30p

♦ 12 hours van hire, 120 miles included, initial cost £63 and cost per extra mile is 30p

It is cheaper to hire the van for the whole day when the extra mileage accounts for the difference in price between the vans. The difference in price is £16. Dividing this by 30p gets 53.3 extra miles so it cheaper to hire for the whole day when we need 40+53.3=93 miles of driving. The minimum whole number distance is therefore E.

Question 50: C

This is another numerical question that relies on the fact that we must work with whole numbers. In a 10m roll, a 2.5 section will contain 4 patters plus an extra portion of 10cm. As we need identical drops, we can only get 3 sections from each roll. There are 6.2m of wall width to cover with each drop being 50cm. This requires just over 12 drops so we actually require 13 drops. 4 rolls would get 12 drops but we need a final extra roll to cover the last bit of the wall giving us the answer 5.

END OF SECTION

Section 2

Should we care more about the survival of animal species or the welfare of individual animals?

This question concerns animal welfare and seems to ask what the best way of looking after animals is. There are two key things we must first clarify before trying to answer this question: why should we care about animals and who does this "we" refer to. In general, when a question uses the pronoun "we", it is referring to humanity as a whole and not a specific group of people.

Now we must consider why we should care about either the "survival of animal species" or the "welfare of individual animals". Here, there are many different ways of looking at the question and it is therefore wise to look at a few different reasons for caring. We can then decide which is the most important based on reasoned arguments. Finally, the TSA essay does not test specific knowledge; markers look for the coherence of your argument and general essay style. It is therefore not an issue if you do not have specific examples of animal conservation; your argument is much more important.

Potential reasons for caring about animals:
➢ They provide a useful source of food
➢ They are an important part of the ecosystem (e.g. bees pollinate plants)
➢ It is our moral duty to look after all life-forms

Introduction:
➢ Define the key terms of the question; in this case, we should define: survival and welfare
➢ List some of the potential reasons for caring
➢ Come down on a side of the argument

Arguments for caring about the survival of animal species:
➢ Caring about the survival of the whole species will have a greater impact- it is all very well to care about the treatment of each individual animal but such a focussed policy will not be as effective as one looking at a species as a whole. As an example, we can take the survival of bees, whose population has been decreasing in recent years. When there is such a large population, there is no gain in looking after the welfare of each individual bee; there will only be an effect if we look at the population as a whole. An example of such a policy

would be banning herbicides that are harmful to bees. Such a policy is important because bees are vital for the pollination of much of our ecosystem. This point shows that we do not need a strong example or even quote an endangered species; we need to explain a relevant point with good justification. A counter-argument to this would be the first point on the next section; by thinking about counter arguments, you show to the examiner that you can structure an essay properly.

➢ Approaching this question from a very primitive perspective, it is possible to argue that we should only care about animals because they are a useful source of protein and other nutrients. We therefore should not care about the welfare of individual animals, we only require there to be a stable population of animals to feed our needs. This is clearly a controversial point which again is fine for the TSA; it just needs to be explained clearly and carefully. When making this point, it must be explained why animal welfare does not concern us e.g. humans are at the top of the food chain for a reason

Arguments for caring about the welfare of individual animals:

➢ It is only by caring for the welfare of each individual animal that we can ensure the survival of a species. There are certain protected species such as giant pandas whose populations have been threatened by poachers. The only effective way of preventing this from happening was to introduce strict punishments for those involved in poaching. Methods such a breeding in captivity would be fruitless if poaching were allowed to go on unpunished.

➢ We can also make a broad ethical point about our moral duty to protect life on earth e.g. it could be suggested that as a civilised society the welfare of all animals concerns us all. The overall survival of a species is irrelevant if there are animals being mistreated. This point here does not really need an example- we are simply making a broadly philosophical point.

Conclusion

This is arguably the most important part of a TSA essay as we must demonstrate to the examiner that we have clearly answered the question. This is easy to do if our previous two paragraphs have addressed the different sides of the question. We must then explain which priority is more important and arrive at a conclusion e.g. on balance, it is clear that the welfare of individual animals is more important. By ensuring the welfare of individual animals, we ensure the welfare and therefore population of animals as a whole.

Do people vote in line with their personal economic interests?

This question is fairly straightforward but we must consider what "personal economic interests" really mean. In order to understand this phrase fully, we will consider the term "personal" and the term "economic" separately. Please note that you are not expected to know the definitions of any technical vocabulary but you must be able to make a reasoned guess at any words you do not fully know.

The word "personal" can either refer to oneself or a close group including oneself. We will take the definition to be the latter in this case as it allows for more argument. For this question, we will define "economic interests" to be related to the net-worth of an individual. This question can now be read as do people vote for the party that would increase their net wealth. Finally, the TSA essay does not test specific knowledge; markers look for the coherence of your argument and general essay style. It is therefore not an issue if you do not have specific examples of animal conservation; your argument is much more important.

Introduction:
➢ It is important to remember that the introduction should be structured in three key parts: introduce the question, introduce your points and introduce your final argument- this means that you need to plan your whole essay before writing your introduction
➢ Introduce the question: define what is meant by all of the key terms in the question as we have done above
➢ Introduce your points: we will discuss some points below, these should be included here
➢ Introduce your argument e.g. "it is clear that economic interest do play a large part in how people vote"

Arguments:
➢ If someone's aim in life is to get more money, then the optimal strategy would involve voting for the party that gives you the most money. In the UK, there is a clear link between income and the chance of voting labour/tory. Labour is the more "left-wing" party in the UK and they have a higher proportion of low income voters. This is because labour traditionally have policies supporting those on lower incomes by taxing those with slightly more money. With this question, it is very easy to get stuck in a very detailed example but the point of the TSA is not to discuss one topic in a lot of depth. In this case, we have made the point of labour/conservative in the UK and we must analyse the principle: income bracket is correlated with how people vote in the political spectrum.

> Counter argument for above point- we need to consider the fact that other demographics may be a confounding variable. In the case US, it can be shown that individuals with higher levels of formal education generally vote Democrat (left-leaning party). Once again, it is important not to spend the whole essay discussing American politics. We have made our point regarding education linked to wealth and we must now explain why it is a counter-argument. If education level is the true driving factor behind how people vote, then they are not basing their vote on their income. This means that their vote might not align with their own personal economic interests

> People vote in alignment with their political beliefs and not their own economic interests- a feature of a more right wing government is that they believe in less state intervention (no "nanny state") and that individual should be able to get on with their own lives- this can be seen most clearly with the Republican party in the US who believe in small federal government. Among certain agricultural workers, there is huge support for the Republican party as these workers do not want the state meddling in their affairs. However, such workers are already on quite low incomes so may actually financially benefit from increased federal spending. In these areas of the country, there is a certain pride with voting Republican even if it is not in their best interests. Here, we have once again given a specific example but we must extract the broad principle to form a coherent argument: political philosophy and self pride are more important than economic self interest when determining who to vote for

Conclusion

This is arguably the most important part of a TSA essay as we must demonstrate to the examiner that we have clearly answered the question. This is easy to do if our previous two paragraphs have addressed the different sides of the question. We must then explain which priority is more important and arrive at a conclusion. As the conclusion is more weighing up both sides of the argument it is important to not get tied down in specific examples and compare larger themes. In this case, we could argue that there are two main reasons for people's voting patterns: their philosophy and the benefit they get from that party. The balance between these two factors is determined by an individual's circumstance so we cannot really come down on either side of the argument.

Is it possible to over-regulate the banking system?

This is a TSA essay that will be more suited to economist students but it should be accessible to anyone with the required interest in current affairs. This question is particularly relevant now as the Trump administration is weighing up whether to repeal the Dodd-Frank act. This question will admittedly be hard to answer if are not familiar with certain aspects of the banking system but there are still three other accessible questions in this case.

As always, it is important to define the key terms of the question in the introduction. In this question, the two key terms are "banking system" and "over-regulation". Although these terms seem fairly obvious, it is always good practice to provide a clear definition. This will allow the examiner to follow your line of argument, even if you slightly misinterpret one of the terms in the question. We define a bank as an "establishment that takes deposits from customers and invests its returning it to customers when requested along with interest". The "banking system" is a collection of retail, investment and other types of bank. Regulation can be defined as legal restrictions placed on the banking system and we will define over-regulation as excessive regulation

Introduction:

➢ Introduction should be tripartite: the question should first be introduced and key terms should be defined (as mentioned above); the points of the essay should be introduced and then you should hint at your conclusion
➢ As your introduction needs to address the points that you will make in your essay, you will need to plan your whole essay before writing the introduction
➢ With the technical nature of this question, it might be worthwhile to introduce some of the key pieces of legislation

Key pieces of legislation:

➢ Glass –Steagall act (1932) and Banking Acts of (1933)- These were introduced by FDR in response to the Great Depression and aimed to separate the retail and investment arms of banks. Although the act has a lot more technical content, knowing the broad principles is more than enough here.
➢ Gramm-Leach-Bliley Act- this act is not as well know but was passed into law by the Clinton administration of the 1990s- this essentially repealed some of the key statutes of the Glass-Steagall act and arguable led to the spread of the financial crisis.

➢ Once again, it is not necessary to know the details of the act or even the name but it is certainly worth knowing the deregulation of the banks may have precipitated in the financial crisis.

➢ Dodd-Frank act- signed into law by Barack Obama in response to the financial crisis of 2008- this was named the "modern Glass-Steagall" and once again separated the investment and retails arms of banks

Arguments:

➢ Over-regulation is most definitely possible and this could have a negative effect on the banking industry- one example of this is the "bankers-bonus tax" proposed by Ed Miliband in 2015 or even the gender quotas in boardrooms suggested by some on the left. Regulation could also relate to the operations of the bank itself. It is now necessary to explain why these examples are "excessive" I.e. we must show that these negatively impact the banking industry. One way to explain this is that with the international nature of banks, this kind of regulation would force banks to relocate to other countries with less regulations which would ultimately harm consumers. Furthermore, the separation of investment and retail arms would reduce returns to investors.

➢ On the other hand, we could argue that the banking industry cannot regulate itself because those at the top are motivated by money. These people therefore cannot be trusted to make decisions about the safety of deposits so government regulation is needed. To explain this, we could argue that bankers can take risks with their investor's money without being personally liable and this breeds a dangerous mindset.

➢ Finally, in this question it is necessary to consider a financial crisis and two seem most relevant: the Great Depression and the Financial Crisis of 2008- both of these led to loss of credit availability severely harming the whole economy- in fact, it could be argued that deregulating the banks led to the 2008 crisis so there is no such thing as overregulation.

Conclusion:

➢ Although you may have your own personal beliefs, for the TSA essay, it may be best to choose the side with easiest line of argument

➢ Here, it is easy to argue the over-regulation is not possible because the risks of too little regulation are far too great

➢ When there has been deregulation, a crisis has followed therefore any regulation reduces this risk and is therefore a worthwhile piece of legislation

With easy access to vast amounts of information through the Internet, what advantage is there to remembering facts?

This is a very general essay question so could be answered if you have no specific knowledge needed for some of the other questions. It is also a very broad question that has a wide range of possible answers. As the question is so broad, it is important not to list lots of examples but have substantial points and then use examples to provide evidence for these points.

Although it is usually necessary to define all the key terms of the question, since this essay title is very self explanatory, it is not needed. If you however want to focus on a specific aspect of the topic, then it is definitely worth stating this clearly in the introduction.

Introduction:

➢ It is important to remember that the introduction should be structured in three key parts: introduce the question, introduce your points and introduce your final argument- this means that you need to plan your whole essay before writing your introduction.

➢ Introduce the question: usually we would define the terms of the question but as this is not necessary for this question we could start off with a controversial statement: "Some people say that knowledge is not as useful as being able to use Google search"

➢ Introduce your points: we will discuss some points below, these should be included here.

➢ Introduce your argument e.g. nothing matches the speed, flexibility and robustness of the human brain.

Arguments:

➢ Speed of recall- if one already knows a fact, then a significant amount of time is saved as the person no longer has to go on the internet, search for the correct webpage and find the answer. This time could be vital in the case of an emergency e.g. a random bystander might witness someone faint and decide to put them in the recovery position- if they already know how to do this, they will save time compared to looking this up on Google and completing the task potentially saving someone's life- although this is quite an extreme example, it is simple and illustrates the point; this is sufficient for the TSA

➢ Robustness of recall- the term robustness is essentially a measure of how a system reacts to small perturbations from normal operating conditions. This is quite a general description but it definitely the case that the human brain is much more robust than a computer at fact recall e.g. if there is a power cut, or problem with the internet, or the person searches for the wrong item on the internet, the computer will not be able to tell the user the correct piece of information. The internet relies on the correct information being supplied exactly and is therefore not robust. A robust system can deal with changing environments and can best adapt to current conditions- this could arguably provide an evolutionary advantage

    ○ This point is quite broad and could be framed as a counter argument to the amount of knowledge that a computer can store. Using a counter argument approach is definitely a good thing to for this question

➢ Interconnected nature of the brain- the brain is a complicated network with many billions of neurons. This means that the brain is uniquely able to gather information and group facts together. This may allow new facts to be discovered or it could allow for the consolidation of facts. For example, it may be possible to memorise the locations of all the stations on a train line but the brain has a unique ability to connect these stations together. This could provide new information on the route itself. Note that this is not a concrete example but such is the nature of the question- do not be afraid to adapt your essay style to best suit the question.

➢ The question specifically asks for advantages of memorising facts so only one side of the argument needs to be presented- it is however wise to consider counterarguments and dismiss them e.g. it could be argued that the internet is more accurate but we pay a cost in robustness. Robustness is arguably more important because it allows us to work in very different environments

Conclusion

➢ It is first worth summarising the broad nature of the points e.g. there are three clear advantages of learning facts: speed, robustness and interconnected nature- this shows the examiner that you have thought about your essay and not just written down a list of facts.

➢ To come to a conclusion, it is not necessary to continue with your argument from the main body- in fact, it is particularly easy to argue that as the internet grows in size it get the knowledge of more and more humans- this is clearly better than the knowledge of one human so memorising large amounts of facts is a fruitless exercise.

END OF SECTION

2017

Section 1

Question 1: E

The key sentence here is that:

"The label "mad" is cynically used as a way of dehumanising and discrediting leaders of countries with whom we are in dispute." None of the other answers capture that the passage is defending those normally characterised as "mad"

Question 2: A

There are 3 stages to this question. The first is the sale of pizzas and flapjacks before the end of lunchtime, the second is the sale of pizzas and flapjacks during the afternoon when the prices is halved and the third is the remaining pizzas and flapjacks being given away for free.

In stage 1, 40 mini pizzas are sold (as 10 remain) and 35 flapjacks are sold (as 15 remain) at a price of $2 and $1: 40x2 + 35x1 = 115

In stage 2, 8 mini pizzas are sold (2 remain) and 14 flapjacks are sold (1 remains) at a price of $1 and $0.5: 8x1 + 14x0.5 = 15

In stage 3 the remainder are given away for free

Therefore final addition: 115+15 = $130

Question 3: E

The concern raised in the passage is that as time goes on not enough people will vote to be able to bestow a mandate upon the government. This problem is solved if, as time goes on, the people who are currently not voting begin to do so with age

Question 4: B

The passage firstly states that the media environment is one of celebrity influence, then goes on to state that celebrities are role models and that to deny this is "unrealistic and irresponsible" implying that they ought to act responsibly due to their being inevitably role models

Question 5: B
All of the concerns raised in the passage arise from the importance of appointing the best person to the job of being head of the company. If this were not important, then the fact that the sons of owners are less good candidates in general would become irrelevant.

Question 6: D
In order to calculate the total height we need to calculate the height of the picture, the added height of the mount at the top and bottom of the picture and the added height of the frame at the top and bottom of the picture

Height of picture: 40cm
Height added by mount: 6cm (top) + 9cm (bottom) = 15cm
Height added by frame: 2cm (top) + 2cm (bottom) = 4cm

Total height = 40 + 15 + 4 = 59cm

Question 7: A

Difference compared to the previous month:

	Jan	Feb	Mar	Apr	May	Jun	Jul	Aug	Sep	Oct	Nov	Dec
2013	-5	-17	-19	**27**	-24	16	18	-11	18	-54	15	-17

Largest **increase in 2013**: 27 – Apr 2013

Question 8: A
Total area of garden: 25x10 = 250m^2
Total area of patio: 2x3 = 6m^2
Total mowed area = 250-6 = 244m^2
Time taken to mow with old mower = 244 ÷ 1 = 244 minutes
Time taken to mow with new mower = 244 ÷ 2 = 122 minutes
Time saved = 244-122 = 122 minutes

Question 9: A

The passage states that few people are unhappy with their bank service because they do not have a tendency to change banks, which would be expected if they were unhappy and wanted to find a better alternative. The low statistic of 11% means that examining the large proportion of people who have changed banks and the significant proportion who have changed repeatedly significantly weakens the above argument as it seems to be the case that this 11% are anomalous and have found a suitable bank for them in childhood.

Question 10: C

The passage claims that the initiative will increase awareness of poetry, which is likely true, but then asserts that this will improve appreciation of poetry. There is no justification provided for this step in the reasoning and it is not necessarily true if children simply learn poems robotically in order to win the competition

Question 11: D

The passage focuses on responses to the increasing popularity to health clubs and therefore this must be present in the answer. The answer must also reflect the negative conclusion reached by the passage centred on self-deception.

Question 12: C
Using algebra:
Number of 19p coupons: X
Number of 12p coupons: Y
Number of 7p coupons: Z

Where X+Y+Z = 7
19xX + 12xY +7xZ = 100

Since there are at least one of each then X, Y and Z are at least 1

Therefore, we already have at least 19 + 12 + 7 pence = 38p

To find the remaining coupons:

19xX + 12xY + 7xZ = 62p
Where X+Y+Z = 4

We can't use any Zs as the total that we need from 4 coins is too high for them to be useful

Only possible way to get 62 from Ys and Xs is with 2 of each (19x2 = 38, 12x2 = 24, 24+38 = 62)

Totals: Xs (19p) = 3, Ys (12p) = 3, Zs(7p) = 1

Question 13: D
Follow each row to see which teams have no games in which they scored 0 goals at home (first number). This leaves us with Amazon, Ganges, Nile, Rhine and Volga. Check these columns only for which team did not score 0 goals in any game as the away team (second number). This leaves us with Rhine.

Question 14: A

Initial shape looks like this, the shapes 1, 2 and 5 fit together as shown to emulate This 'L' shape

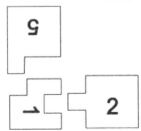

Question 15: E

The passage initially raises single use plastic bags but does not focus on them throughout, the change in focus to the production methods of alternative bags makes this relevant and means that it must be included in a summation of the conclusion as the single use plastic bag discussion was only a set up to this conclusion.

Question 16: A

The Passage focuses entirely on the issue of congestion and evaluates the policy only relative to its effect on congestion. If this were not relevant, the argument would suffer.

Question 17: C

The possibility of posting information anonymously adds a new dimension to the issue of censorship mentioned in the passage. This might, for example, reduce the ability of the government to censor individuals through the threat of prosecution if that prosecution could not happen in practice due to anonymity.

Question 18: A

Total surface area of walls and ceiling =
8x4 = 32 (ceiling)
(4x3) x2 = 24 (2 short walls)
(8x3) x2 = 48 (2 long walls)
Total area = 32+48+24 = 104m^2

Area to paint = 104-10 = 94

Area possible to paint with one tin: 8x12 = 96

Tins of paint needed = 94/96 = <1 = rounded up to 1

Question 19: C
Note that the number of points per improvement in performance increase as the performance gets better.

Test each of the possible answers in turn by calculating the difference in score between that score and the score for jumping 18cm shorter.

Start in the middle and if the difference is too small then try the higher jumps, if it is too large then test the smaller jumps.

Testing the middle score gives us 903 points (1.74m) – 689 points (1.56m) = 214 points

Answer found!

Question 20: D
Difference:

Jan	37.1
Feb	10.1
Mar	77.4
Apr	29.9
May	25.8
Jun	35.1
Jul	33.6
Aug	18.7
Sept	60.1
Oct	18.3
Nov	10.2
Dec	16.7

January is approximately half of March – eliminating A, B, C and E

Question 21: B
As is a common fault in argumentation, this passage attempts to generalise among all unlicensed moneylenders. Since the conclusion of the passage can only be made if the moneylenders are indeed harmful in general, it is necessary to not just extrapolate a very small amount of data more generally

Question 22: C

The passage presents us with two possibilities and then very explicitly eliminates one of them to leave us with only one choice. While B appears to do the same, it is not quite as definitive in its elimination of one of the two options.

Question 23: B

The passage raises the points that there is a risk in everything and that there is also such a thing as personal responsibility meaning that an individual need not be controlled by the state unduly and should be allowed to be responsible for their own choices. These arguments are also applicable to the legalisation of drugs since the risk of drugs can also be defended by claiming that an individual has personal responsibility over their own body despite the risk of drugs.

Question 24: B

Total mass of chemical: 6.0kg

Total mass of X in the mixture = $6 \times \frac{1}{4} = 1.5$

Total mass of Y in the mixture = $6 \times \frac{3}{4} = 4.5$

In order to reach a 40% - 60% ratio, it is necessary that there is 2/3 the quantity of X in the mixture than there is of Y as $40 \div 60 = 2/3$. Therefore, 3kg of X are needed in total so 1.5kg needs to be added.

Question 25: E

	1st choice	2nd choice	3rd choice
Jo	Portugal	France	Greece
Mel	Portugal	France	Tenerife
Kim	Majorca	France	Tenerife
Lexy	Greece	Tenerife	France
Naz	Tenerife	France	Majorca

Totals:

Portugal: 6

Majorca: 4

Greece: 4

Tenerife: 7

France: 9 (**BUT NO FIRST CHOICES**) – therefore the answer is Tenerife

Question 26: C

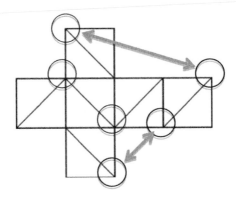

Relevant corners indicated

Question 27: A

The passage makes reference both to the fact that the HRA is important to those soldiers not in battle but also that it ought not to apply when soldiers are in battle. Both of these elements are separate and clearly relevant and so need to be included in the answer.

Question 28: D

The only answer that is explicitly mentioned in the text is D where it is said that: "the aquaculture sector has yet to devise effective methods for rearing some commercially popular predator species, such as tuna, without having to feed them wild-caught fish, which contributes to the pressure on our oceans" which is relevant since the point of aquaculture is to reduce pressure on the oceans.

Question 29: E

The experiment measured in the passage purports to measure the effect of chocolate on Alzheimer's disease but does not actually clearly measure any symptoms of the disease itself, only those things tangentially related to the disease.

Question 30: C
Solve using simultaneous equations:
X = number of majors scored
Y = number of minors scored

For the Red team: 5X+3Y = 77 where 2X =Y
Therefore, 5X + 6X = 77 so X=7

For the Blue team 5X+3Y = 52 where 2Y = X
Therefore, 10Y +3Y = 52 so Y = 4 and X=8
Total Majors = 7+8 = 15

Question 31: D
Using fat or calories (due to their larger number of significant figures)
Amount of fat per oatcake: 2.2g
Amount of fat per 100g: 17.6
Number of oatcakes per 100g: 17.6÷2.2 = 8
Number of oatcakes per 300g packet = 8x3 = 24

Question 32: E

C

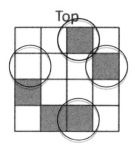

From examining the other 4 answers, they all have these four circeld squares in common, meaning that they must form part of the correct solution. This solution does not have the top left square coloured meaning that one of the other two coloured squares must also be part of the correct solution as only one mistake could have been made. The answer is therefore E as it is the only solution to colour the four circled squares and one of the two squares in this answer that are not circled.

Question 33: C
In summation, the passage is claiming that the parents of more than two children are being irresponsible, this is further true if parents are having children that they did not intend or wish to be born when these children go on to have significant effects on the environment.

Question 34: B
The stated conclusion: that television dampens people's ability to think for themselves, does not necessarily follow from the fact that television causes an individual to be entertained rather than to think and discuss. This assertion is therefore not relevant to the previous claims made in the passage.

Question 35: E
This passage states its main aim initially by saying that we ought to change science lessons in order to give a correct view of modern science and then all other arguments after this point are made in support of that initial conclusion. The closing line that the traditional view is giving children a false, unscientific, view of the universe, is supporting evidence that the science lessons ought to be changed.

Question 36: C
In total, the boat takes 45 minutes from setting off before it is ready to set off from the other end. Therefore, the boat setting off from the mainland at 5 past will be ready to depart back when the boat is next scheduled at 55 minutes past from the island.

None of the other 4 times before 9.55am can be made by another boat travelling from the other destination so at least 5 boats are needed in total for the first journeys.

All journeys from one side have another journey leaving from the other side 50 minutes after that journey therefore there is **no need for other boats** as the turnaround for each boat is 45 minutes so the same boat can fulfil one journey and then the next 50 minutes afterwards = 5 boats.

Question 37: D

Approximate the ratios of each area:

England N	20:1
England Mid	20:1
England E	18:1
England LDN	20:1
England S	18:1
Wales	20:1
Scotland	15:1
N Ireland	17:1

Scotland is the clear answer

Question 38: C

Two identical pieces which when they fit together do not form a complete circle:

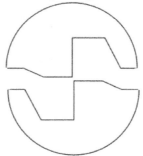

Question 39: A

The passage provides significant evidence that there are many benefits to assigning individual caseworkers to the most vulnerable homeless people. All of the other answers are slightly too tenuous to be clearly drawn from the passage while the benefits of this pioneering scheme are obvious and therefore this conclusion can be clearly drawn.

Question 40: E

There is a lot of information in this passage but in summary it focuses on how to best promote health attitudes among drinkers: with simple instructions or more complex ones. This would not happen if the complicated guidelines were in fact not read and understood at all.

Question 41: A
This passage makes the very broad statement that regardless of the cause of an extinction level event; the planet would be able to recover swiftly. This is a very difficult claim to be able to make without knowledge of exactly what would happen in the instance of every possible extinction-level event. A global nuclear holocaust for example has never been witnessed and therefore may have an effect that this argument has failed to account for.

Question 42: B
Cost each day from local pet shop:
2 sachets at $1 = $2
25g at $1 per 100g = 25p
Total = $2.25

Cost each day from online distributor:
One sachet = $62.40÷96 = approximately 66p
1kg of dry food = $8, 25g of dry food = $8÷40 = 20p
2 sachets = 1.32
25g of dry food – 20p
Total = $1.52

Difference is approximately 75p

Question 43: A
Only Arps and Urps have tails and they have one each, since there are 33 tails there must be a total of 33 Arps and Urps. Therefore the remaining 12 animals are Orps.

Subtracting the total 48 legs and 24 horns from the 12 Orps from the total leaves 174 legs and 75 horns. Since only the Arps have horns out of the Arps and Urps, the remaining 75 horns must come from the Arps. Therefore there are 75/3 Arps = 25 Arps.

Therefore the remaining 8 animals must be Urps

Question 44: A

The sections on the net in A circled (below left) do not cover the side on the completed shape circled (below right)

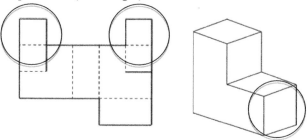

Question 45: C

The passage focuses on the social effects of the Buy-to-let policy on both oneself and the wider public. The unaffordability of houses and the lack of individual benefit due to the increase in rent far above wages, and the risk of investment, has shown that there is no social benefit available to anyone

Question 46: B

This passage claims that a particular characteristic inevitably implies the absence of two other things; in this case the freedoms of speech and assembly. This parallels the idea that a constant amount of energy in the body implies a lack of light and heat being emitted.

Question 47: B

The passage states that in a given situation it is always possible to act for the greatest good for the greatest number and also clearly states that this is what we ought to do. 'Ought' then implies that the action which benefits the most persons is the right action and therefore is the best possible action.

Question 48: D

The difference between RAT and TEAR is only the letter E; therefore the difference in points between the words is the value of the letter **E**.

Now that we know the value of the letter E, we subtract 2 times this amount from TREE to find the value of TR. The difference between the value of TR and RAT is then the value of the letter **A.**

Now that we know the value of TR and E, we subtract this from RITE to find the value of **I.**

No further letters can be found

Question 49: D

Start with the earliest time zone (San Diego) at the earliest available time (8:00). At this time Barcelona (the second latest time zone) is at 17:00 and therefore will be available for **3** more hours.

When London (second Earliest time zone) is then at 8:00, Nairobi (latest time zone) is at 10:00 and available for 10 more hours.

These 2 periods crossed over for 2 hours, totalling 11 hours.

Question 50: D

It is not possible to rotate the tables on the left to create the shape on the right

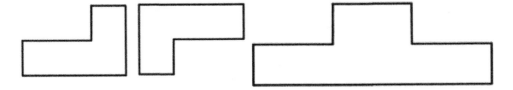

Section 2

Are 'drone strikes' morally different to military campaigns fought on the ground?

Introduction
ADVICE:
> This is a complex question that can be approached from a significant number of directions, and which will produce a variety of valid answers depending upon which ethical viewpoint one adopts. I would stress that, given the limited amount of space available to TSA candidates for their essay, they ought to think very carefully about whether it is worth spending all of their time attempting to establish a case for a particular ethical view when they have so little space within which to do it.
> One approach to this question would be to consider a variety of ethical viewpoints and how the practicalities of this policy might affect them, in order to make this answer approachable and easily comprehensible I would recommend the following approach:
>> o Consider this policy in terms of moral absolutes i.e. 'killing is wrong' since both clearly do kill, and both also clearly breach the sovereignty of a nation
>> o Consider this policy in terms of Utilitarianism which is likely to claim drone strikes to be ethically superior

WHAT TO INCLUDE:
> Include a very brief description of your main points
> Set out what your conclusion will be
Philosophical theory
> Ensure you are confident with a moral viewpoint if you want to include them in your essay – it is better not to ascribe an idea to a thinker than to ascribe a false or erroneous one.
> Moral absolutism: The fact that both forms of military intervention (drone strikes and 'boots on the ground' invasions both lead to the outcome of death of enemy combatants means that both might be regarded as morally indistinguishable by a moral absolutist who believes that killing is wrong. This is also true for those who uphold the sovereignty of nations as an absolute. Since the sovereignty of the nation is being breached in both the case of a drone strike and a full military invasion, both methods breach the sovereignty of the nation affected.

> Another ethical theory to explore would be utilitarianism and how fewer troops on the ground would mean that individuals were less likely to die during the invasion. Less death would therefore mean less loss of utility. This argument can also be made with regards to the greater accuracy of drone strikes and the ability to avoid collateral damage.

Alternative possibilities to explore (slightly more difficult or less persuasive)
> Is it morally differentiating to kill an individual using a drone as opposed to using a weapon
> Might drone use psychologically affect pilots, removing from the situation enough that they might be able to carry out actions that would otherwise be uncontainable to soldiers on the ground.

Conclusion
> Summarize the main points made on each side of the argument the essay.
> You may wish to come to a decision either way, or it is equally fine to sit somewhere in the middle, so long as this is fairly justified

Is reducing inequality always a good thing?

Introduction
> Equality is something of a 'buzzword' but, as with many topics in philosophy, unless you actually consider the theory carefully then what might seem like a question you feel you could easily answer is in fact more challenging than you thought. Consider that if two persons each were almost entirely equal except that one of them had a piece of chocolate then if we always prioritise equality we ought to take the chocolate away from this person even though it does no harm to the other individual by the first person having this chocolate. This is the levelling down objection.
> Ultimately, this question comes down to whether equality has any inherent value – it needs to discuss whether there is any value to reducing the happiness of one person to make them equal with another in abstract in order to reach the very highest level

Arguments for:
- Equality is something that we strive for in all different parts of life. It is certainly something that we wish to apply to all humans at the point of birth and it might be said that this desire for equality should continue forward.
- There is inherent value to equality between individuals, consider the example of two children who live as perfectly equal siblings until their mother gives one of them a lollipop and not the other one – the average person would see this as unfair and would prefer no lollipops over an imbalance of lollipops between the children

Arguments against:
- The levelling down objection shows that a reduction in one persons welfare for no reason other than to make them more equal with a second person is in fact not defensible
- Arguments in support of equality actually misinterpret what it is to accurately discuss the levelling down objection, as there is often a misconception that achieving equality might make one of the parties happier. In fact, this is not the case in the levelling down objection as in order to consider the inherent value of equality in abstract; it is necessary to consider whether it is justified to lower the happiness of one person only for the sake of achieving equality. When one consider arguments for equality with regards to this it becomes clear that the levelling down objection does in fact discredit the idea of equality having inherent value

Conclusion
- A summary of levelling down arguments and objections
- Either a stated conclusion on the value of equality or some degree of uncertainty and an explanation of why you feel that you cannot come to a conclusion

Is a referendum a good way to decide a major question facing a country?

Introduction
- ➤ This question is a really good opportunity to bring in examples of current affairs that you think are relevant – this does not mean however that examples are a replacement for analysis and you need to makes sure that you state why examples you choose are directly relevant to the question.
- ➤ A common fault with questions like this is just talking about all of the things that you know about referenda rather than actually attempting to focus on what the question is asking

- ➤ *Arguments for:*
- ➤ Applying a democratic decision making procedure means that the electorate are given an opportunity to engage with issues affecting them in a way that equally values all citizens of voting age
- ➤ Referenda create a very energised political atmosphere – seen especially around the Scottish and EU referenda. This motivates individuals to engage in politics, including after the referendum itself and also means that more persons attempt to educate themselves on relevant issues
- ➤ If significant decisions need to made and it is in the middle of a government's term and therefore a general election cannot be held on that particular issue, a referendum allows the government to obtain a mandate to carry out action without the need for an election

Arguments against
- ➤ Referendum campaigning is a prime opportunity for fear mongering and populist arguments rather than the reasoned argument that is more prominent in a parliamentary debate – this would be a great time to bring in examples from recent referenda
- ➤ The cost of a referendum is very high and it takes an extremely long time to carry out meaning that quick decisions are very difficult and costly to make through the use of referenda.
- ➤ Referenda can be counterproductive if they are not carried out properly – the EU referendum seems to provide a mandate for the government to leave the European Union but since the result there have been a huge number of people who have changed their minds. The 'mandate' is therefore arguably out of date and counterproductive to what the public now may want

Conclusion

➢ Summarize the main points made on each side of the argument the essay.

➢ In this essay in particular, it might make sense to argue that the value of referenda varies considerably based upon the state of the country, the conduct during the campaigns and the question being asked

➢ You may wish to come to a decision either way, or it is equally fine to sit somewhere in the middle, so long as this is fairly justified

Can we learn about intelligence by studying how humans and other animals learn?

Introduction
- ➢ This question is asking whether there is value in the study of humans and animals learning and as such, this question is quite challenging for those who do not have any notion of psychological theory
- ➢ Despite this, there are general arguments that can be made regarding learning and intelligence but they are unlikely to allow a candidate to access the higher marks without the addition of specialist psychological knowledge
- ➢ This question raises two points – the first is whether intelligence can be directly linked to learning and the second as to whether in practice it is possible to learn using studies of learning
- ➢ Historically there has been a separation of the study of learning and of intelligence which is an anomaly in scientific psychology
- ➢ Increasingly though, there is a claim that there are no clear distinctions which can be made between the cognitive processes that contribute to individual differences in these two areas

Arguments for:
- ➢ Intelligence is expressed relative to the ability of the individual to learn. Smart people tend to learn faster and also learn more than less intelligent people. Intelligence is also clearly manifest in the ability to acquire complicated skills and excel in their performance through practice and progressive improvement.
- ➢ The results of recent analysis are consistent with the conclusion that performance on learning tasks and conventional tests of intelligence, e.g. IQ tests, both reflect common factors, for example Spearman's g, or the general factor common to all cognitive abilities. For this reason the historical separation between learning and intelligence as psychological concepts ought not to be so rigorously enforced.
- ➢ Since learning is dependent upon the existence of systems through which information can be interpreted and translated into skill, systems that we understand as intelligence, the two concepts are fundamentally linked
- ➢ By examining differences in the learning processes of intelligent and less intelligent individuals we can then see the difference that intelligence makes to the learning process

Arguments against:

➤ It is extremely tempting to equate knowledge with intelligence and this needs to be avoided in order to accurately gather information on intelligence through the process of learning. It is accepted that knowledge and intelligence are entirely separate things and that, to an extent, an individual in possession of one is not necessarily in possession of the other

➤ In terms of examining animals, it is extremely important not to adopt an anthropocentric standpoint when attempting to evaluate the intelligence of animals through their practices and their ability to learn. It is accepted that animal abilities differ considerably to human abilities and what might indicate a genius intellect in a human might be a skill possessed by all members of a particular animal species. As such there is a certain amount of discretion that needs to be applied when attempting to acquire information about the intelligence of an animal from their learning practices.

Conclusion

➤ Summarize the main points made on each side of the argument the essay.

➤ In this essay in particular, it might make sense to argue that the value of referenda varies considerably based upon the state of the country, the conduct during the campaigns and the question being asked

➤ You may wish to come to a decision either way, or it is equally fine to sit somewhere in the middle, so long as this is fairly justified

END OF PAPER

2018

Section 1

Question 1: B

A is incorrect because the passage suggests technology has made us live longer, not enabled us to choose when we die. C is incorrect because the passage describes a 'new' fear, not a worse fear. D and E are not relevant to the passage and therefore B most accurately expresses the idea that people should be allowed to be euthanised if they wish to.

Question 2: D

If we say there are y girls and x boys in the class.

$$3x + \frac{y}{3} = 24$$
$$x + y = 24$$

By solving these equations simultaneously we obtain x=6 and y=18. Then 18-6=12 and so D is the correct answer.

Question 3: E

The structure of this argument is as follows: let maize be A and soybeans be B. A is preferred to B yet A is unavailable so the farmer settles for B. E is the only statement which mirrors this because the bank is better than the hotel however the bank was unavailable so they had to use the hotel.

Question 4: D

A is incorrect because the statement does not suggest fish farmers should switch, it simply states that carnivorous fish are less environmentally friendly to farm. D is correct because the statement says that salmon can only be farmed by depleting wild fish stocks which means they are worse for the environment than non-carnivorous silver carp.

Question 5: B

B is correct here because the statement suggests that in order to solve the problem of failing to hire talented researchers and lecturers, the new policy will help to 'improve recruitment' by using independent HR in hiring committees. For this to be effective the HR consultants must be able to spot suitable candidates, if they are unable to do this, they will not improve recruitment procedures and so the argument is flawed.

Question 6: D

After the spillage, the 400ml is still 4/5 water and 1/5 concentrate. Therefore, 320ml water and 80ml concentrate. Adding 100ml of concentrate means the final amounts are 320ml water and 180ml concentrate.

$$\frac{180}{500} x100 = 36\%$$

Question 7: C

If we calculate the net loss of professionals by looking at the P column under professionals.

2017: 65-44= 21 out
2016: 67-45 = 22 out
2015: 68-44 = 24 out
2014: 50-55 = 5 in
2013: 51-59= 8 out

Therefore we can see that 2015 had the greatest loss of professionals.

Question 8: C

This is the correct answer because if we look at the top of the platform clock, the first number must be a 1 and the second must be a 4. In the minutes section the first number must be a 5. Therefore automatically we know the time is 14:5?, whatever the final digit this rounds to 3 o'clock.

Question 9: E

E is the correct answer because the main conclusion of the argument is that shooting overpopulated species can have very positive conservation effects. However, E suggest that the reintroduction of top predators is more effective and so weakens the statement in the argument.

Question 10: D

D is the correct answer because B and E are irrelevant to the passage. C is not necessarily true as the mother seems to be implying good grades may have been achieved despite taking the holiday not as a result of it. A is not related to the content of the argument. D is correct because the mother suggests the law is unnecessary simply from her own experience.

Question 11: E

E most accurately expresses the main conclusion of the argument because the argument highlights several flaws in the idea: not only that it punishes single parents but also subverts incentives and punishes those who have not found a partner. Therefore, E is correct as it is the most representative.

Question 12: D

From 2011-2012, we can round down 4.2 to 4, $\frac{4}{3}$ is roughly a 33% increase.

From 2012-2013, 6.3-4.2=2.1 so he increase is 50%.

From 2013-2014, 9.45-6.3=3.15 another 50% increase.

From 2014-2015, approximating the figures, 15-9.5=5.5 which is greater than a 50% increase.

From 2015-2016, approximately 22.5-15=7.5 which is roughly a 50% increase.

Therefore, overall, from 2014-2015, the percentage increase is the biggest.

Question 13: D

Let us calculate the costs with each wall paper type.

Woodchip- 27 rolls at £25 each, 5 rolls are free, so the total is $22 \times 25 = £550$

Vymura- 18 rolls at £35 each, 10% off is applied, so the total cost is $18 \times 35 \times 0.9 = £567$

Anaglypta- 18 rolls at £40 each, 20% off is applied so the total cost is $18 \times 40 \times 0.8 = £576$

Embossed: 14 rolls bought at £50 each, 25% off is applied, so the total cost is $14 \times 50 \times 0.75 = £525$

Fabric effect: 11 rolls at £100 each, buy one get one free is applied so the total cost is $6 \times 100 = £600$

Therefore the cheapest overall is D, embossed at 525.

Question 14: C

As there are 8 folded sheets on each block, on each half of the block the following page numbers will be shown because each page is double sided:

Block 1 Half 1 - P 1-16
Block 1 Half 2 - P 17-32
Block 2 Half 1 – P 33-48
Block 2 Half 2 – P 49-64
Block 3 Half 1 - P 65-80
Block 3 Half 2 - P 81-96

Therefore, the centre of the block will show pages 48 and 49

Question 15: C

C is the correct answer because the statement says that by awarding a Nobel Prize within Economics, this wrongly categorises it as an exact science and further gives examples of why economics does not have the same certainty and predictive power associated with the exact sciences and therefore cannot be treated as one.

Question 16: B

B is the correct answer because the argument states that injuries/deaths due to tiredness are preventable by not driving if extremely tired. However if drivers cannot recognise they are dangerously tired, this mechanism will not work to reduce deaths/injuries therefore making the argument invalid.

Question 17: B

B is the correct answer here because A may be true but the argument is still valid as people may not use such open spaces, so A is not correct. The article states an increase in the number of children with rickets and so this may be true even if the incidence is rare, therefore C is incorrect. D and E are not relevant to the argument. Therefore B is the correct answer.

Question 18: B

If 4 girls have 22 shells each, let us say that the youngest girl has x. The 4 girls each lose 3 shells so now 4 girls have 19 shells each and the youngest has $x + 12$. If they all have the same it must be true that $x + 12 = 19$ and therefore $x = 7$

Question 19: D

If we look at training, we can tell that Graham cannot win the prize.
Analysing penalties, David and Colin are also excluded from winning.

John and Mike are the only two left, so by looking at the goals column, Mike scored the most so Mike wins the prize.

Question 20: B

Immediately we can see that cube 2 is possible as if the W is folded round, it will resemble cube 2. Therefore C,D and E are incorrect. Cube 3 is also possible as if the A and D are folded down the net will resemble 3. Therefore B is correct.

Question 21: A

A is the correct answer because the argument states that phones are supposed to keep teenagers safe but due to cyber bullying and stalking, they have now become unsafe. But phones still make teenagers safer than they were before, in other words, cyber bullying and stalking does not undermine the respects in which mobile phones ensure safety. Therefore A is correct.

Question 22: B

B is the correct answer because the structure of the reasoning is as follows: customers are rewarded if they achieve X, you have not achieved X and so do not get the reward. In B the dessert is the reward and the condition of achievement is completion of the main course and so this exactly mirrors the above reasoning.

Question 23: E

E is correct because the argument shows the negative impacts of the media on the general public. Magazines are another media form which can have negative impacts on young people and so reflects the principle of the argument.

Question 24: D

If we model the time as ab:cd and we want to maximising the number of segments in d, remembering we can only choose between numbers 0-9, 8 has the most segments (7). Maximising c, between numbers 0-5 , 0 has the most segments (6). Maximising b, we between numbers 0-9, 8 has the most segments (7). Maximising a, between numbers 0-5, 0 has the most segments with 6. Therefore, the time 08:08 is shown which has 26 segments in total.

Question 25: D
Round all the valued to the nearest thousand, by adding them up we find that Val and Pat have the two most votes. By adding up each of their scores using long addition (discounting the two scores where they apply to both people). We find that Pat has roughly 600 more votes than Val and therefore Pat is elected president.

Question 26: E
From Amy's view point let us label the lines (rows) of piles x,y,z,a. Row x has one pile with 5 boxes; the tallest pile in row y has 6 boxes; the tallest pile in row z has 7; the latest pile in row a has 5.
The far left column from Ben's view must therefore have 6 boxes or less, so E cannot be Ben's view. Therefore E is the correct answer.

Question 27: D
The statement says that unemployed people all respond differently to different solution measures. Therefore in order to solve the problem there must be more skilled staff in order to tailor solutions to each individual person. D is the correct answer.

Question 28: A
A is the correct answer because the statement makes several points which imply prime ministers should sack ministers to show integrity and to remain In power as well as reflect high moral standards.

Question 29: A
A is the correct answer because the librarian pledges to increase the number of computers in the library as a result of student complaints. The librarian need not respond to this in such a way, but they are aiming to cater to the students preferences, therefore A is correct.

Question 30: C
Let x equals the number of 9p coupons and if y is the number of 14p coupons, and z the number of 20p coupons. As a result, we have the equation $14y + 9x + 20z = 150$.
We also know that $x > y > z$. We will start by finding combinations of multiples of x and y which are equal to 130.
Starting off with $x = 8$ and $y = 4$, $14(6) + 9(4) = 120$, this is too small.
Next with $x = 8$ and $y = 2$, $14(8) + 9(2) = 130$ so z must therefore equal 1 giving the combination of $8+2+1=11$

Question 31: E
'Beginner's guide to history' and 'All about history' are not relevant because we are looking at 1900-1950.
The cheapest book therefore is History of the 20th century and so she withdraws £45.

Now working out 20% off, History of the 20th century is 45x0.8=36, The 'illustrated guide to history' is 50x0.8=40 and 'History for all' is 60x0.8=48, so she buys The illustrated guide to history at £45 leaving £5 left.

Question 32: E
The left item has one large diagonal edge and the item on the right has a larger and a smaller diagonal edge. In combination E, we can see both the large diagonal sides for each item, therefore the longest horizontal side on the item to the right is connected to the item on the left, but then the small diagonal side must also be visible. Since it is not visible, combination E is not possible.

Question 33: C
C is correct because the new health guidelines suggest 7 portions rather than 5 should be the norm, however a change in target would not result in a change in behaviour as previous evidence has shown. Therefore, current guidance should be maintained.

Question 34: C
C is the correct answer because the statement says that the tougher restrictions on eligibility resulted in a fall in the number of recipients. This is an example of confusing correlation with causation and therefore undermines the argument which suggests that tightening these restrictions even more will result in the same effect.

Question 35: D

D is the correct answer due to the fact that the author states 'More likely this status derives from a small number of his plays, the four great tragedies' rather than the plot development/skill with language.

Question 36: B

Profit = TR - TC, and revenue = P(price)xQ(quantity sold). Let us find the profit for each item. Always round up for wholesale packs bought leaving some leftover.

	Revenue	Wholesale Packs bought	Total Cost	Profit
Crayon	180x10=1800	180/12=15	15x48=720	1800 - 720 = 1080
Felt tips	150x12=1800	150/12=12.5=13	13x72=936	1800 - 936 = 864
Pencils	200x6=1200	200/24=8.3=9	9x24=216	1200 - 216 = 984
Pens	150x15=2250	150/36=4.1=5	5x36=180	2250 - 180 = 2070
Rulers	40x30=1200	40/12=3/3=4	4x60=240	1200 - 240 = 960

Pens and Crayons produced the highest profit out of the five items sold

Question 37: A

It is not necessary to look at the photo development time of the first five people beause they are able insert their money while the photos are being developed. Therefore, the first person is finished in the booth after 3 minutes, the second is finished after 6 minutes and if we continue this we can tell that the 5th person is finished after 15 minutes. Therefore, although you have wait after having inserted your money for your photos to be developed, the total waiting time before you can insert your money is still 15 minutes in total.

Question 38: B

The answer is B because the smallest x value is Hilltop, so the point furthest left is 763613 . Since Longwood is 787634, it is 2 right and 1 up from the square that Hilltop is in. Therefore it has to be W, so B is the correct answer.

Question 39: A

The statement implies that problems occur when autopilot systems hand responsibility back to the pilot and this can lead to crashes. Therefore by developing autopilot so that this does not occur, this will reduce the incidence of crashes. Therefore A is the correct answer.

Question 40: E

E is the correct aswer as the author wants children to enjoy poetry rather than analyse it and suggests the way to do this is by requiring children to learn and recite poems by heart. But if this does not increase their appreciation for poetry, it will not achieve the author's objective.

Question 41: C

C is the correct answer because the statement suggests that unpaid internships mean that less wealthy students are unable to support themselves and then this prevents them from gaining entry into industry. However, if unpaid internships last a few days, students will not have a problem with supporting themselves for this duration.

Question 42: E

To reach our total of 10 digits, 4 numbers must have 2 digits and 2 numbers must have a single digit. Let us think of the optimal scenario, the largest number should ideally end with a 0 and the smallest number should ideally end with a large digit. Since the largest number has 2 digits, this leaves 3 other numbers with 2 digits and 2 numbers that have a single digit. Therefore, the 2 single digit numbers should be as large as possible, 8 and then 9. The next 3 numbers which are all 2 digits will have the first digit ascending and the second digit descending. Therefore, we are left with; 8,9,17,26,35,40.

So the smallest range is 40-8=32

Question 43: C

One 8h ticket = £6.20.

Returning increasing quantities of smaller length tickets, one 7h + one 1h ticket = £6

6h + 2h = £5.40

5h + 3h = £5.20

4h + 3h + 1h= £4.90

4x 2h = £4.80

(2x 3h) + 2h = £4.60

Therefore, £4.60 is the cheapest amount for parking for 8 hours, the minimum amount of time valid for a 7.5-hour period. Therefore, £6.20 - £4.60 = £1.60

Question 44: D

All 3 faces have 1 triangle shaded and all 5 possibilities only have the middle 3 cubes shaded so there is only one possible orientation for each one. If you look at the two squares on top of each other in each net, and look for the connected edge of those two squares, the connected left vertex of that edge is where all the all the one triangle faces meet and as shown in the picture, 2 triangles meet at this corner. Therefore, we can discount 5 and 2. Also we discount 3 as none of the triangles meet across faces. So we are left with 1 and 4. By visualising 1, we cannot turn this net to match the one in the question and therefore the answer is D.

Question 45: D

This is the correct answer as the chain of reasoning in the statement goes as follows. Charities do not attack the root of the problems that market economies create, therefore it is immoral to support them as in doing so this makes the problem deeper. Therefore giving to charity is immoral.

Question 46: D

If we label – understanding Pushkin's poetry as A and having a mastery of Russian as B. A only applies conditional on B. B is necessary for A. The second part of the statement states that A is true, therefore B must be true. Therefore D is correct because it follows this structure with A being having a bypass and B being creating pedestrian only high street for shoppers.

Question 47: A

A is correct because the main point of the statement is the abuse of power of rail contractors by using inmates as cheap labour and this resulting in an infringement of their rights. The point about safety is more of a sub-point and therefore is not the general principle of the argument.

Question 48: D

Let us analyse the first leg of the journey, remembering that speed = distance / time, we can calculate the time as: $\frac{15}{60} x \, 60 = 15$ minutes.

Now, if we look at the second leg of the journey, this took a total of 5 hours.

And finally the third leg the duration of which we can calculate: $\frac{20}{40} * 60 = 30 \, minutes$, therefore the total time of the journey was 5 hours and 45 minutes. We know that the destination was reached by 12:00 midday, so the journey must have begun at 6:15am.

Question 49: C

Firstly, the shelves must be at least 40cm in depth, so we know 30cm wood cannot be used. We should look at the longer lengths to find the cheapest option. Consider a 4m long piece, which can be used to make two 1.8m long pieces. This can make 4 of the selves if we buy 2 x 4m at 45cm because this is the cheapest option. If we buy a 2m piece at 45cm, this account for the shelf left over.

$$£9.30 + £9.30 + £4.95 = £23.55$$

Question 50: C

Combination A will be symmetrical because the pattern changes such that the bottom line becomes horizontal and the others will cross in the middle making them symmetrical.

Combination B, the bottom two lines on the left will create a symmetrical cross at the bottom. The top line on the left will be horizontal and the middle lines will form another symmetrical cross making B. If we think about combination C, we only need to consider the top line, this line will be diagonal linking the top left and bottom right and there is no line to symmetrically match this. Therefore, C is not symmetrical.

END OF SECTION

Section 2

Is humanism a religion?

This essay should contain:

> - Humanism is a moral ideology which posits positive attitudes centred around our common humanity
> - What is a religion? How can we define religion? The answer must define religion with certain criteria and test whether humanism adheres to such criteria
> - Consider both sides of the argument and weigh them up to reach a final conclusion
> - Should be less superficial than a simple science vs religion argument, it should delve deeper into the psychology behind religion and human belief.

Suggested points:

> - Humanism suggests a moral code to live by, a feature of religion is the creation of a code of conduct to live by, normally which involves revering/respecting a deity
> - Even through humanists do not agree with religion, it is a system of beliefs itself and so can be regarded as a form of a religion
> - Religions have many supernatural elements but humanism is based on the real world
> - Humanism only makes scientific claims and does not require belief without concrete proof
> - Student could may suggest texts like JSM's 'On Liberty' and Richard Dawkins/ Bertrand Russell literature as a 'religious text' of humanism

Should journalists only be allowed to follow their profession if licensed to do so, like medical doctors?

This essay should contain:

> - Meaning of lisencing: under what conditions?
> - The answer should explore what licensing entails and comparisons between the implications of licencing for both medicine and journalism
> - Introduction which defines key terms and identifies line of thought for their argument in a concise way
> - Conclusion which summarises the argument, opening up avenues for new research

Suggested Points:

> - Journalists need to be able to retrieve information from reliable news sources and present stories with strong evidence and transparency
> - Fake news has become a growing problem in society, which can result in the mis-education of the public. Licensing of journalists may reduce the potential for this to occur
> - Licensing could allow government capture to occur within the media industry – as who would they be licenced by? It must be an independent body, but who would fund them?
> - Licensing may deter potential journalists if they cannot afford to obtain a licence
> - It seems unnecessary to provide journalists with licences because the responsibility associated with the occupation is not as important as that of a doctor

Should a government impose a legal maximum ratio between the highest and lowest pay of individuals in companies?

This essay should include:

- ➤ Technical economic analysis and chains of thought, as this question is geared towards economists
- ➤ Introduction should outline the argument and introduce the candidates reasoning
- ➤ Conclusion should accurately summarise the argument
- ➤ Essay should consider whether this is a viable economic policy and what the potential effects could be
- ➤ What would be the motivation for the introduction of this policy

Suggested points:

- ➤ A maximum ratio could result in lower productivity within firms as shareholders are unable to incentivise greater performance from the highest-earners within the firm
- ➤ However, this may not necessarily the case, as evidence has shown that firms which have an employee-centric business model may grow faster than others
- ➤ Inequality within a firm may lead to new recruits becoming disillusioned when comparing their salaries to those of the CEO/managers
- ➤ Firms may move to a different country to avoid this policy and it will therefore result in 'brain drain' and hence, lower GDP growth
- ➤ The ethical motivation for this policy should be considered- is this fair?

non-human animals have opinions? Do they have beliefs?

This essay should include:

➢ An introduction which outlines the key points within the candidates essay
➢ Confirms the definition of words in the statements: i.e opinions could be interpreted as expressing like/dislike towards certain things
➢ The argument should follow on the basis of this definition (i.e the argument depends on the definition the candidate chooses), the candidate may explore multiple definitions to show breadth
➢ The conclusion of the essay should state the candidate's final viewpoint on the question and perhaps suggest opportunities for greater research on this topic

Suggested Points:

➢ Observations amongst elephants and certain animals have shown a trend towards family units and groups rather than acting alone. This could be interpreted as an opinion
➢ Are animals conscious? Perhaps pronounce religious viewpoints on this
➢ Animals have been shown to express empathy in the wild – documented account of a humpback sweeping a seal onto its back away from killer whales
➢ Animals can communicate and this, in itself, is a form of expression
➢ Given that we have evolved from animals (apes), many species have an extremely similar genetic makeup to humans and so, they are
➢ Can animals tell the difference between right and wrong? Does this indicate that they have moral codes of conduct

END OF PAPER

Afterword

Remember that the route to a high score is your approach and practice. Don't fall into the trap saying that *"you can't prepare for the TSA"*– this couldn't be further from the truth. With knowledge of the test, time-saving techniques and plenty of practice you can dramatically boost your score.

Work hard, never give up and do yourself justice.

Good luck!

About UniAdmissions

UniAdmissions is an educational consultancy that specialises in supporting **applications to Medical School and to Oxbridge**.

Every year, we work with hundreds of applicants and schools across the UK. From free resources to our *Ultimate Guide Books* and from intensive courses to bespoke individual tuition – with a team of **300 Expert Tutors** and a proven track record, it's easy to see why UniAdmissions is the **UK's number one admissions company**.

To find out more about our support like intensive **courses** and **tuition**, check out **www.uniadmissions.co.uk/tsa**

YOUR FREE BOOK

.anks for purchasing this Ultimate Guide Book. Readers like you have the power to make or break a book – hopefully you found this one useful and informative. *UniAdmissions* would love to hear about your experiences with this book.

As thanks for your time we'll send you another ebook from our Ultimate Guide series absolutely <u>FREE</u>!

How to Redeem Your Free Ebook

1) Either scan the QR code or find the book you have on your Amazon purchase history or your email receipt to help find the book on Amazon.

2) On the product page at the Customer Reviews area, click 'Write a customer review'. Write your review and post it! Copy the review page or take a screen shot of the review you have left.

3) Head over to www.uniadmissions.co.uk/free-book and select your chosen free ebook! You can choose from:

- ✓ The Ultimate TSA Guide
- ✓ The Ultimate Oxbridge Interview Guide
- ✓ The Ultimate UCAS Personal Statement Guide
- ✓ The Ultimate Medical Personal Statement Guide
- ✓ TSA Practice Papers

Your ebook will then be emailed to you – it's as simple as that! Alternatively, you can buy all the above titles at **www.uniadmissions.co.uk/our-books**

TSA ONLINE COURSE

If you're looking to improve your TSA score in a short space of time, our **TSA Online Course** is perfect for you. The TSA Online Course offers all the content of a traditional course in a single easy-to-use online package- available instantly after checkout. The online videos are just like the classroom course, ready to watch and re-watch at home or on the go all with our expert Oxbridge tuition and advice.

You'll get full access to all of our TSA resources including:

- ✓ Copy of our acclaimed book "The Ultimate TSA Guide"
- ✓ Full access to extensive TSA online resources including:
- ✓ 6 complete mock papers
- ✓ 300 practice questions
- ✓ Fully worked solutions for all TSA past papers since 2008
- ✓ 20 hours of TSA on-demand lectures
- ✓ Ongoing Tutor Support until Test date – never be alone again.

The course is normally £99 but you can get £20 off by using the code "*UAONLINE20*" at checkout.

www.uniadmissions.co.uk/product/tsa-online-courses/

Printed in Great Britain
by Amazon